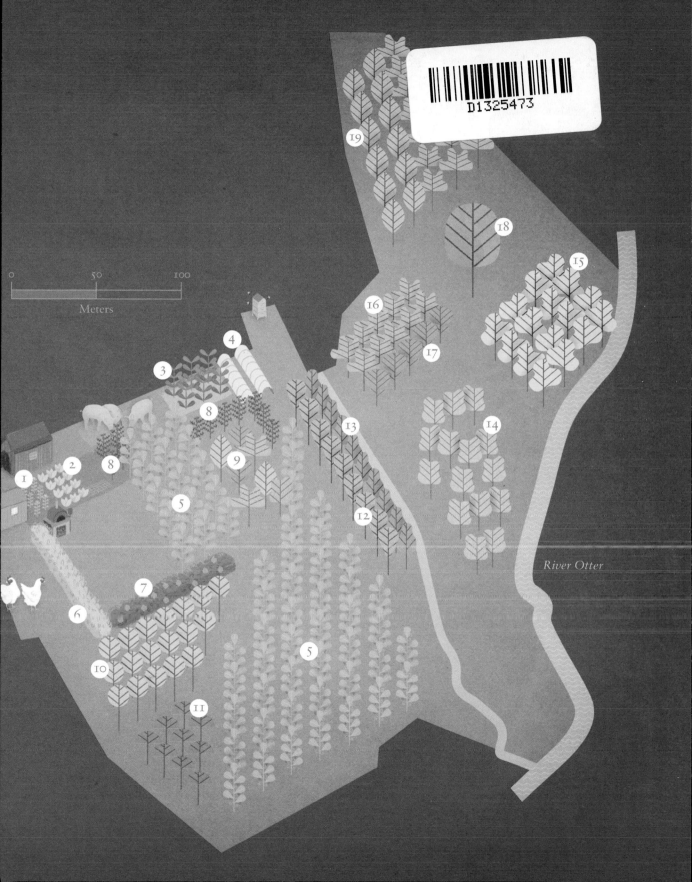

0   50   100
Meters

River Otter

1
2
3
4
5
6
7
8
8
9
10
11
12
13
14
15
16
17
18
19

A YEAR AT OTTER FARM

MARK DIACONO

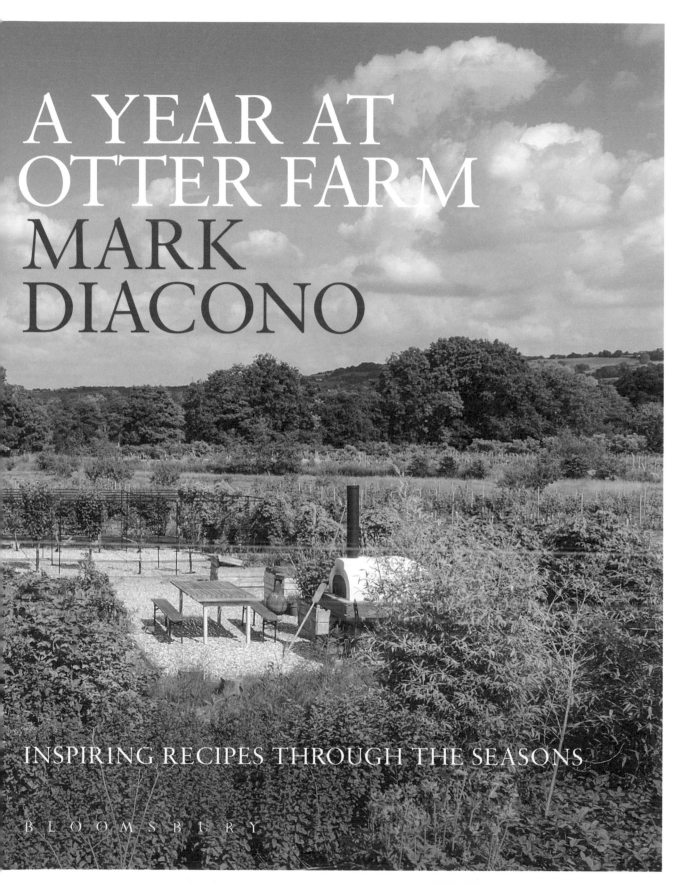

A YEAR AT OTTER FARM

MARK DIACONO

INSPIRING RECIPES THROUGH THE SEASONS

BLOOMSBURY

Contents

Starting out

It wasn't meant to turn out like this; I had plans for idleness. If I hadn't been painting the ceiling of a friend's shop when the woman who became my wife walked in, if I hadn't had that first mulberry just before the millennium changed, if the mortgage adviser hadn't given me artistic licence when moving here, there would be no Otter Farm and I would be a whole lot less tired. I'd also be a whole lot less happy.

Picking Szechuan pepper

WE GOT MARRIED IN A FEVER, if not quite hotter than a pepper sprout then certainly with a sense that we'd better get it done before we realised what we were doing.

A month from the question, we were wed. Instead of a honeymoon, Candida and I gathered twenty close friends in Dorset for an early-summer long weekend of walking, eating and a drink or two. In the few weeks between the wedding and the Dorset weekend, a house we had hoped to buy fell through. It was a huge stretch, needed much work and the land was prone to the odd bit of flooding, but we were still flat that it wasn't to be. The estate agent tried to soften the blow with news of 'a curious proposition' that was coming up for sale: an end of terrace, extended former cider barn, with eight acres attached. We picked up the details on the way to Dorset, and booked to see it on the way back.

I don't remember much about my first impressions of the house; my mind was on what was out the back. We had two and a bit acres where we lived in mid-Devon, but I couldn't imagine what eight might look like. The land rumbled away steadily from my feet, with the odd gentle rise and fall, to the curve that joined the boundaries either side together: a river.

It was summer, sunny and we all wanted to walk. We crossed the river into another nine-acre field, a huge ancient oak at its centre. The owners were to keep this, they said. Their field was partly defined by another river, the Otter, which met with the tributary we had crossed in the corner of 'our' field.

We followed the Otter downstream from the highest point of the field, a six-metre cliff formed by it tearing at the ground as it turned sharply below. A kingfisher, only the second I'd ever seen, flashed orange-blue just above the surface of the water, calling brightly.

It wasn't without its compromises. The house that had fallen through was detached and more beautiful. Here the A30 was within earshot if the wind was just so, but I was sold. And so was Candida. But I wanted both fields; the whole seventeen acres.

The fields had belonged to one of the local authority smallholdings established after the Second World War, when Britain had been vulnerable to being starved into submission by having food imports cut off. Sixty years later, this smallholding had been sold off in pieces by the local authority: a quarter of it, already purchased from the council, was to come with the house, and it seemed wrong to separate it any further.

The raw ingredients were there for a lot of fun, and the second field had a few hundred yards of trout fishing. I imagined fishing rods bending into the water, beer cooling in the net, fire waiting for the fish. We put in an offer for the house and the whole seventeen acres. Eventually the owners agreed to part with the second field.

We moved in early in winter, which gave me time to think about what I wanted to do. I had plans: I just didn't know what for yet.

✿ ✿ ✿

THE SEED FOR OTTER FARM was hidden inside the first mulberry I ate, the summer before we came here. Eaten perfectly ripe from a friend's tree and followed by several mulberry vodkas made from the previous year's fruit, it blew me away. It was the finest fruit I'd ever tasted, yet never in the shops. Imagine a blackberry, a raspberry and a handful of blackcurrants with a teaspoon of sherbet and you'll have the mulberry – the perfect fruit.

I have no idea why we aren't planting mulberry trees in our town and city parks and on our roundabouts instead of those waves of imported flowers. I couldn't believe that such a fine fruit wasn't for sale everywhere, but discovered they're too delicate when ripe to make the journey to the shops. There was no alternative: I had to grow mulberries.

I'd started growing food a couple of years before, when we were living in mid-Devon, and had done everything wrong. I'd cultivated too much land, grown too much on it, chosen predictable varieties of common vegetables: in short, I'd dedicated my weekends and evenings to growing mountains of unspectacular food. Our first pigs were very grateful.

The experience taught me that there are many things I'd rather be doing than growing ordinary food. Those mulberries, eaten at the end of that initial veg-heavy summer, showed me there was another way.

A few weeks later, I paid my first visit to Martin Crawford's forest garden near Totnes, Devon. It was one of those rare moments when your usual pattern of thought about something turns a right angle. His two-acre patch flipped the idea of a kitchen garden on its head, adding the third dimension and modelling the growing space on a natural forest. From there grew the idea of a largely perennial, diverse farm, with every inch dedicated to flavour.

When we moved here a few months later, I made a list of everything I loved to eat or liked the sound of. Whenever I got sidetracked by plants, the recipes in *Jane Grigson's Fruit Book* reminded me to think with my stomach. I should grow whatever made me hungry.

The wish list of possibilities was long and not limited by practical limitations of growing in Britain – partly because I wanted to make a dream list and partly because I hadn't the faintest idea what was viable here. I was all enthusiasm and little knowledge. I read like crazy. Books, newsletters, journals and the internet threw up so many possibilities – plants that might work well in this spot or that. I had breakthroughs, 'genius' plans and then doubts, quickly overridden by the next apparently 'fabulous' idea.

I whittled the possibilities into a short list with three categories: the best of the familiar, 'forgotten' food that was once popular here, and climate change food.

The first list included the most delicious varieties that had done well for me in my first few years of growing – Hurst Green Shaft pea, Sungold tomatoes and Annie Elizabeth apples were familiar favourites. The 'forgotten' list comprised fruit, herbs and vegetables that had once

River Otter tributary

The perennial garden

been popular and sounded wonderful to me but had either gone out of fashion or fallen out of favour as they didn't suit the supermarket supply chain – parsley root, Chilean guava, mulberries, quince and medlars among them.

The climate change list was perhaps the most exciting but also the riskiest. With the expected rise in temperatures over the coming decades, I wondered whether peaches, nectarines, apricots and other foods that thrive in neighbouring, slightly warmer, countries might become viable to grow in Britain.

I liked the idea of nurturing food that was on the margins, that climate change might just nudge into possibility. It struck me that if we could take advantage of the climate change – to which we are already committed – to grow low-carbon food that is normally sourced from overseas, we would be opening up possibilities. Together with other growers, we might help to reduce food's huge contribution to the acceleration of climate change. It seemed a beautiful virtuous circle.

Seventeen acres is a vast space. Half an acre, less even, is plenty to keep a family in fruit, veg and herbs. It presented the opportunity for growing some from that wish list on a small commercial scale, but what?

I decided on a range of small harvests rather than dedicating the whole farm to one or two, the idea being that in any given year – wet and windy, sunny and dry and everything in between – I could hope for seven or so out of ten crops to be productive. I liked the model: it built in some edible insurance against imperfect conditions and made the idea of failure less absolute.

So, a plan of sorts. And a piece of land to try and turn into a farm.

❀ ❀ ❀

THE FARM IS BOUNDED to the east and south by the River Otter and split into two fields by a tributary that flows into it. To the north is a small farm of cattle and apple trees; to the west, a line of houses, including ours.

Within those boundaries I've planted orchards, a vineyard, a forest garden and a perennial garden, put up polytunnels and created a veg patch. A few unplanted acres await either the next new idea or the expansion of an orchard or vineyard.

Most of what is planted has chosen its own spot. I look around and can convince myself that I've guided the shape and order of this place but I'm largely kidding myself. The vines took the most well drained area, the medlars and quince would be happiest in a seasonally damp lobe of the far field, while the pecans might do best near the river, mirroring where they thrive in the southern states of the USA. The almonds had to be distant from the peaches to avoid cross-pollination and there was only one place where the soil was well drained enough.

And in general, the more a plant, animal or garden needs attention, the nearer to the house it is.

Summer in the veg patch

The veg patch

A winding and increasingly effective hornbeam hedge encloses a number
of slightly raised beds, a fruit cage, a strawberry patch and a daffodil bed,
and although, clearly, much of it isn't 'veg' we refer to it all as the veg
patch. The true veg patch within is home to what I think are the finest
varieties of the familiar veg – International Kidney potatoes, Barbabietola
di Chioggia beetroot, Uchi Kuri squash among them – and those lesser
knowns whose flavour I can't be without, such as salsify, agretti and
Romanesco. I'm no slave to rotation, so I don't assign each plant group
to a quarter of the plot and move them around each year, though I tend
not to grow the same thing in the same place two years in a row.

The forest garden

A forest garden turns the idea of a normal vegetable garden on its head.
Rather than being predominantly annual veg, planted and grown almost
in two-dimensional plan view, with exposed soil between the plants,
a forest garden mimics a natural woodland. It is designed in integrated,
complementing tiers, from the subterranean, through the ground cover
and low herbaceous layers, to shrubs and up into the tree canopy, each
linked by climbers and interplanted to maximise mutual benefit.

   Forest gardens are mainly comprised of perennials – essentially,
plants that live longer than a year – which does away with the usual veg
patch cycle of sowing, hoeing and watering. Once established, perennials
tend to grow strongly and usually very early in spring – they're not busy
trying to grow and establish a root system as annuals are. This, and their
inclination to draw low in the soil profile for their nutrients and water,
makes perennials (and a garden in which they dominate) more resilient
and less demanding than annual veg.

   Many forest gardens, including ours, are essentially edible forests
that provide for most of their own nutrients through mineral-accumulating
plants, such as comfrey, and nitrogen fixers – including autumn olive and
clovers. It is a beautifully low-input system for growing food – I spend
perhaps a day and a half a year weeding the quarter-acre forest garden
here, and it never gets watered.

   The key to a fully functioning forest garden is to position the
plants as if they are fully grown. That two-year-old pear may look lonely
six metres from its neighbours when it's planted, but as they start to
spread you'll be glad you left room for them to do so. It takes vision and
confidence to plant a forest garden.

   Our forest garden is now four years old and starting to lose its
ridiculousness. Spring seems to be the tipping point, where plants begin
to relate to each other. The strawberry, comfrey, trefoil and Nepalese
raspberry ground cover is knitting together, the walnuts lining one side
are touching fingers, the mirabelles, pears, Cornelian cherries and other
trees are spreading above the lower layers. It's evolving from a sea of
unrelated plants into a place, a garden.

The perennial garden

I love the complexity of the forest garden, of seeing something planted in tiers gradually developing a personality, and it gave me the idea for something that takes the spirit of a forest garden and its multiple tiers and shrinks it to the allotment or garden scale. The perennial garden is just that, with the canopy layer sacrificed to allow more light in beneath, and with the focus on high-flavour harvests. I also wanted it to be a place where everything relates intimately as well as productively, without the usual bare spaces found in the typical veg patch.

It is now three years old. There are ones, twos, sometimes more, of sweet climbing kiwis and grapes, succulent dwarf apricots and peaches, spicy Nepalese pepper and cool Eastern mint, aromatic Japanese quince, crisp bamboo shoots, luscious mirabelles, sweet American bladder nuts and vanilla-scented musk strawberries – my daughter Nell's favourite. The plants are becoming quietly impressive.

Even in early spring, when the veg patch is still rubbing the sleep out of its eyes, the perennial garden is flourishing. Six kinds of chives will be pushing up flavour and colour in their hollow stems and flowers, the dwarf kiwi and Japanese quince will be in blossom, and the flowers of the Himalayan rhubarb will be well on their way to reaching around four metres high.

Anything not edible is still wonderfully productive: New Zealand flax for tying thread, mock orange and buckbrush for soap, bamboo for canes (as well as young, tender edible shoots), beautiful purple-flowering phacelia to draw in the pollinating insects, with trefoil, Italian alder and northern bayberry amongst the many plants naturally fertilising the soil.

Never mind the individuals though, the garden itself has started to come together. The plants are growing towards and even into each other. Relationships are being formed. The *Rubus spectabilis*, with its sweet-tart berries, is giving the glad-eye to the Moroccan mint, the Scottish lovage is giving the same to the blue honeysuckle, the Japanese parsley is getting over friendly with the creeping strawberries, while the young American bladder nut enjoys a little protection in the shade of the Himalayan rhubarb. The perennial garden is slowly developing its own identity.

The orchards

The field furthest from the house, which I persuaded the previous owners to part with, is home to young orchards that need little of my time – perry pears, quince, medlars, almonds and sweet chestnuts.

On the near side of the river, I planted a 'Devon' orchard of local pear, plum and apple varieties along with four Devon sorbs. There are fifty or so trees in this condensed culinary county that give a long season of fruit, a source of fruitwood for grafting new trees and, in another year or two, somewhere to hammock my bony backside. Between it and the vineyard is an orchard of Japanese plums, covered in early blossom and, with luck, midsummer fruit.

cking Annie Elizabeth apples

Drying Szechuan pepper

Rows of pecans and persimmons border the near side of the river. At their southernmost end, the pecan trees benefit from full sun, so they're twice the height of those at the shady north end, with a steady gradient in between. In addition, sixty or so Szechuan pepper trees are scattered in the near field – some lining the path to the polytunnels, others in mini-orchards where a little space has presented itself, and a few in the perennial garden.

The vineyard

I planted the vineyard six years ago. By 'I', I mean a team of highly experienced, hardworking vineyard planters with expensive equipment. Somehow, with their laser-guided tractor, they managed to plant 3,500 vines in perfectly straight lines on a north–south axis in under four hours. A further two weeks of driving metal posts into the ground and stringing wires between (30km in total) and the newly planted vines had a trellis to grow up. Dry sticks in the winter, they miraculously take only a few months to fill the lines with leaves and ripen their grapes. We grow five varieties: Pinot Noir, Seyval Blanc and Solaris, plus a few Sauvignon Blanc and Gerwurtztraminer.

The polytunnels

We put up two tunnels soon after we arrived. One holds all the plants yet to find their home outside – from tiny seedlings to shrubs and trees – along with a couple of raised beds for the summer Mediterranean veg and winter leaves. The other is a mini forest garden, under cover, with kiwis, peaches, nectarines and persimmons among the plants that fruit earlier in life and earlier in the year, with the extra warmth and protection of the plastic.

In extending the season and the range of flavours we eat, as well as providing somewhere under cover to start plants off, they are invaluable.

The hedges

Around the fields these are a mix of hawthorn, hazel, blackthorn, elder, blackberry, ash, willow and oak, to which I've added Italian alder and autumn olive as fast growing, nitrogen fixing windbreaks here and there.

I've also planted hedges within the fields, for structure, shelter and food. Lines of autumn olive, rosa rugosa, small-leaved lime, Szechuan pepper and Jerusalem artichoke provide delicious foraging, to go with the nettles, berries, haws, hazelnuts and elderflower from the older boundaries.

The animals

The farm comes alive with animals. It has movement. Chickens are ever-present: when they're not busy laying, they're overwintering in the veg patch, clearing weeds and picking off as many leatherjackets and other soil pests as they come across.

Most years we have pigs; originally breeding sows and their young, and now introducing young piglets to raise from spring into early autumn. Their home is one of a line of three fenced enclosures, each with an ark (a semi-cylinder with entrances at each end) to keep them warm and sheltered. The pigs draw me outside when I don't feel like it. They need feeding twice a day, their water needs topping up and when I'm on my rounds, often as not, I see something I wasn't looking for: a sparrowhawk taking a bird mid-flight a few metres from my head; the first daffodils, a fortnight ahead of usual; a lamb being born earlier than it should.

Having had sheep here for a few years, we've had to let our small flock of Devonshire Longwools go. As orchards, gardens and vines have covered more of these seventeen acres, space for the sheep has diminished. In a year or two, once the orchard trees become established enough to bear their rubbing and leaning, we'll have more again. In the meantime, mowing is done by tractor rather than teeth. I don't like it one bit.

✿ ✿ ✿

I SHOULD COME CLEAN: I'm not a proper gardener, and I'm certainly not a chef. I've just discovered that I love to grow, cook and eat. I've had no training in horticulture or cookery but I've been nosy enough to read, listen, ask and experiment.

I have been inspired by urban roof gardens, permaculturists in Canada, the home gardens of Kerala, community gardens in Britain, and by cooks, books and friends galore. I bend the ear of anyone who loves food because there's always something delicious and new to try, and someone who knows an interesting way to grow or cook it.

Otter Farm is more than a collection of influences though: it is the result of mistakes, brilliant ideas, the fluke of weather, the need to work elsewhere and distractions. Happy accident has played its beautifully creative part.

There has been no master plan executed with precision, nor a bucketful of money to invest. I've learnt and added things as I've gone along, and planted when money and opportunity allowed. In return, we have enjoyed homegrown peaches, almonds, apricots, sparkling wine, Szechuan and Japanese peppercorns, the finest asparagus and much more besides. Slowly, everything is getting established, and there is, I hope, plenty more to come.

In truth, it feels like I've just started. The first three years were spent finding my feet, making obvious mistakes, learning and deciding what to grow, three more were consumed in making larger mistakes and undoing some of what I'd done in years one to three, and the last three have gone pretty well.

I hope seeing how easy and rewarding it can be will persuade you to grow something. There's no need for seventeen acres: a few herbs grown by the kitchen door can change every meal you eat. It is largely very simple – I know just as much as I need to for plants to flourish, and with that in mind, I offer only the advice you need to grow something well and no more. For chillies and tomatoes, there are particular steps to get the best from your plants; with chervil root or peaches, there's very

uckoo Marans chickens

little. As friend and gardener Michael Michaud said, 'Gardening is the art of knowing the compromises you can make and still get a good crop.' Amen to that.

Growing even a little can lead to much more than a few interesting harvests. Those first new potatoes made me more inquisitive about where the rest of my food came from, about the people who were growing it and the impact of my food spend.

Cooking and growing draws people together: other gardeners, cooks, growers and enthusiasts. In short, it builds communities, but as much as anything it is life-enhancing. I've become more awake to the seasons and to the subtleties within each one. Clichéd as it sounds, when you are out there growing and eating, you become more aware of the little things – the changing light, the first blossom, the buzzard passing overhead that does so most days at that time.

Scents too, can switch on with little notice, often as the weather changes – the quince blossom, hawthorn and elder in spring, through to *Elaeagnus ebbingeii* in late autumn – but you have to be out there to be caught in their invisible cloud.

It is these tiny things as much as the changing flavours that quietly mark out the year and make the grower even more attached to their patch, even if that's just a few square feet by the kitchen door.

The four sections that divide this book are not seasons as such, but transitions – winter into spring, spring into summer, and so on – reflecting how harvests and the recipes that use them often flow across seasons, gradually being replaced as the new season's conditions dominate. The harvests in each month are chosen for no other reason than they are personal favourites that in some way mark the time of year, and that I look forward to eating. It is the same with everything I grow here.

The recipes are intended as starting points for you to take where you will. Most of them are adaptable – the mulberry bakewell tart is as fine with blackberries as it is with apple and quince slices. And, although I love every single recipe as it is, I hope you'll use them as diving boards for your own ideas. I've been precise where accuracy is needed, and loose when I can. This book is, after all, about eating happy-making, great food with loved ones.

When it comes down to it, Otter Farm is all about flavour. It starts and ends with the question: what do I really want to eat?

harvesting almonds

Seasonal harvest

Below are a hundred of the foods I love most and when you can expect to harvest them. Add to this most of the woody herbs – bay, rosemary and thyme among them – that can be picked all year, and those fruits, herbs, nuts and vegetables that can be stored or dried, frozen or otherwise preserved, and you have the basis for a pretty spectacular larder.

	Jan	Feb	Mar	Apr	May	June	July	Aug	Sept	Oct	Nov	Dec
Agretti				✿	✿	✿	✿	✿	✿	✿		
Almonds (including green almonds)					✿	✿				✿		
Apples							✿	✿	✿	✿	✿	
Apricots							✿	✿	✿			
Asparagus				✿	✿	✿						
Aubergines								✿	✿	✿		
Autumn olive										✿	✿	
Babington's leek		✿	✿									
Basil							✿	✿	✿	✿	✿	
Beetroot							✿	✿	✿	✿	✿	
Blackberries								✿	✿	✿		
Blackcurrants (including leaves)					✿	✿	✿					
Blue honeysuckle					✿	✿						
Borage				✿	✿	✿	✿	✿	✿	✿		
Borlotti beans								✿	✿	✿		
Broad beans				✿	✿	✿	✿	✿	✿			
Brussels sprouts	✿	✿	✿	✿						✿	✿	✿
Cabbages	✿	✿	✿	✿	✿	✿	✿	✿	✿	✿	✿	✿
Carrots						✿	✿	✿	✿	✿	✿	
Cauliflower	✿	✿	✿	✿	✿	✿	✿	✿	✿	✿	✿	✿
Celeriac	✿	✿	✿						✿	✿	✿	✿
Celery								✿	✿	✿		
Chard & perpetual spinach	✿	✿	✿	✿	✿	✿	✿	✿	✿	✿	✿	✿
Cherries								✿	✿	✿		
Chervil	✿	✿	✿	✿	✿	✿	✿	✿	✿	✿	✿	✿
Chervil root	✿	✿								✿	✿	✿
Chicory	✿	✿						✿	✿	✿	✿	✿
Chilean guava										✿	✿	
Chillies							✿	✿	✿	✿	✿	
Chives				✿	✿	✿	✿	✿	✿	✿		
Coriander					✿	✿	✿	✿	✿	✿		
Courgettes							✿	✿	✿	✿		
Cucumbers & gherkins							✿	✿	✿	✿		
Edible flowers			✿	✿	✿	✿	✿	✿	✿			
Elderflower (including American elder) & elderberries					✿	✿	✿	✿	✿	✿	✿	
Figs								✿	✿			
Florence fennel						✿	✿	✿	✿	✿	✿	
French beans					✿	✿	✿	✿	✿	✿	✿	
Garlic (including green & scapes)					✿	✿	✿	✿				
Globe artichokes					✿	✿	✿	✿	✿			
Good King Henry			✿	✿	✿	✿	✿	✿	✿			
Gooseberries					✿	✿	✿	✿				

	Jan	Feb	Mar	Apr	May	June	July	Aug	Sept	Oct	Nov	Dec
Grapes								✿	✿	✿	✿	
Herb fennel	✿	✿	✿	✿	✿	✿	✿	✿	✿	✿	✿	✿
Japanese wineberries								✿	✿			
Jerusalem artichokes	✿	✿	✿							✿	✿	✿
Kale	✿	✿	✿	✿	✿	✿	✿	✿	✿	✿	✿	✿
Kiwi fruit	✿									✿	✿	✿
Lavender					✿	✿	✿					
Leeks	✿	✿	✿	✿	✿				✿	✿	✿	✿
Lemon verbena				✿	✿	✿	✿	✿	✿	✿		
Lettuces	✿	✿	✿	✿	✿	✿	✿	✿	✿	✿	✿	✿
Lovage				✿	✿	✿	✿	✿	✿			
Medlars										✿	✿	
Mexican tree spinach					✿	✿	✿	✿	✿	✿		
Microleaves	✿	✿	✿	✿	✿	✿	✿	✿	✿	✿	✿	✿
Mint				✿	✿	✿	✿	✿	✿	✿		
Mulberries								✿	✿			
Nasturtium					✿	✿	✿	✿				
Oca										✿	✿	
Onions					✿	✿	✿	✿	✿	✿		
Parsley	✿	✿	✿	✿	✿	✿	✿	✿	✿	✿	✿	✿
Parsley root	✿	✿							✿	✿	✿	✿
Parsnips	✿	✿	✿					✿	✿	✿	✿	✿
Peas & pea shoots				✿	✿	✿	✿	✿	✿	✿		
Peaches & nectarines							✿	✿	✿			
Pears								✿	✿	✿	✿	✿
Pecans										✿	✿	
Plums, damsons & gages							✿	✿	✿	✿		
Potatoes					✿	✿	✿	✿	✿	✿		
Quince										✿	✿	
Radish				✿	✿	✿	✿	✿	✿	✿		
Raspberries							✿	✿	✿	✿	✿	
Redcurrants & white currants							✿	✿				
Rhubarb (including forced)		✿	✿	✿	✿	✿	✿					
Rocket				✿	✿	✿	✿	✿	✿	✿	✿	
Romanesco	✿	✿	✿							✿	✿	✿
Runner beans					✿	✿	✿	✿	✿			
Salad burnet	✿	✿	✿	✿	✿	✿	✿	✿	✿	✿	✿	✿
Salsify & scorzonera										✿	✿	✿
Scented geranium	✿	✿	✿	✿	✿	✿	✿	✿	✿	✿	✿	✿
Shallots								✿	✿	✿		
Small-leaved lime				✿	✿	✿	✿	✿	✿			
Sorbs	✿	✿										✿
Sorrel			✿	✿	✿	✿	✿	✿	✿	✿	✿	
Spinach	✿	✿	✿	✿	✿	✿	✿	✿	✿	✿	✿	✿
Spring onions		✿	✿	✿	✿	✿	✿	✿	✿	✿		
Sprouting broccoli	✿	✿	✿	✿								
Squash & pumpkins									✿	✿		
Strawberries (early mini)					✿	✿	✿	✿	✿			
Strawberries						✿	✿	✿	✿	✿		
Sweet chestnuts										✿		
Sweet cicely			✿	✿	✿	✿	✿	✿	✿			
Sweetcorn							✿	✿	✿			
Szechuan pepper							✿	✿	✿	✿	✿	
Tarragon (French)				✿	✿	✿	✿	✿				
Tomatoes							✿	✿	✿	✿	✿	
Walnuts (including green walnuts)						✿	✿			✿	✿	
Wild garlic			✿	✿	✿	✿	✿					
Yacon										✿	✿	

January

I love New Year's Day. It windscreen wipes the previous year – I get to leave the mistakes behind, the plans that time ran away from, I get to start again and be a genius this time. On the day itself, I want to be by the sea. I feel nauseatingly positive, like I've pedalled over winter's hill and that it'll be a freewheel into spring.

January's peak harvest

Cabbages

Celeriac

Chicory

Hyssop

Jerusalem artichokes

Swede

Sorbs

Of course, there is no freewheel into spring. January will seem two optimistic weeks long and February like a month and a half of icy winds but, at least for the early part of January, I'm happy.

I pay for December's fireside idleness with icy fingers – pruning the vines and most of the dormant fruit takes up much of January. It is not the most welcoming time to spend outside. You never quite know what you are going to get with March or April in Devon, but January is pretty reliable: it is almost always cold and wet, often relentlessly so. Snow can make a welcome change from the rain.

From the end of the garden, the vineyard looks closer at the start of the year. The fields are largely bare – skeletons of trees and shrubs where greenery and movement used to be. There's nothing to obstruct the view of lines of steel and stem. The four acres of potential wine looks vast.

Each of the 3,500 vines is assessed: how strong does it look; has it progressed well this year; how much fruit-producing wood shall I leave? The answers guide the pruning. A thick-stemmed vine with the woody remnants of this year's vigorous shoots will be left (to varying degrees) with plenty of potential fruiting buds for the following year; any that are seriously struggling will be allowed to strengthen rather than fruit. It is the start of a little dance with the vines that ends in autumn and these are the most crucial steps. It is this simple, seasonal intervention that gets you most attached to your vines and their peculiarities, and that sets everything on its way in the hope of wine.

A day set aside for pruning the vines. We have to become close friends. What I have to do is encourage the right balance between fruit and leaves. Simple. Except today it isn't. I start and the wind picks up. I carry on and the clouds gather. I continue and it rains. And in combination with the wind, it's just enough to take the feeling out of my secateur hand. It's slow going: 350 pruned in 6 hours. There are 3,500 vines. Even I can do that maths. And my boots are leaking. I stubbed the same toe that had a good solid skirting-boarding a fortnight before and was only just returning from purple to white.

I opened the barn door which set off a pool of water in a perfect arc from the roof down the back of my neck. Two minutes later, I discovered that only half had gone down my neck – the other half was sitting in my hood, waiting only for the rain to start again and me to put my hood up. Rather than driving me into the warm arms of a lazy bath, all this incremental tedium makes me more determined to at least get one thing ticked off the list. I clear the sleeping beds and the paths between of weeds. I deserve cake, but I finished that yesterday. Nice to get one thing actually done though. Perhaps today, as Howard Devoto sang, 'My irritability keeps me alive and kicking', although I bet his toe wasn't as sore as mine.

— 14 January, 2009

TAKING A FORK to the ground beneath the Jerusalem artichokes' tall dry stalks is the end to an autumn of wondering. There isn't the reassurance that the tubers are developing through the summer and autumn that comes with above-ground harvests like apples and cabbages. Until I dig, there's no way of knowing if the trug I've taken to load with artichokes will return empty or need to be replaced with a wheelbarrow.

It's a bit of a moment for me every year. The earthy, mushroomy flavour of the Jerusalem artichoke is one of my winter favourites – hearty and unmistakable without being loud – and this is where I discover if I'll be eating them in the weeks ahead.

Jerusalem artichokes were made for winter. They are easily transformed into a fine soup, a wonderful risotto or a fabulous purée, and they are delicious roasted (which draws out their earthy sweetness without making them crisp) or cooked as a gratin, made into crisps, pickled raw in slices and even in the heart of a cake. I've never been able to tell varieties apart for flavour, so I grow Fuseau as it's the least knobbly and makes for easy peeling.

Jerusalem artichokes come from the river basins of North America – they love plenty of sun and a moist soil – so I've planted them by the river, together with pecans, which love similar conditions and hail from the same region. The moisture, Devon can guarantee; the sun less so.

Having originally planted two lines of tubers in spring a few years ago, the Jerusalem artichokes have evolved into an untidy hedge, slowly expanding and thickening from any tubers I left in the previous year.

In late spring stems emerge, growing rapidly as the temperatures rise, producing a rash of striking yellow sunflowers in summer. They attract hoverflies, bees and ladybirds that help to maintain a natural balance of pests and predators, and are prolific enough for me to be able to cut handfuls to light up the house – they'll easily last a week or so in a vase.

As the frosts hit, the top growth dies back. Hopefully the tubers will have matured. Although I may dig a few in late December, I harvest most in January when the farm is producing less abundantly – they're perfectly happy left underground until we're ready to eat them, which is handy as they don't store well.

In a good year, they will often return a couple of kilos for each tuber planted. And when they've been lifted, the stalks are added to the compost heap, making every centimetre from the tops of the flowers to the subterranean tubers useful.

Jerusalem artichokes have a reputation for two things other than their earthy flavour: being invasive and causing flatulence. 'Invasive' is mostly a state of mind – as with potatoes, any left in the ground will regrow the following year, which, if planted in a permanent home means you can buy tubers once and eat them forever. If not, just dig them up every year, as you would potatoes.

Flatulence is more of a state of stomach – the starch contained in Jerusalem artichokes is indigestible to some, which leads to wind. Eating

JERUSALEM ARTICHOKES

Site	Sunny and moist
Sow	December–March
Harvest	October–March
Notes	Cutting the flowers directs the plant's energies towards the tubers

them with lovage or parsley seems to solve it for most, and many people find that if they eat them regularly the problem vanishes. In any event, Jerusalem artichokes are delicious enough to be worth a bit of farting.

Driving the fork into the soil isn't the tricky part; lifting the sodden earth is. A year of rain has left no air in it. It's weighed down into itself. The ground sucks at my boots like it wants them for itself. Such little sun for the Jerusalem artichokes this past year – a roasting week in March, a long weekend in June and I remember having to wear that ridiculous straw hat in August for a couple of days, but little else. Still, surprisingly, in the sludge, like potatoes in a stew, there are tubers. And they've largely escaped the slugs – perhaps it was too wet even for them to make much progress under the surface. There aren't too many, perhaps three or four under each stem, but they are huge, more like small sweet potatoes. Time to make root crisps.

— 3 January 2013

CELERIAC

Site Not too dry or shady

Sow Under cover, in modules February–March, planting out in May, 40cm apart

Harvest September–March

Notes I find varieties indistinguishable in flavour but Giant Prague is reliable and stores well

OF THE PLANTS that take up space in the veg patch for most of the year, celeriac is the one – along with January King cabbage – I least begrudge its long tenancy.

Superficially, celeriac is as ugly as a heavyweight with a weak defence yet I find it strangely beautiful too. It grows largely above ground as a gnarly fist topped with a gonk of serrated leaves, giving the grower little confidence through the summer as it tends to swell quite late, especially in a dry summer (ha!) when it should be watered regularly.

There is a ghost of celery in celeriac's flavour, but I think of it as more of a cross between lovage and potato, with all of the loveliness that implies. It is unequivocally savoury – how could potato and lovage not be? Yet there is a faint underlying sweetness that works beautifully in ice cream and crème brûlée, however unlikely it sounds.

Once a plant has established and the leaves are growing well, you can pinch off the odd few leaves – don't go overboard. Use their savoury bitterness in place of celery or lovage to lend depth and character to soups, stews and stocks.

Although distinctive in itself, celeriac borrows readily, taking on chilli, garlic and other strong flavours without losing its identity. I love it cubed, roasted and puréed, or raw in rémoulade, and it is (like Eric Clapton) perhaps at its best with cream.

Celeriac: Prinz

Chicory: Radicchio Palla Rossa

SOMETHING ABOUT THE DEEP, cold heart of winter makes me crave bitterness. I want dark chocolate, strong coffee and bitter leaves in a wholly different way to the warmer months and I'm not sure why. I guess I don't need to know: coffee and chocolate I can buy; the bitter leaves come courtesy of the veg patch.

I grow chicory and a few endive for their gentle bitterness, almost as hardy lettuces to pick through the winter. Most of the chicories are radicchio, or red chicory, varieties such as Rossa di Treviso, that just get on with it largely unattended. They look relatively unspectacular until late October when the cold arrives to flush the acid-green leaves deep red. I also grow Variegata di Castelfranco and a line or two of Sugar Loaf and Palla Rossa, each with its own character and all fabulous for cut-and-come-again leaves or leaving to form hearts.

Hearts tend to be sweeter than the leaves, but the bitterness in cut-and-come-again leaves somehow suits the weather and whatever else is in season. Happily, whether grown for hearts or leaves, chicory thrives in the cold and produces well through the lean weeks of winter.

Remembering to sow for winter harvests, however much they might be a favourite, is not something that comes easily to me. When the sun's shining, the winter seems as distant in time as Antarctica is in space, so I anchor my seed sowing to important dates. With chillies, it's Valentine's Day; with chicory, it's our wedding anniversary (mid-May).

I sow seed direct in a well-drained corner of the veg patch or raised bed in the polytunnel, and thin the seedlings to 25cm or so. They tend to grow well with little attention other than watering through dry periods   pretty good value considering they can provide 3 or 4 months of fabulous leaves in winter.

Raw chicory leaves are really good used sparingly to complement other leaves or on their own, as a single-variety salad with a honey mustard dressing contrasting (rather than diluting) their bitterness. Those chicories I allow to form hearts are usually braised or griddled to caramelise and sweeten the surface while leaving the centre gently bitter, and eaten with lamb, venison or roast vegetables and greens.

Chicory can be forced in much the same way as rhubarb (see page 49). I love a palaver as much as the next man, but with all the digging up and mess about involved, this is one for idler times when I'm old and (more) cantankerous.

CHICORY

Site Well drained

Sow Direct May–July, thinning to 25cm

Harvest August–February

Notes Slugs don't seem to like chicory – perhaps because the leaves are bitter

Lamb chops with chicory & Jerusalem artichoke purée (page 66)

SORBS

Site Not waterlogged or too sandy

Harvest December–February

Notes Prune out crossing branches etc.

Sorb jelly (page 83)

Sweet chilli dipping sauce (page 262)

THE YEAR AFTER WE CAME HERE I planted four Devon sorb apples in the Devon orchard and they were mightily demoralising. Slow to grow and reluctant to fruit was about the best I was able to say about them. A couple of years ago, at long last, they came good. If not an ugly duckling turned siren, then certainly a plain Jane turned foxy – beautiful leaves, a gorgeous shape and colour and (most gratifyingly) fruit.

Sorbus is an under-appreciated genus of trees and shrubs – rowans, whitebeams and service trees among them – many of which hybridise easily. The Devon sorb apple is one such cross, likely the result of a wild service tree and a whitebeam becoming over-friendly. Small in stature yet prolific once established, sorbs have much in common with medlars (see page 311) in that their fruit is astringent until the frost softens and draws out their winey sweetness. The 'apple' part of their name is a touch generous – the fruits of the Devon sorb apple are perhaps 1.5cm across, but they are full of flavour when picked on the edge of decay.

John Peel once said that if The Fall brought out an album that he didn't like he would presume that he just didn't know how it was good yet. What a fine way to look at music, life and indeed food. I have christened this The Fall Principle. It applies perfectly to sorbs – hard and unpalatable when apparently in their prime, they only become special when the frost breaks down the cell structure and brings on a gentle collapse, a process known as bletting.

There has been precious little cold this year – two frosts to speak of and here we are in the middle of January. Half an hour with Candida and Nell in the orchard today relieved the trees of their load – maybe half a basket's worth of soft and still firm sorbs. It gave a grand total of 2.4 jars of the most amazing coloured jelly. All that anticipation for such a small reward, but it's incredible stuff. After a few spoons of tasting that's now two jars. Or rather one jar as I promised Alys Fowler a jar.

I saw The Fall a few times. Once, the floor in front of the stage collapsed (almost certainly due to the weight of snakebite and black ingested by those watching): cue much standing around and looking into the abyss while The Fall carried on. They played for 40 minutes. Including the encore, which was the first two songs of their set played again. They were very fine indeed. This leads me to The Fall Principle No.2, which states that a little of something truly marvellous – even a single jar of Devon sorb jelly – can give an awful lot of pleasure.

— 13 January, 2012

February

*February is a slap in the face. The harshest frosts
hit and the wind blows the enthusiasm out of me,
yet slowly things are waking up. There's the relief
of spring around the corner, tempered by what needs
to be done before it arrives. It is a month of cold,
windy panic.*

February's peak harvest

Babington's leek

Chard

Chervil root

Parsley root

Sprouting broccoli

Winter lettuces

The snowdrops come whether there's snow or sun, so, lovely as they are, I don't take them as a sign of changing seasons; it's when the first of the forced rhubarb pokes its nose out of the ground that spring feels close. It'll turn on and off like a faulty bulb for a few weeks yet, but slowly plants and birds are waking up, and there are more days that get me going. But for these few weeks, the wind, at least, belongs to winter.

The farm appears dormant but looking closely there are buds beginning to swell, firstly those under cover, then the ones in the most sheltered spots, followed by those robust enough to bear a little harshness. The peaches, apricots and nectarines in the polytunnel may even have burst into blossom by the end of the month.

Every February I hope for an orderly procession into spring – a gradual easing of the chill and upping of the light. It rarely happens: more often, there's a week of early warmth, followed by a blast of Siberia. Any plant taken in by an unseasonably sunny week can find its buds and early blossom pinched, and with it the chance of fruit later in the year. It is a month, frankly, that I could do without.

The best that I can say about it is that when it's cold it gives me a little extra time to prune the vines or plant a tree or two if the ground isn't frozen, and when it's warm I'll be dry in the polytunnel, busy with a soft brush moving pollen from blossom to blossom in the absence of bees.

When I'm rich, I'll spend Februarys in Sri Lanka.

At last…the final few hundred of the 3,500 vines pruned this morning. Cold, snow everywhere – crusty with a second freezing overnight – and glorious sunshine. Tired hands and back, cold fingers and toes, but the flask and the odd nip of a single malt provides the antidote.
— 7 February, 2009

To keep on digging the holes and planting on these cold days, I have to remind myself that this leafless stick in my hand is a few short weeks away from springing into life and perhaps only a few months away from filling a basket with fruit. As numb hands claw back the soil around the roots, it helps to tell myself that inside this uninspiring stick is an Asian pear waiting to come out, that there's half a chance of one or two of its crisp, lightly russeted fruit in September, by which time I will have forgotten that I can't feel my fingers today. And besides, I have to do it now, in a week or two it will really be too late. It'll be spring.
— 28 February, 2013

Babington's leek

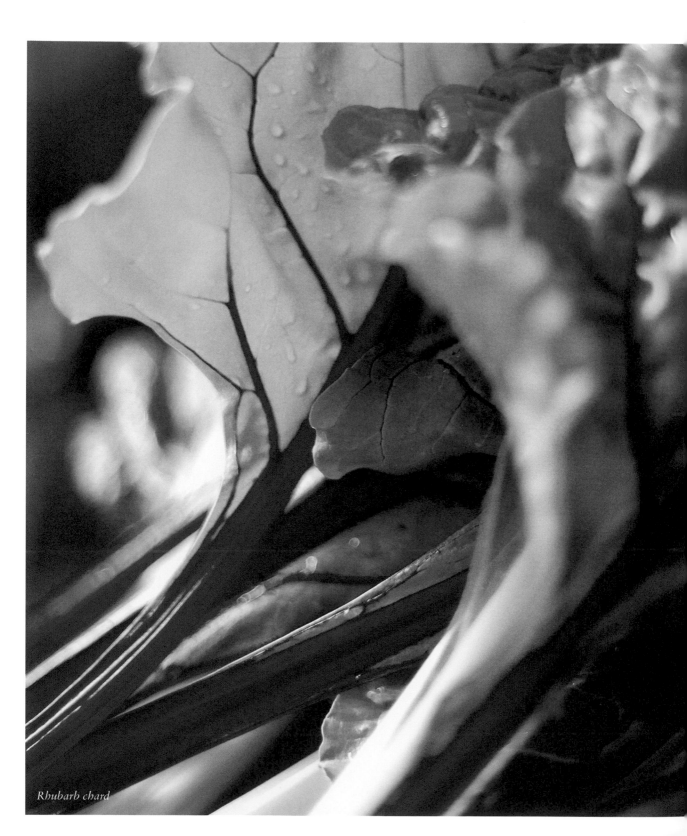

Rhubarb chard

I'M WELL AWARE that chard seems almost too dull to enthuse about. There's no instant pleasure as with freshly picked peaches, no slap of flavour like rocket, nor either the anticipation and sweetness that comes with asparagus. I'm not going to tell anyone that it lights up a meal like chilli, coriander or basil either.

I do love its dreary little vegetable ass though. It quietly produces reliably all year round without asking great skill of the gardener, and if you take a knife to harvest it an inch or two above the base, it will grow fresh leaves almost indefinitely. It is pretty much the perfect backing band to all the other harvests that come and go through the year.

It's weirdly beautiful too. Enjoying a coffee in the height of the colour, flower and life of the mid-July veg patch last year, I kept returning to the chard. A beautifully clean block of unnibbled leaves is a rare pleasure – there's always a flea beetle or a slug perforating the greenery – and dull as it may sound, that perfect square of chard was the finest sight in the garden. That may have been the moment I passed into middle age.

Something that can be eaten all year round can easily be taken for granted without recipes to suit the seasons. In spring, I'll use the young chard leaves raw in salads; in summer, shredded and stir-fried with chilli and garlic on bruschetta; in autumn, I use it in hearty pasta sauces and as a side veg; in winter, often as not it will be with lamb or chicken, in pies or instead of the Savoy cabbage in the recipe on page 64.

It is, in the kitchen at least, two vegetables, as the stalk and leafy parts have very different flavours and textures. Although great together – soften the stalks ahead of wilting the leaf – I often use the stalk one day and the leaf the next. Pickling the stems might seem like a pointless palaver, but trust me enough to try it once and you'll do it all the time – its texture and vinegar/sweetness are lovely with lamb.

CHARD

Site Unfussy but prefers rich, moisture-retentive, free-draining soil

Sow March–September

Harvest All year

Notes Early sowing under cover, plant out 6 weeks later. Sow direct in April, then again in August for winter picking

Picked chard stems (page 82)
Stir-fried chard leaves (page 80)

CONTRARY LITTLE VEG that it is, Babington's leek starts growing in October, flourishing around New Year, and is usually ready to harvest from late February when it looks like a slim leek. The flavour is a little sweeter than regular leek, and is balanced with a gentle garlickiness.

It is a perennial and native to our seashores, which means it's as tough as old boots and very easy to grow – once the plant is established in a well-drained, sunny spot, it can either be split into smaller plants or left to clump up. I tend to leave mine to get on with it, then dig up part of the tight little colony and move some to other areas I'd like them to inhabit.

Harvesting is a wintry affair. I pick most, slicing above the base to allow them to regrow, in February and early March. Any left will throw up long arcing stems in May, on the end of which glorious flowers and seed heads develop in summer to be revealed when the papery outer sheds. The bees love them as much as I do. The little florets are very good scattered over pizzas and salads, providing tiny, intense, garlicky onion punctuation.

BABINGTON'S LEEK

Site Sunny, most soils

Harvest February–March

Notes Florets in summer are wonderful for pizzas, salads and mayo. Outermost leaves are sometimes tough

Babington's leek, walnut & goat's cheese tart (page 69)

CHERVIL ROOT AND PARSLEY ROOT

Site Not too dry or shady

Sow Direct in October–November or March

Harvest September–February

Notes Sow either closely in lines to thin later or spaced 8–10cm apart and just cover with fine soil or compost

Root crisps (page 60)

WHEN I WAS A NIPPER, I'd put a handful of crisps in my pyjama pocket whenever the possibility presented itself, in the hope of a sneaky under-duvet midnight feast. I was rather overfond of Frazzles and Bacon Wheat Crunchies. And of course salt and vinegar crisps. It is a peculiarity of that flavour that most love it up to the age of thirteen, go right off it until their mid-thirties and then remember how great it is.

Were I the sort to still wear pyjamas to bed (and unless you're Morecambe and Wise that's only one step away from tucking your shirt into your pants), I would be smuggling two new flavours of crisp to bed.

Firstly, chervil root. Another of those vegetables that is inexplicably unknown in Britain yet well loved across the Channel. I tried it for the first time only recently and it is as good as any vegetable I've eaten: sweet (but not in the way that squash can sometimes overdo), chestnutty and gently earthy.

Secondly, parsley root. Also known as Hamburg parsley, it is as old as the hills yet has somehow slipped off the culinary map. The flavour is a far superior version of the offspring you would expect from a carrot and celery.

Roasting brings out the best of these two roots beautifully, and both make a fine purée, as with Jerusalem artichokes (see page 66). The first thing I did with them was make crisps and I still think this shows them off at their best. They were equally, differently delicious.

They are easy to grow too. Chervil root needs around 8 weeks of cold to germinate so I either sow direct in autumn or store the seed in the fridge before sowing in March. I sow parsley root from early March when the soil is just thinking about warming up. Both are ready to lift from September to early February. Parsley roots tend to be the size of small parsnips/medium carrots, while chervil roots are more like small Jerusalem artichokes or baby new potatoes. Both will keep for a month or more in a cool, dark room, with chervil's flavour often improving for a period in storage.

Parsley root

March

March may not be a wild time of high harvesting, but what there is – largely shoots and leaves, part foraged, part domesticated – is particularly fine. After February's unwelcome cold, I feel I get the place (and my energy for it) back in March.

46

The perennial garden wakes up with garlic cress, sorrel, Egyptian walking onions, sea kale and sweet cicely coming through, the nearby woods begin to fill with early wild garlic, and the field boundaries flush with the first nettles. In a warm year the first forced rhubarb will be on its way to go with the last of the stored apples and pears, Purple Cape cauliflower and the end of the sprouting broccoli.

More often than not March is where the baton hands over between winter and spring, the end of last year's food and the start of this. As the days lengthen, the hens return to laying, the dawn squawk becomes a chorus and the evenings become ours. I want to be outside again.

March is a little random in Devon. Spring can arrive early and hot enough to eat outside then vanish under a cloak of frost, or conveniently step through the gears from winter into early spring. Either way, the tractor will come out of the barn for the first time since October, the grass will be shorn and the strimmer will deal with the edges the mower can't reach.

I have a love/hate relationship with the strimmer. The prospect of giving an overgrown area a haircut gets me disproportionately excited, yet something invariably goes wrong. Today, all went well – I cleared a vast area around the Szechuan peppers – until I failed to observe the third of the simple rules of strimmer operation.

1 Wear the appropriate safety equipment (goggles, ear defenders, harness), even if strimming for a short time.

2 Always take the petrol can with you... You WILL run out of fuel with approximately half a square metre left to cut.

3 Never strim so quickly or enthusiastically that you breathe at all heavily, or you'll breathe through your mouth at precisely the same time that you strim an unsuspecting frog or slug.

— 26 March, 2009

I scribbled an inventory of the polytunnel, which holds so many of the plants I have yet to get out from last year, even the year before, and some I've dug up over winter for relocating. The apricot is covered in about-to-burst blossom and the daylilies are ready to plant out. I counted the Szechuan pepper plants (40 large, 35 small) and spiked myself in the finger with one of the prickles that had fallen into the compost in its pot. I'm not sure why but they hurt more than most other prickles.

But there is a malady that can afflict the gardener which while not painful is a little weird. Phantom Hat Syndrome occurs when you've been wearing a hat all day, come in, remove the hat, go to make a cup of tea and reach up to take your hat off, only to find you're clutching a mop of your own hair – the hat, though removed, has left a trace of itself on your head. For hours it can feel like it's still there.

— 8 March, 2010

Tomato seedlings in the polytunnel

Rhubarb forcers

MANY POCKETS of the farm have a spiritual 'home': the pecans from the river deltas of the southern states of America, the peppers from Szechuan province in China, the Mexican tarragon, the Japanese wineberry and so on. For a few weeks in March it is Yorkshire that dominates.

In a frost pocket between Wakefield, Rothwell and Morley lies the Rhubarb Triangle. Within its three sides, the combination of landform, soil, climate, water and ingenuity has for a couple of centuries produced the world's finest rhubarb. As well as the rhubarb we know and love, there is an early form grown in the triangle, where stalks are 'forced' from the heart of the plant. Dormant in the winter's cold, the plants are dug up and relocated to warm dark sheds. The warmth convinces the plant that spring has arrived, but the absence of light for photosynthesis confuses it into using its own starch stores to drive growth. Long, pale pink stalks with lemon coloured leaves emerge, the stalks sweeter than 'normal' rhubarb, because the plant's starches have been converted to sugars in the process.

It is one of the year's most precious harvests and I wouldn't be without it. A warm shed I don't have, but ceramic rhubarb forcers – tall pots with lids – partially replicate the ideal conditions by excluding light and keeping off the worst of the cold. This creates a microclimate within that hurries the stalks into emerging – a pile of fresh manure around the outside speeds things up by releasing heat as it breaks down. The result is sweet and delicious rhubarb, one of the highlights of the year, and a welcome return to fresh fruit after the stored apples and pears through the cold months.

Our clutch of rhubarb plants (Timperley Early, Champagne, Raspberry Red and Victoria) produce over a long period from early to late season, but the earliest – Timperley Early and Champagne – are best suited to the rhubarb forcers. The process depletes the plant of reserves, so it needs to recover for the rest of the season and only be harvested as 'regular' rhubarb (rather than being forced again) the following year.

We use the stalks simply, cooking them gently – a slow, low roast with orange zest to go with pannacotta, or simply with yoghurt, brings out their best.

FORCED RHUBARB

Site	Sunny, well manured
Harvest	February–April
Notes	Divide large plants in winter – creates more and reinvigorates them

Pannacotta with orange & rosemary roasted rhubarb (page 87)

Rhubarb daiquiri (page 92)

Spring into summer pudding (page 175)

A FEW YEARS AGO I planted three sweet cicely plants in different corners of the perennial garden and I soon had thirty or so joining the dots between. Sweet cicely self-seeds like crazy, which to my mind is a very fine thing.

The seeds are deliciously aniseed, sweet and particularly beautiful – narrow 2–3cm batons, star-shaped in profile and full of flavour. The plants spread less every year as I come up with more recipes for the seeds. As with the fern-like leaves, they have the ability to sweeten and enhance while not dominating with their aniseed. Any sharp fruit – rhubarb and gooseberries, in particular – is complemented perfectly by sweet cicely,

SWEET CICELY

Site	Semi-shade
Sow	March–October
Harvest	Leaves: April–September; Seeds: July–October
Notes	Seeds only viable for a year – buy fresh

50

allowing you to use less sugar than you might otherwise. The seeds and leaves also lift the wonderful early shoots and leaves that are around in spring – Good King Henry, asparagus and bamboo, along with any of the early spinaches and other leaves, make a fine lunch.

There are a few aniseed herbs – fennel, anise hyssop and sweet cicely are my favourites – and though aniseed may not be everyone's cup of tea, I have a theory, based on highly unscientific studies of those trying it while on one of my courses, that as with beetroot, aniseed is one of those flavours that people set themselves against at an early age and surprise themselves by liking when older. I mean, who doesn't like aniseed when they taste it in basil?

Stir-fried asparagus & Good King Henry (page 158)

Sweet cicely shortbread (page 180)

WILD GARLIC

Site Shade/semi-shade

Harvest March–July

Notes Leaves at their most succulent before you can feel the front and back of the leaf move separately when rubbed between your fingers

Spring herb omelette (page 155)

Wild garlic ravioli (page 70)

Wild garlic risotto (page 72)

THERE IS A SHARP HILL not far from here where the Gruffalo lived when my daughter was young and the most perfect light runs through the autumnal beech. In March, sometimes even late February, this has a swathe of wild garlic that draws us with basket and knives.

A quarter of an hour picking, in the early spring light with that bright scent in the nose, is one of those family moments I hang the year on. We might only gasp up the hill two or three times each spring but it sticks in the memory like bonfire night. Nell rolls wads of leaves into her pockets as much as the basket, nibbling on the odd leaf as she picks. She's as distracted by a gadget as the next eight year old but the adventure of a wild harvest, especially something she can eat while she picks, has excited her from an early age. The rest of the day is swallowed up with making pesto and wild garlic ravioli, Candida and me as kitchen assistants to Nell as she reads the recipe and orders us about.

Wild garlic is easy to identify: a few plants (including Lily of the Valley) look superficially like it, but none have its characteristic smell. The bulb, leaves and flowers are all edible, but the young leaves have the best texture and flavour.

I use the leaves raw or with minimal cooking – they lose much of their flavour if cooked for too long and become bitter on drying. I find wild garlic bulbs disappointing in flavour, size and texture, so I cut the leaves and leave the roots undisturbed to grow again. The flowers are very good tempura-ed or for adding a little punch and contrast in leafy salads.

I immerse the leaves in cold water for 5 minutes (essential before eating, unless you're happy – as my daughter seems to be – to play Russian roulette with the local weeing dog population). As with salad leaves, it also conditions the leaves, giving them a longer shelf life. Drained, spun-dry and bagged, they will last at least a week in the bottom of the fridge.

Wild garlic can be tamed – it is easy to grow from bulbs or young plants, favouring a damp, shady spot, as it does in its natural woodland habitat. The deeper the shade, the longer it will crop for – into July with luck. As soon as the heat strikes, it retreats into its bulb until early spring.

wild garlic

Rocket micros

MICROS ARE A REAL TRIUMPH of flavour and pleasure over heft. Grown to just 5–6cm, with only the first leaves showing, they have an intensity of flavour far beyond their fully-grown selves.

Rocket, radish, fennel and coriander, in particular, are the ones I grow most of. Each has its own characteristic flavour, yet more intense and cleaner as a micro than at the size it's usually harvested.

I grow them throughout the year in the polytunnel, with some on a sunny windowsill, in a metre-long length of guttering, three-quarters filled with compost and with parcel tape at either end to stop the compost washing out when watered. I dedicate a quarter each to rocket, radish, coriander and one other that takes my fancy at the time. Sown in winter, they're ready in around a fortnight, half that when sown in the summer.

Coriander takes longest to germinate but it is the prince of them all. When it reaches 6cm in height, a single seedling, its roots brushed free of compost, is an airbag of flavour, releasing what would take a mouthful of regular coriander to impersonate. The flavour is simply better when the plant is so tiny: it has everything of regular coriander in bright abundance yet without that occasional, unpleasant soapiness that gets in the way when the plant reaches full size. The fresh, intense flavour from that single micro will easily last 15 minutes of gentle chewing.

Micros are best uncooked, so I use them to liven up a leafy salad or as a garnish – especially for baked fish.

MICROLEAVES

Site Seed compost

Sow All year

Harvest All year

Notes Coriander good plucked from the soil – the roots have a lovely intense flavour

Baked mackerel with coriander micros (page 144)

Cauliflower pakoras with raita (page 58)

WE BEGAN KEEPING CHICKENS on a chilly early spring day at a local auction, bidding, as newcomers often do, for the prettiest birds. Those three adults came here in a cardboard box to find the grass on its way up, the temperature warming and the days lengthening.

Since then, we've added to them with chicks, more adults and the odd clutch of eggs to be incubated under a broody hen or in the incubator. Raising chicks from eggs is hugely rewarding – just 3 weeks under the hen or in the warmth of the incubator is all it takes for wet feathered chicks to emerge. After a period in a brooder – essentially a warm box in which they can develop safely – they are ready for outdoor life.

Hatching eggs aren't guaranteed for fertility and there is no way of predicting which sex chick will emerge. As with sowing seedlings, if you anticipate a few not emerging you are unlikely to be surprised.

Like many who raise chickens from hatching eggs, we over-order intentionally. Not all will hatch, and (assuming the law of averages) around half of those that emerge will be cocks and half hens – the girls will lay eggs, the boys clearly not. What you will do with the males is something to decide before you order the eggs.

Of course, a cockerel can do wonders for a flock – chickens enjoy a hierarchy, and the cockerel provides the domineering apex of that pyramid – but two cocks will almost certainly fight, often seriously.

CHICKEN

Source As eggs to incubate, or as chicks or adults

Feed Pellets, occasional corn and some access to grass

Notes Early spring is the perfect time to start with eggs, chicks or adults, with the grass growing, days lengthening and laying rates increasing. Chicken house required

Some varieties (including some of the Maran hybrids) have good laying hens as well as cockerels that grow well for meat, which gives you the option to give the males a full and happy life before a gentle roasting. This is, to my mind, the best option of all. It may be the most practical too, as chickens are usually hard to sex until a few months old.

Raising chicks to eat on a domestic scale is rarely rewarding financially but in every other sense it is. The cockerels are unlikely to become aggressive towards each other (or you) before they have grown large enough to eat, by which time they will have had a fine life scratching about and playing and entertaining anyone with idle time to watch. The flavour and texture of a home-raised bird is incredible.

If you're a vegetarian who eats eggs, let me encourage you to consider raising the cockerels for someone else to eat. Those born in commercial egg production are usually dispatched, so whether you buy eggs from the supermarket or raise chicks yourself, cockerels are in the equation. Raise them yourself for others to eat and they have the chance of a happy life, and live much longer than they might otherwise have.

If you do keep a cockerel for your flock, do bear in mind that they can, as can all us males, grow into cantankerous old buggers, often with little warning.

Dear Henry

You are magnificent. With your fine squawk, splendid plumage and confident swagger, you cut an impressive figure. You rule the roost. I take my rather knackered straw sun hat off to you Henry.

You have, like many before you, become too enchanted with your own magnificence. Your manly demeanour started to give way to random aggression, your evocative calling of the dawn turned to day-long wailing, your occasional not-entirely-successful attempts at the amorous arts replaced by digging your sharp spurs into the ladies. You started scaring my daughter with unpredictable charges, then my wife. Charges became rabid attacks, throwing yourself into the fence repeatedly in an attempt to get at anyone passing by.

Henry, you've become a pain in the arse. I wonder what has turned you this way. Can it be the dawning of spring and the rising of the sap? Perhaps you're feeling a little more frisky than normal in this unseasonal sunshine Henry. You wouldn't be the only one. But you know what Henry, when my daughter can't collect the eggs, my wife can't clean out the hen house and you're starting to hurt the egg-laying ladies, things cannot stay like that.

Henry, the living daylights were strangled out of you last night while you were snoozy. I'm truly sorry. It was, however, the best of a short series of options. Tonight you rest in the fridge awaiting red wine, perennial herbs and Gas Mark 4.

Bye bye Henry. It was fun before you became a total bastard.
— 31 March, 2012

Recipes for

January, February & March

Cauliflower pakoras with raita

I could eat these pakoras every day, they are so good. The batter works equally well coating Romanesco, calabrese, sliced onions and most root veg. I usually eat them with the minty, poppy seed raita, below, and/or sweet chilli dipping sauce on page 262.

Serves 3–4

1 medium cauliflower

3 onions

140g chickpea flour

1 tsp bicarbonate of soda

1 tsp ground cumin

1 tsp ground turmeric

1 tsp ground ginger

1 tsp garam masala

1 tsp salt

About 100ml water

Sunflower oil for deep-frying

For the raita

300ml natural yoghurt

A handful of mint leaves, finely shredded

2 tsp poppy seeds

To serve

Sea salt and freshly ground black pepper

A good sprinkling of coriander microleaves, or a half-handful of coriander, finely chopped

For the raita, combine the yoghurt, mint and poppy seeds in a bowl.

Remove and discard the outer leaves and stalk from the cauliflower, then cut it into 1cm pieces. Finely slice the onions.

To make the batter, sift the flour, bicarbonate soda, ground spices and salt together into a large bowl. Add most of the water and mix into the flour with your fingertips, adding more of the water a little at a time, if needed, to form a thickish batter (think pricey emulsion).

Heat the oil for deep-frying in a suitable large, deep, heavy pan (it should fill no more than one-third of the pan) to about 170°C. To test the temperature, drop a small cube of bread into the oil – it should fizz and brown in around a minute.

Toss the onions and cauliflower together in a bowl. Add the batter and turn the vegetables to coat well.

You will need to cook the pakoras in batches to ensure you don't crowd the pan; I usually cook three at a time. Carefully ease a spoonful of the mixture into the hot oil. When it begins to cook, add a couple more. Turn the pakoras occasionally so that they cook and colour evenly. This should take 7–10 minutes. When they are golden brown and cooked through, lift them out with a slotted spoon onto kitchen paper to drain. Keep hot while you cook the rest.

Sprinkle the pakoras with a little sea salt, pepper and coriander, and serve with the minty raita.

Root crisps

The fact that most of us don't know who invented crisps is, frankly, a failure of the school syllabus. It seems it was either George Crum or Eliza Acton (depending who you believe), as recently as the mid 1800s. It makes you wonder what people ate for centuries before with their chosen brew.

Crisps are simple to make. Potatoes, celeriac, parsnip, Jerusalem artichokes and salsify all work well, but nothing touches chervil root and parsley root. Whatever the veg, the process is the same.

Root veg of your choice (see above)

Sunflower oil for deep-frying

To serve

Caster sugar

Ground cinnamon, mixed spice or garam masala

Sea salt and freshly ground black pepper

Wash the root veg and pat dry with kitchen paper, then pare into long, fine strips, using a vegetable peeler.

Heat a 5cm depth of sunflower oil in a fairly wide, heavy pan over a medium heat to about 170°C; the oil should come no more than a third of the way up the side of the pan. To test the temperature, drop a small cube of bread into the oil – it should fizz and brown in around a minute. If the oil is too hot, the crisps turn very dark and bitter, so turn down the heat and let it cool a little if you need to.

Carefully add a handful of the vegetable strips – not too many at once, as they need some room. Fry, turning them once in a while with a slotted spoon, until they're lightly browned all over. Lift them out onto kitchen paper to drain, keeping chervil root and parsley root crisps separate.

When most of the oil has drained but a trace remains, dust the chervil root crisps with salt and black pepper, and the parsley root with caster sugar and cinnamon or mixed spice. Try them the other way round if you like, or with garam masala, or whatever else you fancy.

Chorizo, borlotti & cabbage soup

A hearty lunch or a warming supper that's full of flavour and a contrast of fabulous textures – as much a stew as a soup really. It's very adaptable to what's around so throw in some cooked pasta or rice, and/or serve with good bread. If there's some left over for a lunch after supper the night before, it's the sort of thing I'm looking forward to all morning.

If you're using dried borlotti beans – a fine winter staple for soups and stews – soak them in cold water to cover overnight. Drain and place in a saucepan with plenty of fresh water. Bring to a simmer and cook for about 45 minutes until the beans are tender.

Serves 4

3 tbsp olive oil

90g cooking chorizo, sliced

2 large red onions, sliced

130g carrots, cut into batons

1 celery stick, finely sliced, or a good pinch of ground lovage seeds

3 garlic cloves, chopped

1 bay leaf

A handful of thyme sprigs

700ml chicken stock

400g tin chopped tomatoes

260g fresh borlotti beans (or use cooked dried or tinned beans)

½ Savoy cabbage, cored and sliced

Sea salt and freshly ground black pepper

To serve

A handful of parsley, finely chopped

Heat the olive oil in a large pan over a medium heat, add the chorizo and cook until it starts to crisp, flipping each piece over as it cooks. Remove and set aside on kitchen paper.

Add the onions, carrots and celery, if using, to the pan and cook for 7 minutes or so, stirring occasionally. Add the garlic, bay leaf, thyme and lovage seeds, if using, and cook for a couple of minutes, stirring often.

Pour in the stock and the tomatoes and bring up to a simmer. Add the fresh beans, if using, and simmer for 15 minutes.

Add half of the cabbage (with the cooked dried or tinned beans, if using) and simmer for 5 minutes. Add the chorizo and the rest of the cabbage, and cook for a further 4 minutes. Remove the thyme sprigs.

Season the soup with salt and pepper to taste and serve, scattered with chopped parsley.

Chicken & Savoy cabbage in cider

I love a Savoy cabbage as much for its crinkled looks – deep seaweed green, to pale and purpled – as its flavour. Beautiful as they are, the wrinkly leaves can be a refuge for those little maggoty, pale grey slugs, so shred them and give them a decent soak in a sinkful of cold water. Any slugs will float up – to be skimmed off and fed to the chickens.

If I'm feeling lazy, I add the cabbage to the casserole 50 minutes into the cooking, rather than adding it to the cidery liquid at the end.

Serves 4

25g butter

About 6 tbsp olive oil

1.6kg chicken, jointed into 8 pieces

150g pancetta or unsmoked streaky bacon, cut into small cubes

400g red onions, finely sliced

8 garlic cloves, chopped

A large handful of thyme sprigs

4 bay leaves

4 tbsp brandy (apple brandy if you have it)

750ml dry cider

½ Savoy cabbage, shredded

50–100ml double cream

Sea salt and freshly ground black pepper

To serve

A handful of parsley, finely chopped

Heat the butter and half of the olive oil in a frying pan, and colour the chicken pieces in batches on both sides, seasoning with salt and pepper as you go and adding more oil to the pan as necessary. When golden, lift the chicken pieces out onto kitchen paper to drain, then into a casserole dish large enough to hold them all in a single layer.

Fry the pancetta in the pan until lightly coloured, remove with a slotted spoon onto kitchen paper to drain briefly, then add to the casserole.

Add the onions to the pan and cook gently for 15 minutes until fairly soft, stirring frequently to ensure they only colour lightly. Add the garlic, thyme and bay and cook for a couple of minutes, then add to the chicken.

Add the brandy to the frying pan, stirring and scraping to deglaze, then add to the chicken and pour in the cider. Cover and simmer gently for an hour. Check that the chicken is tender and the juices run clear when you pierce the thickest part of the thigh with a skewer. If not, cook for another 10 minutes and check again. Once cooked, lift the chicken, pancetta and onions out into a warm serving dish and cover to keep warm.

Bring the cooking liquid to a simmer, add the shredded cabbage and cook for 5–8 minutes until just a little firm still. Lift it out of the liquid and add to the chicken in the dish. Reduce the cidery liquid a little, then discard the herbs. Whisk in a little cream – how much depends on the amount and strength of the cooking liquid you have in the pan. Allow it to bubble over the heat for a couple of minutes, stirring occasionally.

Pour the sauce over the chicken and serve, sprinkled with chopped parsley.

Chicken, celeriac & leek pie

You need a pie or two in January and February to get you through. This one is easy, quick and delicious and one of my favourite ways of using leftover roast chicken. The cider can be replaced with wine, the celeriac with other root veg – parsnip works particularly well.

Serves 4

2 good-sized leeks, well washed

500g celeriac

25g butter

1 tbsp olive oil

1 onion, chopped

3 garlic cloves, finely chopped

Finely grated zest of 1 unwaxed lemon

160ml dry cider

2 tbsp plain flour, plus extra for dusting

320ml chicken or vegetable stock

400g cooked leftover chicken

130ml double cream

500g packet puff pastry

1 free-range egg, lightly beaten

Sea salt and freshly ground black pepper

Cut the leeks into thin slices. Peel the celeriac and cut into 1cm cubes.

Heat the butter and olive oil in a large pan and gently fry the onion and leeks until soft, stirring frequently. Add the garlic and cook for a further few minutes, stirring to prevent burning.

Add the celeriac, lemon zest and cider and simmer until the liquid is reduced down to a quarter of its original volume.

Sprinkle in the flour and then stir into the reduced liquor. Add the stock gradually, stirring constantly. Season with salt and pepper, then add the chicken. Cover and simmer gently for 10 minutes, stirring a couple of times. Add the cream, stir, and cook uncovered for 7–8 minutes, stirring once or twice.

Transfer the filling mixture to a 22cm round pie dish, about 6cm deep (or other dish with a similar capacity) and leave to cool.

Preheat the oven to 210°C/Gas 6–7.

Roll the pastry out on a lightly floured surface until slightly larger than the pie dish. Brush the rim of the pie dish with beaten egg, lay the pastry on top, trim off the excess and press the pastry against the rim.

Use a knife to make a small hole in the centre of the pie to allow steam to escape, and brush the pastry with beaten egg. Place in the oven and cook for 10 minutes, then lower the oven setting to 190°C/Gas 5 and cook for a further 20–25 minutes until the pastry is crisp and golden brown. Delicious served with mashed potato and kale.

Lamb chops with chicory
& Jerusalem artichoke purée

I like chops pretty much any way, but this may just be my favourite. They are so good with the sweetness of the Jerusalem artichokes and the gentle bitterness of the chicory. For the purée, you can use celeriac, parsnip or even potato in place of the Jerusalem artichokes.

Serves 4

100g plain flour

4 free-range eggs, lightly beaten

100g breadcrumbs

60g hazelnuts, toasted and crushed

A good handful of thyme, leaves only

8 small lamb chops

About 300ml groundnut oil for shallow-frying

4 heads of chicory, halved lengthways

A little olive oil

Juice of ½ lemon

For the Jerusalem artichoke purée

500g Jerusalem artichokes

50ml chicken or vegetable stock

200ml double cream

30g butter

A good grating of fresh nutmeg

Sea salt and freshly ground black pepper

To serve

A handful of parsley, finely chopped

For the Jerusalem artichoke purée, half-fill a large pan with water and bring to the boil. Peel the artichokes and cut them into pieces around the size of a pound coin, then add to the pan. Simmer until tender – usually around 15 minutes, though this can vary.

Meanwhile, put the flour and eggs into separate shallow dishes. Mix the breadcrumbs, hazelnuts and thyme together in a third shallow bowl. Season the chops, then dip each in turn into the flour, the egg and the herby breadcrumbs so that both sides of the chops are coated.

Drain the artichokes, return to the pan and add the stock, cream, butter and a good seasoning of salt, pepper and nutmeg. Stir and warm slowly to a gentle simmer, cooking for 5 minutes or so. Cover and keep warm.

Add the oil to a frying pan to a depth of around 1cm, and place over a medium heat. When the oil is hot, hold each chop by the bone and lay it carefully into the oil, away from you to avoid splashing yourself. Don't crowd the pan – better to cook the chops in batches and keep them warm while the rest cook. Cook steadily but not too quickly – it should take 7–8 minutes to brown the breadcrumbs well. Turn over when brown and cook the other side. Drain on kitchen paper and keep warm if necessary.

While the chops are cooking, put a char-grill pan on a medium-high heat (or use a frying pan). Lightly coat the chicory halves in olive oil, season with salt and pepper and place them cut side down in the pan. Once char-lined and slightly wilted, turn them over and cook the other side.

When the chops are cooked, purée the artichokes with their creamy sauce in a blender. Taste and season further if needed. Spoon a generous dollop or two of artichoke purée onto each plate, add two chops and two chicory halves. Add a generous squeeze of lemon juice and sprinkle with parsley.

Beef in beer

The cold months call for the sort of food that you can put on to cook before you go out and return to a warm, welcoming home full of glorious smells. Most beers work well here – I make it most often with the local Otter Bright, whereas Guinness makes a much darker, richer stew. It's especially good served with celeriac mustard mash (page 73) and stir-fried chard leaves (page 80).

The recipe is very forgiving, so tweak timings and temperatures to suit: cook over the working day on 120°C/Gas 1, and if you leave it too long it'll get beautifully treacly as the onions darken and dissolve.

Serves 4

2 tbsp olive oil

2 large onions, sliced

3 celery sticks, chopped

1 leek, well washed and finely sliced

2 carrots, diced

6 garlic cloves, chopped

8 mild fruity chillies, such as Apricot, halved lengthways, or a few peppers, cored, deseeded and sliced

A splash of Marsala or sherry

500g brisket or silverside, diced

1 tbsp plain flour

400g tin chopped tomatoes

500ml light ale

4 bay leaves

Sea salt and freshly ground black pepper

Preheat the oven to 180°C/Gas 4.

Warm the olive oil in a heavy-based pan over a medium heat. Add the onions and cook for 5 minutes, stirring frequently. Add the celery, leek and carrots and cook until all the vegetables are soft. Stir well and add the garlic and chillies, or peppers if using. Cook for another few minutes. Add a splash of Marsala or sherry and sizzle for a minute, stirring once or twice.

Add the beef and sprinkle in the flour, stir, then add the tomatoes, beer and bay leaves. Season well with salt and pepper. Bring to a simmer, then cover and transfer to the oven.

Cook for 2 hours, then turn the oven down to 170°C/Gas 3 and cook for another hour until the meat is very tender.

Babington's leek, walnut & goat's cheese tart

Babington's leek may have been invented for this tart. The hint of garlic alongside its leekiness is perfect here. This tart is equally, if differently, delicious with regular leeks, though you may want to add a clove or two of garlic in with the leeks when cooking. Either way, the leeks should shine through with the nuts and cheese as little pockets of flavour.

Serves 6

For the pastry

125g plain flour, plus extra for dusting

A pinch of salt

75g unsalted butter, chilled and cut into small cubes

1 free-range egg, separated

3–4 tbsp cold milk

For the filling

25g butter

20ml olive oil

600g Babington's leeks, well washed and finely sliced

A few sprigs of thyme, leaves only

70g hard goat's cheese, such as Village Green, cut into cubes

30g walnuts, broken into pieces

2 free-range eggs, plus 2 extra yolks

200ml double cream

100ml full-fat milk

Sea salt and freshly ground black pepper

Grease and lightly flour a 23cm tart tin.

To make the pastry, put the flour, salt and butter in a food processor and pulse until the mixture forms coarse breadcrumbs. With the motor running, add the egg yolk, then gradually add just enough milk for the dough to come together, stopping the machine as soon as it does. Gather the pastry and form it into a ball on a lightly floured surface. Pat to flatten slightly to a disc, wrap in cling film and chill in the fridge for 30 minutes.

Meanwhile, preheat the oven to 170°C/Gas 3 and get on with the filling. Heat the butter and olive oil in a large frying pan over a low heat. Add the leeks, thyme and a pinch of salt and cook slowly, stirring regularly; don't rush this – you want a creamy sweetness without a hint of browning.

Roll the pastry out thinly on a lightly floured surface and use to line the tart tin. Prick the base all over with a fork and line the case with baking parchment and baking beans. Bake for 15 minutes, then remove from the oven and take out the parchment and beans. Use a serrated knife to trim off any excess pastry. Lightly beat the egg white (left over from the pastry) and brush sparingly over the inside of the pastry case to seal. Bake for a further 5 minutes, then set aside to cool slightly.

Spread the leeks evenly over the base of the pastry case, dot with the cheese and scatter over the walnuts. Briefly whisk the whole eggs, egg yolks, cream and milk together and slowly pour into the tart – it should fill to just under the rim of the pastry. Grind plenty of pepper over the top and bake for about 30 minutes until nicely golden.

Allow the tart to cool just a little before serving. It is also very fine cold. A leafy green salad with a nice sharp dressing is great with it.

Wild garlic ravioli

Ravioli is hugely pleasurable to make – well worth the time it takes – and the flavour and texture leave ready-made pasta in the shade. If I'm thinking ahead, I'll take it a step further and make labneh to use instead of the ricotta. It's so effortless: upturn a pot of yoghurt into a sieve lined with muslin and the liquid will seep through overnight, leaving you with a semi-firm, delicate curd cheese that is utterly delicious.

Serves 4 (for lunch)

For the pasta

250g '00' flour

2 free-range eggs, plus 1 extra yolk

About 1–2 tbsp water

A good pinch of salt

For the filling

500g wild garlic leaves

100g ricotta

1 tbsp freshly grated Parmesan

A good grating of fresh nutmeg

Sea salt and freshly ground black pepper

To serve

Knobs of butter

Parmesan shavings

To make the pasta, put the flour in a bowl and add the eggs and egg yolk. Mix together with your hands until it forms a rough ball. Add a little water to help bring the dough together and make it pliable, but don't worry if it's still quite hard at this stage. Knead for 5–10 minutes until smooth and then wrap in a damp cloth and put aside to rest while you make the filling. The pasta will become much more workable after this.

For the filling, rinse the wild garlic in cold water and drain. Place in a pan, cover and cook in the water that clings to the leaves until only just wilted. Drain very well – rolling the cooked leaves in a tea towel and wringing the water out is very effective. Once drained, chop the leaves quite finely and then mix with the ricotta, Parmesan and nutmeg, salt and pepper to taste.

Divide the pasta into 4 equal portions and roll into sausages. Re-wrap three of these, then roll out the fourth. Use a rolling pin on a floured board to flatten your sausage enough to go fairly easily through a pasta machine. Take the pasta through each setting until you reach the finest setting and then place it on a damp cloth. Repeat this process with the other three sausages. (If you do not have a pasta machine you can roll the dough out very thinly using a rolling pin on a floured surface.)

Place teaspoonfuls of the filling down the length of a pasta sheet, leaving plenty of space to cut and seal the parcels on either side. Dampen the pasta surrounding the filling and lay another pasta sheet on top, pressing all around the filling to seal it. Repeat with the rest of the pasta and filling. Cut into parcels and cook in boiling salted water for 3–4 minutes.

Drain and serve in warm bowls, topped with butter, Parmesan and pepper.

Wild garlic risotto

A perfect winter-into-spring recipe that makes the best of the wild garlic. It is hugely adaptable – beef it up by stirring through steamed sprouting broccoli, a handful of chopped parsley and/or top with a just-poached egg to serve. Alternatively, you can substitute the wild garlic with spinach, kale, Mexican tree spinach or other leafy greens, adding a little chopped garlic with the pearled spelt.

Serves 4

130g butter, cut into cubes
2 shallots, finely chopped
350g pearled spelt or risotto rice
800ml chicken or vegetable stock
120ml dry white wine
120g wild garlic leaves, shredded
60g Parmesan, freshly grated
Sea salt and freshly ground black pepper

Melt 50g of the butter in a heavy-based pan and cook the shallots gently, without browning, until completely soft and translucent. Add the pearled spelt and cook for a couple of minutes, stirring constantly. Meanwhile, heat the stock in a saucepan; keep it at a gentle simmer.

Add the wine to the spelt and continue to stir. When the pan is almost dry, add a ladleful of stock and let it simmer, stirring frequently, until most of it is absorbed. Continue to add stock in this way, a ladleful at a time, stirring often and allowing each addition to be almost all absorbed before adding more, until you have used about two-thirds of the stock.

Now add the wild garlic and 100ml stock, stirring until the leaves have wilted. Try the spelt: it may need a little longer – it should be cooked but still firm to the bite – and you may need some of the remaining stock. Season with salt and pepper to taste.

Once cooked, allow the risotto to rest for a minute, then add the remaining butter and the Parmesan, stirring it in vigorously – this has such an influence over the risotto's creamy lusciousness. An enthusiastic grinding of black pepper should finish it off perfectly.

Celeriac mustard mash

I guess I make celeriac mash about three times more often than I do potato mash and if you make it once, I suspect you might too. This is a perfect partner for many, many things – from fish to roast veg, to sausages or the beef stew on page 68. If you only have semi-skimmed milk, add a splosh of cream for velvetiness, and by all means stir chopped parsley through if you like.

You can use a regular masher rather than a blender – both can take the heat out of the mash, so return it to the pan for reheating if needs be.

Serves 4

1kg celeriac

60g butter

4 garlic cloves, finely chopped

450ml whole milk

Freshly grated nutmeg

3 tbsp grainy mustard

Sea salt and freshly ground black pepper

Peel the celeriac and cut into 7–10mm cubes. Melt the butter in a pan and cook the celeriac over a medium heat, stirring often, until lightly golden. Add the garlic and cook for a few minutes longer, stirring frequently. Season with salt and pepper, and pour in enough milk to just cover.

Bring to the boil, then lower the heat and simmer gently for 15–20 minutes, until the celeriac is just tender. Drain, reserving the milk. Put the celeriac into a blender and return the milk to the pan over the heat.

Purée the celeriac, adding a little of the hot milk to make a creamy mash with a little looseness to it. Add a good grating of nutmeg and the grainy mustard, and blend briefly. Taste for seasoning and add more salt and pepper if needed.

Crisp kale, beetroot, blue cheese & walnuts

Kale, crisped in the oven, is to my mind its finest incarnation. The flavours intensify and the texture is fabulous. It makes a very fine snack on its own; with beetroot, red onions and walnuts it becomes a great side; and the addition of cheese turns it into a superb lunch.

Serves 4 as a side

200g kale

2 tbsp sesame oil

1 tsp salt

4 tbsp sesame seeds, or 2 tbsp each sesame and hemp seeds

450g cooked beetroot (roasted or boiled), peeled and cut into chunks

2 red onions, finely sliced

80g walnuts, broken into pieces

A handful of parsley, main stems removed

40g Dorset Blue Vinny or similar cheese, broken into small pieces (optional)

A few twists of black pepper

Honey mustard dressing (page 164)

Preheat the oven to 180°C/Gas 4.

Tear or chop the kale into pieces and toss in a bowl with the sesame oil and salt. Spread the kale evenly between two baking sheets, keeping it in one layer. Bake until crisp, about 12–15 minutes.

Meanwhile, lightly toast the seeds in a hot dry frying pan.

Now your choice is to either mix the kale, beetroot, red onions, walnuts, parsley, cheese if using, seeds and seasoning in a large bowl and lightly coat in the dressing, or – as I mostly tend to – create a bed of the crispy kale and then layer on the remaining ingredients, scatter over the seeds and dollop with dressing to serve.

Zlatan's temptation

Jansson's Temptation is a simple, fabulous thing from Sweden, classically made with potato. My version is with celeriac and I have re-christened it after the mercurial footballer Zlatan Ibrahimovic, another thing of great wonder from Sweden, as he scored a ridiculous goal against England on the night I first cooked this. As you would imagine, this works beautifully as a side to lamb or beef but is perfectly capable of being a main with either sprouting broccoli or a leafy salad.

Serves 4

30g butter, plus a little for greasing the dish

8 anchovy fillets, plus a little of their oil

3 medium onions, very finely sliced

800g celeriac

300ml double cream

A little milk (if required)

Sea salt and freshly ground black pepper

Preheat the oven to 200°C/Gas 6.

Slowly melt half the butter in a saucepan. Add 1–2 tbsp of the anchovy oil. Add the onions and cook over a low heat, stirring occasionally, until they are very soft and without a hint of browning – this can take 20 minutes or more, so don't rush it. Watch that Zlatan goal on the internet a few times while they're cooking.

Butter a fairly shallow ovenproof dish, about 20 x 15cm. Peel the celeriac and cut into very fine slices. Layer the celeriac slices in the prepared dish up to halfway. Spoon the onions over evenly and space the anchovies on top. Carefully pour on half of the cream. Season with salt and pepper. Add the remaining celeriac in layers, followed by the rest of the cream. Season the surface and dot with the remaining butter.

Bake for 30 minutes, pressing down the top layer of celeriac into the cream a couple of times. Add a little milk to top up if needed, then turn the oven down to 180°C/Gas 4. Cook for a further 20–30 minutes, until golden, again pressing the surface down a few times to prevent the top layers drying out.

Roasted Romanesco, shallots & celeriac

The first time I made this, I ate most of it with a fork straight from the pan, in quiet self-congratulation, and had to make some more to go with the pork belly still in the oven. Thankfully slow-cooked pork belly is perfectly happy to sit where it is for another half an hour. Depending on what you're having with it, a little chilli (fresh or dried) and/or chopped garlic is good, as is lime instead of lemon, and thyme in place of rosemary.

Serves 4 as a side, or 1 hungry, impatient person

1 Romanesco

½ celeriac

16 shallots, peeled and halved

A good splosh of olive oil

2 tbsp balsamic vinegar

A few sprigs of rosemary

Juice of ½ lemon

Sea salt and freshly ground black pepper

Preheat the oven to 190°C/Gas 5.

Break or cut the Romanesco into florets. Peel and cut the celeriac into 8–10mm dice. Put the Romanesco, celeriac and halved shallots in a roasting tin and add a few tablespoonfuls of olive oil – enough to coat the veg without leaving a pool in the tin.

Splash with the balsamic vinegar, add the rosemary and toss well. Roast for 25–30 minutes, agitating the tin once or twice to lightly toss the veg in the oil and flavourings. Remove when everything is cooked and lightly charred, but still firm. Squeeze over the lemon juice and season with salt and pepper as you like.

Brussels, celeriac & red cabbage slaw

I'll eat coleslaw pretty much anytime in the year, tweaking the veg to whatever's around. With just a little cheese and/or nuts this version is substantial enough to have as a light lunch; it also makes a great side, especially with sausages or leftover chicken. The apple needs a little sharpness to it and the cheese should be lively and/or salty to punctuate the coleslaw. Crushed walnuts, hazelnuts or sultanas – thrown in just before serving – all make delicious additions.

Serves 2

150g Brussels sprouts, outer leaves removed

90g red cabbage, core removed

1 apple

50g celeriac

2 tbsp honey mustard dressing (see page 164)

30g Cheddar

A good squeeze of lemon juice

Sea salt and freshly ground black pepper

A handful of fennel tops or dill leaves

Finely slice the Brussels sprouts and cabbage and set aside.

Grate the apple into a large bowl, avoiding the core. Peel the celeriac and coarsely grate into the bowl. Immediately add the dressing and toss to coat the celeriac and apple to prevent them discolouring.

Add the Brussels sprouts and red cabbage and toss well. Crumble in the cheese, add salt and pepper and stir to combine. Taste and adjust the seasoning and add lemon juice to suit. Scatter with fennel or dill to serve.

Stir-fried chard leaves

As quick and easy as a tasty side veg gets – I make this all the time. The thick central ribs can be included if you slice them finely and stir-fry them for a few minutes before you add the leaves. And you can save the stems for pickling (see overleaf). You can sweeten the stir-fry a little or add more zing if you like – 1 tbsp balsamic vinegar or 1 tsp ground ginger and 1 tbsp soy sauce in with the chilli and garlic both work a treat.

Serves 2

25ml vegetable oil

8 good-sized chard leaves (stems removed), shredded

1 garlic clove, finely chopped

½ small medium-strength chilli, finely chopped

Sea salt and freshly ground black or Szechuan pepper

Heat the oil in a wok or large frying pan over a high heat. Add the chard leaves and stir-fry for a minute or two. Add the garlic and chilli and stir-fry for another couple of minutes.

Salt and pepper is all it needs. The result is gently, gorgeously iron-y – perfect with beef stew and anything creamy.

Pickled chard stems

Chard is pretty much two veg in one – the stiff, crisp central rib and the iron-y green leaf. If you plan to use the leafy part as leafy greens, this is my favourite way of enjoying the crunchy stems. It's delicious the day after it's made and even better after a week. If you use one of the coloured chards, such as rainbow, it will colour the vinegar beautifully.

Serves 6–8

8 good-sized chard stems

75g caster sugar

2 tbsp salt

300ml white wine vinegar

½ tsp coriander seeds

½ tsp fennel seeds

½ tsp Szechuan or black peppercorns

1 cardamom pod, bashed

1 bay leaf

Wash the chard stalks and cut them off flat at both ends.

Dissolve the sugar and salt in the wine vinegar in a saucepan over a medium heat. Add the spices and bay leaf, increase the heat and simmer for 10 minutes.

While the spicy vinegar is simmering, cut the chard stems into narrow batons – to a length that suits the jar you're using, which needs to be sterilised (see page 170). Put the chard batons in the jar.

Pour the spicy vinegar over the chard stalks and seal the jars. The pickled chard with keep for a month or so in the fridge.

Sorb jelly

I only make a few jellies – medlar, redcurrant and sorb, usually – and this is the only one I do every year, without fail. It has the perfect balance of sweet with an edge of sharpness that goes beautifully with blue cheese, pork and that enormous goose I have in the freezer for Christmas.

A blend of firm and bletted (frost-softened) fruit is perfect for making jelly – the soft fruit gives up its structure readily in a pan whereas the harder fruit gives you more pectin, which is needed to achieve a set. The core principle works for medlars and other fruit but needs tweaking depending on the fruit – redcurrants need much less simmering, for example. It is an inexact recipe even for sorbs, as the fruit is never the same, varying with the harshness of the winter and the time of year. Thankfully, however, it is a pretty forgiving process. Let this be all the encouragement you need to acquire a jam thermometer; they are hugely useful and take the guesswork out of things.

Makes about two 225g jars
About 1kg sorbs
About 500g caster sugar

Wash, de-stalk and de-leaf the sorbs. Place them in a pan, add just enough water to cover and bring slowly to the boil. Simmer for an hour and check whether they are soft. Depending on the degree of bletting, you may need to simmer them for a further hour, adding a little water to keep the fruit covered.

When the fruit starts to soften, you can use a potato masher to carefully encourage the fruit into a good mashed consistency.

Scoop the mush into a muslin, suspend it from the legs of an upturned chair or similar, and allow it to drip through into a large bowl overnight. Don't squeeze the mush through the muslin as this makes the liquid cloudy – just let it drip.

Measure the liquid. To every 600ml, add 450g caster sugar. Dissolve in a pan over medium heat, then boil until setting point is reached (105°C on a jam thermometer). Immediately pour into warm, sterilised jars (see page 170) and seal.

This jelly will keep in a cool, dark place for 12 months. Once opened, store it in the fridge and use within a month or two.

Poached pears in a spiced syrup

Poached pears are good at pretty much any time of year, especially for making the best of any stored pears that you are unlikely to eat fresh or that are reluctant to ripen – under-ripe pears are best for poaching. The cooking liquid and spices can be varied, according to what you prefer or have to hand: a bottle of dessert wine can replace the sugar, perry and water, or you can use a dry white wine with the sugar, or a mixture. The cooking time varies depending on the variety of pear and its degree of ripeness, so test them during cooking.

For a simple chocolate sauce to accompany the pears, break 170g dark chocolate into pieces and melt with 85g butter in a heatproof bowl over a pan of simmering water, stirring until smooth.

Serves 4

250g caster sugar
350ml water
350ml perry
8 firm pears
1 cinnamon stick
½ tsp cloves
1 vanilla pod, split lengthways
½ tsp black peppercorns
½ lemon
2 star anise

Dissolve the sugar in the water and perry in a large saucepan over a medium heat. Peel the pears, leaving the stalks intact, and add them to the pan, along with all the other ingredients. Make sure the pears are fully submerged – top up with water if necessary. To help keep them submerged, lay a cartouche over the surface (a piece of baking parchment a little larger than the diameter of the pan with a small hole cut in the centre to allow steam to escape).

Turn up the heat until the liquid is at a very gentle simmer – an occasional blip rather than anything too active. Let the pears cook for 12 minutes, then test with a sharp knife. Simmer them for a few minutes longer if needed and retest.

Once cooked, remove the pan from the heat and allow the pears to cool a little in the liquor. Taste the liquor: if you prefer a sweeter, more intense syrup, lift the pears out into a warm bowl using a slotted spoon and cover. Reduce the liquid by simmering for a few minutes. Sweeten if you like.

Serve the warm pears whole, or halved and with their seeds scooped out, bathed in a few spoonfuls of the aromatic syrup. Accompany with a jug of chocolate sauce (see above) or double cream and shortbread (see page 180) if you fancy.

The pears will keep in their liquid for 4–5 days in the fridge.

Pear & parsnip ice cream

I know it's cold out there, but I still want ice cream in winter and this one somehow manages to be warming, even fresh from the freezer. By all means, add a little cinnamon and/or cloves if you like, but make it without first – it's subtle yet distinctive as it is.

Serves 6

1 vanilla pod

500ml milk

300g parsnips

1 large pear, about 250g

8 free-range egg yolks

150g caster sugar

250ml double cream

Split the vanilla pod lengthways, tease out the seeds and set aside. Put the milk and vanilla pod into a pan and slowly bring up to a gentle simmer.

Meanwhile, peel the parsnips and cut into cubes. Add to the vanilla milk and simmer until tender.

While the parsnips are cooking, halve, core and peel the pear. Whisk the egg yolks and sugar together in a bowl until creamy.

Lift the cooked parsnip out of the milk with a slotted spoon and place in a blender. Add 300ml of the warm milk, the vanilla seeds and the pear, and purée until smooth.

Pour the warm parsnip and pear purée over the egg and sugar mixture, whisking as you go. Pour into a clean saucepan and stir constantly over a medium heat. The custard will gradually thicken. When it is thick enough to coat the back of the wooden spoon, remove from the heat and pour into a clean bowl.

Whisk the cream into the custard and leave to cool. Once completely cool, pour into an ice-cream maker and churn until set. Freeze unless serving straight away.

Pannacotta with orange & rosemary roasted rhubarb

I love this recipe. It makes a silky, luscious pannacotta that threatens to lose its shape but holds steady – just. It is infinitely lovelier than one made with more gelatine. Rhubarb is the perfect partner. Roasted slowly so it retains its shape, the rhubarb is paired with orange and rosemary, which add warmth and depth, while the vanilla lends fragrance.

Serves 4

For the pannacotta

A few drops of vegetable oil

3 sheets of leaf gelatine (each 4–4.5g)

450ml double cream

150ml whole milk

1 vanilla pod

90g caster sugar

For the roasted rhubarb

800g rhubarb

Grated zest and juice of 2 oranges

2 vanilla pods, split lengthways

280g caster sugar

A couple of 20cm stems of rosemary, broken into 5cm pieces

For the pannacotta, lightly oil 4 ramekins. Soak the gelatine sheets in a shallow dish of cold water to soften.

Pour the cream and milk into a pan. Split the vanilla pod lengthways, tease out the seeds and add them to the cream with the pod. Heat gently until approaching a simmer, then add the sugar and stir until it has dissolved. Bring to a bare simmer, then take off the heat and remove the vanilla pod.

Lift the gelatine sheets out of their dish, squeeze out excess water and then stir into the warm cream until fully dissolved.

Pour the mixture into the prepared ramekins. Allow to cool and then refrigerate for a minimum of 4 hours or overnight.

For the roasted rhubarb, preheat the oven to 190°C/Gas 5. Chop the rhubarb into 8cm lengths, spread them out in a roasting dish and sprinkle the orange zest over them. Use the tip of a knife to tease out some of the vanilla seeds and mix them into the sugar.

Sprinkle the vanilla sugar over the rhubarb, then spoon over the orange juice. Lay the vanilla pods and rosemary on top of the rhubarb. Cover with foil and cook in the oven for 30 minutes. Leave to cool down.

To serve, dip each ramekin briefly in hot water to loosen the pannacotta. Invert a plate on top, then turn the plate and ramekin over to release the pannacotta onto the plate.

Lift the rhubarb from the roasting dish with a slotted spoon and place alongside the pannacotta, then spoon the orange syrup over to serve.

Celeriac & lemon thyme crème brûlée

There ought to be a custodial sentence for messing with the traditional crème brûlée, but mess with it I have. Celeriac and lemon thyme sounds an unlikely combination for a brûlée, but it is, I promise, really very fine. If you haven't any lemon thyme, lemon verbena works perfectly well, or you can substitute a couple of sprigs of regular thyme with some finely grated lemon zest. When I made the brûlée opposite, I had an accident that turned into a happy one: the blowtorch used to finish the brûlées ran out of gas on the last one and turned out, as in the picture, partly topped in hot sugar, with islands of solid caramel. It suited the celeriac perfectly.

Serves 6

370g celeriac

50g butter

120ml milk

8 free-range egg yolks

140g caster sugar

500ml double cream

1½ vanilla pods

8 or so sprigs of lemon thyme

120g soft light brown sugar

Peel and chop the celeriac into pieces about the size of a pound coin. Melt the butter in a pan over a medium heat and add the celeriac. Cook over a low heat for about 10 minutes until the celeriac begins to soften. Add the milk and simmer until the celeriac is tender, about 15–20 minutes. Purée the mixture in a blender until smooth.

Preheat the oven to 150°C/Gas 2.

Whisk the egg yolks and sugar together in a large bowl until pale and creamy. Pour the cream into a pan. Split the vanilla pods lengthways, tease out the seeds and add them and the pods to the cream, along with the lemon thyme. Bring just to the boil, then strain the hot cream through a sieve onto the egg and sugar mix, discarding the vanilla pods and thyme. Whisk briefly, then add the celeriac purée and whisk to combine.

Stand 6 ramekins in a roasting tin and fill them with the custard. Pour enough boiling water into the tin to come two-thirds of the way up the side of the ramekins. Cover the tin loosely with foil. Cook for 20–25 minutes, until the custard is just set – it should have a little wobble to it.

Lift the ramekins out of the water and leave the custards to cool, then refrigerate for at least a couple of hours or overnight.

Sprinkle each brûlée with 4 tsp sugar and caramelise with a kitchen blowtorch. If you don't have a blowtorch, use a very hot grill.

Jerusalem artichoke cake

I still remember making a 'what's the matter with chocolate?' face when years ago someone first mentioned the idea of carrot cake to me. I forgive you yours if you are similarly gargoyled at the thought of this. Trust me, it's a smasher. The artichokes lend an almost festive earthiness, adding sweetness and texture.

Serves 8–12

120g raisins

A double brandy

150g butter, plus a little extra for greasing

220g Jerusalem artichokes

3 free-range eggs

150g soft light brown sugar

200g self-raising flour

1 tsp bicarbonate of soda

1 tsp salt

1 tsp ground cinnamon

½ tsp freshly grated nutmeg

90g hazelnuts, toasted and roughly crushed

For the topping

200g cream cheese

Finely grated zest of 1 unwaxed lemon, plus the juice of ½ lemon

50g soft light brown sugar

Soak the raisins in the brandy for about an hour. Preheat the oven to 180°C/Gas 4. Lightly butter a 20cm cake tin.

Melt the butter slowly and allow to cool until barely tepid. Peel and grate the Jerusalem artichokes (you need 200g prepared weight).

In a large bowl, whisk the eggs, sugar and melted butter together until creamy and light. Sift the flour, bicarbonate of soda, salt and spices together over the mixture and fold in very gently – try to avoid knocking out any air. Add the grated artichokes, the raisins with the brandy, and the crushed hazelnuts. Fold in carefully until evenly combined.

Pour the mixture into the prepared cake tin and bake for 30 minutes. To check whether it is cooked insert a skewer into the centre – it should come out clean. If it isn't ready, check again after another 5 minutes. Allow the cake to cool in the tin for at least 20 minutes, then turn out onto a wire rack and leave to cool completely.

For the topping, mix the cream cheese, grated lemon zest and juice and the sugar together until smooth, then cover and refrigerate. When the cake is completely cooled, spread with the topping.

Rhubarb daiquiri

Most rhubarb cocktails use puréed cooked rhubarb, or the syrup that leaks from the chopped stalks when they are slowly roasted. Very lovely it is too. This daiquiri is a little different: using raw rhubarb, juiced, with all the sharp intensity you'd hope it would have. This is definitely a springtime spring-in-your-step cocktail, rather than a warming around the fire kind.

The proportions are approximate – they will vary depending on the strength of the syrups and the rhubarb – so do tweak until you have a cocktail that balances the rhubarb's sharpness with the sweetness of the flavoured syrups. You should be able to pick out all the ingredients.

Per person

Crushed ice

50ml white rum

6 tbsp rhubarb juice

1½ tbsp lemon verbena syrup

1½ tbsp rosemary syrup

1 tbsp lime juice

Make sure all the ingredients are very cold. Put some crushed ice in a glass, cocktail shaker or jug (depending on how many you are making) and add the rum and rhubarb juice. Stir. Add 1 tbsp of the rosemary and lemon verbena syrups and the lime juice. Stir and taste. Add more of either syrup if needs be. Add more crushed ice and serve.

April

April can break your heart like no other month. It is like the best and the worst of young love – the sunshine interrupted by cold winds and showers without any warning. It's not so much spring as half-summer half-winter, often in the same day. It's not unusual to be in the vineyard slathered in sun cream, with hat, scarf and gloves on too. It is a month of layers: coat on, coat off.

April's peak harvest

Asparagus

Bamboo

Broad beans

Buck's horn plantain

Chives

Good King Henry

Lovage

Nettles

Pea shoots

Spring onions

It is traditionally the start of the hungry gap, with little annual veg to pick, but even this soon out of winter the perennials are growing well. Asparagus, bamboo shoots and early spikes of Good King Henry with any number of dressings and sauces, are among my favourites of the whole year. Handfuls of asparagus, especially, may not even make it to the house – eaten instead within a few feet of the veg patch, griddled over the firepit on one of those evenings where you light a fire, certain that summery outdoor eating has arrived, only to be followed around the flames by sharp wet gusts of smoke and drizzle.

The salad bowl begins to fill with cut-and-come-again leaves – or rather pinch-and-come-again, as we tend to pluck the odd leaf (where we dare) from seedlings or self-sown leaves that have sprung up around the veg patch – a bonus thanks to tardy winter veg patch clearing.

Australian Yellow Leaf, Reine de Glace, Giant Red Mustard and Really Red Deer Tongue are usually going well by now, with sweet cicely, the first of the chervil and parsley, plus a few of the woody herbs all able to take a little harvesting.

It's not only the flavours that perk up in April, the early spring warmth loosens the scents. The leaves begin to sprout on the Szechuan, Nepalese and Japanese peppers, the sweet cicely and salad burnet are growing strongly, as are the various mints and chives. A three-minute walk to the polytunnel can take half an hour, with all the rubbing and sniffing en route.

An afternoon for planting and it's raining. Fidgety, I took a few minutes with the plants that were going to go out from the polytunnel – a row (where, I hadn't decided) of Japanese peppers. They used to be very definitely third out of the Nepalese, Szechuan and Japanese peppers I'm growing but they're coming round on me with their soft, almost floral leaf scent. I'm sure there is a hint of white chocolate about it but Candida thinks they smell of cat's pee. She thinks hawthorn smells of cat's pee too. It's like every unfamiliar meat is supposed to taste of chicken; to her, any uncommon plant smell is cat's pee.

— 30 April, 2009

IF YOU HAVE ANY PEA PLANTS in your garden, pop out there now and pinch off the end 15cm of any shoot and have a munch. The flavour of these arching, prawn-like tips is as sweet and bright as the best of the pods, with a crisp succulence to match. They are known as 'Green Gold' in Japan, and with good reason. They are every bit as good as the first peas in the pod, especially if eaten within an hour or two of picking, harvested from young plants of the sweetest varieties. Thankfully the wait for tips is much shorter than for the pods.

Early in spring, when I sow peas and beans in root trainers, I sow a weekly tray of peas early and thick at the same time – they are not for planting out, they'll never reach maturity; they're for snipping and eating when only 15cm tall. I scatter a good handful of seeds (I generally use sugar snaps, for their extra sweetness) into a tray of compost – the seeds can be as close as 2–3cm to each other – and then cover them with 1cm or so of compost. Light is vital to swift germination and growth, so I usually leave them either on a windowsill or in the polytunnel. Watered lightly and often, they germinate quickly and grow with enthusiasm.

I also sow a block or two of peas in the veg patch to grow into an informal low hedge. Pinching out the growing tip from each seedling when it reaches 30cm or so causes the plants to throw out side shoots, thickening the hedge and giving more shoots to pick. I can graze over these for a couple of months at least, often much longer, before they tire or toughen.

Growing peas for shoots has the added bonus of not having to consider pea moth and its tedious larvae that can infest the pods from midsummer. For that reason alone, I usually don't sow peas for pods after early May – most pods can then be harvested before the moth arrives.

With regular sowing, it's possible to be in pea shoots from April to September, bringing life and welcome freshness to spring salads, as a simple dressed side vegetable or wilted into an omelette or tortilla.

PEA SHOOTS

Site Light and sunny

Sow November, February–June

Harvest April–October

Notes Sow a weekly tray in spring, and a row or two in the veg patch as a long productive hedge

Asparagus, pea shoots & borage with elderflower dressing (page 138)
Eggs Gordon Bennett (page 154)

WHEN WE FIRST CAME to look at the house and land we were on the way back from our wedding weekend on the Isle of Purbeck, in Dorset. We go there often – the walks, countryside and coast are as fine as anywhere I know. A few years ago, in mid-spring, we came across the only field of broad beans I've ever seen, or rather ever smelled, while walking there. It seems impossible that such a beautifully intoxicating scent can come from a vegetable.

I would grow broad beans even if I was one of those peculiar souls who doesn't like their flavour. Lay down next to a just-flowering row and look at their everyday, familiar blossom – they are as extraordinary as their perfume.

I'm not someone who clamours after the earliest possible harvest, so it rarely registers on my autumn radar to sow broad beans in November for early-spring picking: thankfully Candida nearly always remembers to

BROAD BEANS

Site Relatively unfussy

Sow Direct in November and direct or under cover February–May

Harvest April–September

Notes Plant out quickly when roots hit the bottom of the root trainer

sow a few rows in the veg patch and I'm glad she does. Ready to pick in the second half of April, well ahead of the first spring-sown batch, they are all the encouragement I need to sow more for early summer eating.

Broad beans need little encouragement to grow – push a seed a couple of centimetres below the surface, 20cm from its neighbour, allowing 60cm between rows and the sun and rain will do the rest. I sow a few direct like this in spring (and all direct in autumn) but I start most legumes off in toilet-roll inners or root trainers. Beans and peas like a long root run, and starting them off indoors allows a good few inches of root system to develop under cover, where it's easier to protect them from the slugs' attentions. When the roots appear at the bottom of the inner or trainer, I plant them out in the garden and away they go. A batch sown every month from late February until the end of May ensures that as one lot of plants tire of producing, there are others to take their place.

Of the different varieties I like Claudia Aquadulce for autumn sowing and Bunyard's Exhibition for spring, and I always find room for a line or two of Crimson Flowered – their flowers are even more beautiful than the usual varieties and their taste is really fine.

Before I planted a hornbeam hedge around its perimeter, the veg patch was a little exposed, so I had to create a string and cane perimeter to keep the plants upright. I'd often grow the dwarfing broad bean variety The Sutton, but as the hedge thickens I increasingly take my chances with the taller varieties.

As those perfumed flowers begin to wilt, I pinch out the top from each stem. This does three fabulous things: it directs the plant's energies to the developing beans, it deprives the aphids of their favourite site and provides me with one of the great unbuyable harvests of the garden.

I might just prefer these delicious tops to the actual beans. Wilted in butter, they add freshness, flavour and succulence to omelettes, risottos and stir-fries.

Once plants are established, pests are few. Aside from aphids, pea and vine weevils may leave their trademark postage stamp notches along the leaves but damage is largely only cosmetic.

For the best of their flavour and texture, I pop the pods early and small – they are sweet and succulent: leave them longer and what I'd gain in size I would lose to bitterness.

Ants on the broad beans. Lots of them, and very busy apparently doing nothing in particular, but they stayed in my mind long enough to prod me into googling and I'm glad I did. The ants themselves aren't causing any harm to the plant, but they are there for a reason – looking for aphids. Aphids secrete honeydew, which the ants can detect in minute amounts, so it seems that my broad beans are about to come under attack from the aphid militia… spray hose at the ready.

— 19 April, 2008

imson Flowered broad beans

WEANERS

Source When aged 8–14 weeks old, usually in spring

Feed A compound, GM-free pig grower feed, plus any veg patch waste

Notes Weaners grow quickly, so be prepared to up their feed intake. And don't be surprised if you find yourself watching them rather than the TV

TEN YEARS AGO, after a decade and a half of not eating meat, I bought some electric fence, a solar charger and three piglets. I wanted to produce more of our food, we had some land to clear for growing and our expanding veg patch was producing more rough outer brassica leaves and peelings than the compost heap could handle: a living dustbin and turf clearer seemed the perfect solution.

If you can fall in love with something that grows into a large, lumbering cylinder with oversized and usually muddy testicles, then fall in love we did. Now, almost every spring, we take delivery of two or three weaners from their birthplace a couple of hundred yards up the road. We usually have Saddlebacks – a rare old breed of characterful pigs that grow slowly, producing what I find the most flavoursome pork with plenty of (but not too much) fat.

A little short of a couple of months old when they arrive, they run around in hysterical, interweaving circles, driven by excitement and shyness, then stop suddenly, randomly, with only their eyes moving to follow you. And then it starts again.

I like the sheep well enough, but they're not overly bright, only a few stand out as individuals and their enthusiasm for acquiring any passing ailment does make it slightly easier to accept their eventual fate. The pigs are entirely the opposite.

Still, and cute as they are, it's hard not to start looking forward to the salamis, bacon, hams, sausages, pâtés, terrines, rillettes and pork that we'll be enjoying late in the year. Nell told me how lovely she thought the last pair were – she named them Alice and Daisy, even though they were boys – then she asked when we could make them into salami.

We have three fenced enclosures for the pigs to grow into over the summer, but if the ground is wet or we need an area clearing, we use a moveable electric fence to contain them. It works a little too well – after a couple of weeks and a few smacks from the charger, you can take the fence down and the pigs will remain within, reluctant to cross the line where the fence was.

I would like to contend that the fastest creature on the planet is not the cheetah. It's the pig. Or at least it's the male pig that backs gently onto the electric fence, while trying to gain purchase on a tasty-looking root. The snap of electric as the fence comes into contact with the pig is enough to make any male, of any species, wince.

— 27 April, 2010

ice, the boy weaner

Asparagus: Mary Washington

I HAD A MEETING with someone from the local planning office a few years ago and I noticed she was looking at me strangely. A glance at the mirror in the loo revealed a man with soil on the right side of his face and in his hair. Just before I drove to the meeting, I'd leant down to look along each asparagus row for the first signs of green nosing through the soil. I found only dandelions and, it would seem, a layer of topsoil more than willing to adhere to an ill-shaven cheek.

Fittingly enough, I start looking along those rows on April Fool's Day. It's almost always too early, often by 3 or 4 weeks in a cool year, but I still do it every year, in hope.

Asparagus is in season throughout May and for a week or two either side depending where in the country you are and how warm spring is. The best asparagus owes everything to time. Once the spear is severed from the plant, its sugars begin their sad, swift descent into starch. The sooner you cook and eat them the sweeter they'll be. I often boil the water it will cook in before cutting it. That's the sort of unnecessarily anoracky behaviour I would be best advised to keep to myself, but you can certainly distinguish between today's asparagus and yesterday's.

It is one of those foods that for the short time it is in season, you simply can't have enough of, and the only way of assuring that you get the best of it is to grow some yourself.

Like many short-season foods, asparagus is expensive to buy, yet pleasingly simple to grow and care for. It can be grown from seed, but is best from young plants known as crowns. I planted them in our first April here, in a well-drained spot alongside the veg patch. Having dug three trenches, a spade-blade deep and 80cm apart, I created a Toblerone-like ridge 10cm high in the bottom of each trench. I lay the crowns along these ridges, around 50cm apart, and spread the roots evenly on either side. Backfilled and well watered in, it was the start of a little wait.

Asparagus asks a little patience of you – the roots need time to develop enough energy to drive springtime spears through the soil – but if you leave the spears unpicked for a couple of years you'll be repaid in luxuriously succulent stems each April for a couple of decades or more. Occasionally, you can find a supplier of two-year-old asparagus crowns to halve the wait. Many of the new varieties are very reliable and productive, but I have to say I still prefer Mary Washington and Connover's Colossal for flavour.

Steaming or griddling for a few minutes is all the cooking this prize vegetable calls for – a little butter, Parmesan, sea salt and pepper, and/or an egg with the runniest of yolks, is all it needs for company.

Asparagus roasts beautifully too. Toss with a splash of olive or rapeseed oil and a little salt and roast in the oven at 200°C/Gas 6 for 10 minutes, then turn and scatter with sesame seeds and roast for another 5 minutes. Squeeze over a little lemon juice if you fancy, and serve. Every year, I eat more asparagus raw, harvesting the spears with my knife as a mini-reward while gardening – they're deliciously nutty, like raw peanuts.

ASPARAGUS

Site Well drained

Sow February

Harvest April–June

Notes Plant March–April. Support the late-season flowers, then cut down to 2–3cm above ground

Asparagus & goat's cheese tart (page 150)

Asparagus, pea shoots & borage with elderflower dressing (page 138)

Sparga siitve (page 151)

Stir-fried asparagus & Good King Henry (page 158)

Veg patch tempura (page 141)

Vignarola (page 148)

ACCIDENTAL SALAD

Site Wherever they like

Sow Self-sown

Harvest April–June

Notes Must remember to sow some early plain leaves, as most of the self-seeders seem to be full flavoured

A FAIR PART of the veg patch never gets dug. From November to April, a 7–10cm layer of compost is added, forming a dark blanket over the whole of the veg patch. By April, the darkness of the compost has been mellowed by the weather and the quiet work of the worms and water in drawing it slowly into the soil beneath. Here, and in the perennial garden and gravel paths, seedlings appear: not all of them weeds. Self-sown salads spring up everywhere, a shameful yet delicious tribute to my tendency to let some of the leafy plants go to seed the previous year.

Tree spinach, callaloo, rocket and Giant Red mustard can pop up by the dozen and, somewhat annoyingly, usually ahead of any I've sown. Some stay to grow into full-sized plants, but if they're numerous or in an inconvenient place, I let them get just large enough to be worth picking before pulling them up, roots and all, in lunch-sized batches as I want them. At this stage they are small, tender and full of flavour.

Self-sown nasturtiums and borage also litter the veg patch and beyond, and I love their random presence. I've never quite got along with the notion of 'invasive' or with the dislike for self-seeders – these are free plants, free food, and I'd rather tear them up from unwanted spots to eat than have to go to the trouble of sowing or planting more. These first flowers are a much-needed early source of pollen, drawing insects in that I hope will help keep a check on pests and, in turn, pollinate later flowers. They are a welcome early source of liveliness in leafy salads, adding peppery honey and cool cucumber to the bright, young, renegade leaves.

GOOD KING HENRY

Site Full sun or semi-shade

Sow Direct in March

Harvest March–September

Notes Good ground cover – allow 25cm between plants

POOR MAN'S ASPARAGUS or Lincolnshire spinach, as it is also called, Good King Henry grows into a tall leafy plant that makes a good substitute for spinach, though I harvest it much earlier, when it's producing succulent spears, to enjoy as one of spring's most delicious early treats.

From late March, the early shoots will be tall enough to slice off the top 20cm – pick off any leaves and steam, or stir-fry it as you might asparagus. It's a really special veg, and provides an early excuse to make hollandaise or soft-boiled dippy eggs before the asparagus arrives.

I tend to let the leaves go unpicked early in spring, using them later in the season. The unopened flower buds are lovely too, cut in summer as an out-of-season sprouting broccoli, and sautéed in butter and garlic.

March is a fine time to start Good King Henry off – I sow seed direct, thinning seedlings to 30cm or so apart. It is perennial, reappearing for years, so I let new plants develop for the first year, taking only a few leaves and flower buds. That uncharacteristic patience is rewarded the following March, when the now-established plant throws up enough of those wonderful spears to pick for a few lunches.

Good King Henry doesn't need a special soil and isn't particularly fussy about sun or shade, so I grow it tucked away in half-seen pockets, where it makes a fine green backdrop.

Stir-fried asparagus & Good King Henry (page 158)

ccidental salad: Mexican tree spinach, parsley, winter lettuce, nasturtium

May

The shoulders of summer are my favourite times of year. Although May hasn't the abundance of September and October, it has a freshness and a vitality of its own. Where the coming of autumn brings slowness, summer's imminence stirs the blood. And the appetite.

May's peak harvest

Green garlic

Lemon balm

Mint

Potatoes

Radish

Tarragon (French)

Early mini strawberries

Blackcurrant leaves

Blue honeysuckle

Daylilies

Elderflower

Gooseberries

Small-leaved lime

I feel most alive in May. My clock moves round, the sun wakes me early and bright, and gives energy to the rest of the day. The asparagus is in full steam in more ways than one, the hedgerow scent of elderflower and hawthorn fills the air and there are enough days of sun for more than the odd meal to be enjoyed in the lengthening grass.

The early peas and beans, sown as a gamble with the cold back in February, are often starting to come good, along with the pea shoot hedge. The lush green of spring is broken by chives – pinky purple and white flowered varieties lighting up the garden and spring-into-summer salads. If I was bothered to sow early carrots and potatoes in tyre stacks in the polytunnel in February (and frankly, some years I'm too idle) they will be ready to lift now.

There's the pleasure, too, of salads, with mini globe artichokes, little-fingernail broad beans, tiny peas taken before their skins touch in the pod, and the earliest of those under-cover potatoes and carrots.

And at last, there is fruit. Musk and Mignonette strawberries and the fruit of the blue honeysuckle need the barest sunshine to ripen way ahead of the pack. In sunny springs, the beautifully sharp, early gooseberries are ready to pair with elderflower. The blackcurrants need more sunshine yet, but their leaves are plentiful enough to steal a few handfuls to make the first, and possibly my favourite, sorbet of the year.

In May, a few plants tell me what they couldn't over the winter – that they've given up the ghost. If there aren't leaves now, they're not likely not be coming. Usually it's a few ones and twos in the perennial garden, finished off by a hard freeze after wet weather, or just reaching the end of their life. It's what you expect and you largely learn to be philosophical about it, but digging them up and replanting adds to the workload of an already busy month.

Pulling nettles around the trunks of the pecans at the end of a long hot day, I lazied into a kneeling position. Everything went dark: I was in the shade of a pecan tree. I may be the only person to have said that on English soil. The leaves formed a small but very definite canopy. And they're rather beautiful leaves at that – double-edged saws, narrow curves like Elizabeth Taylor's eyes in Cleopatra. The thought comes into my head that they're good enough to grow just to look at, followed quickly by the thought that that is exactly how most people choose what to grow.
— 28 May, 2009

WHEN YOU'RE PLANTING TREES in the depths of winter, it helps if you can bear in mind that the seemingly lifeless stick in your hand will, in a few months, sprout leaves and then, in time, yield fruit or nuts. This skinny cane will give me Asian pears, nectarines or almonds, you tell yourself. On the windiest, rainiest days, it helps.

The pecans needed no such strategy. I planted them in the May sun seven years ago, as two-foot trees. Their arrival from Canada gave me childish pleasure and they were the fastest holes I've ever dug. Native to the deep, well-drained, moist river-basin soils of the southern USA, pecans wandered their way slowly northwards as optimistic growers tested their range, gradually planting seedlings from thriving trees a little further north until they crossed into Canada with a similar climate to our own. And then they crossed the Atlantic to be planted in this country for the first time.

The pecans gave me little encouragement for a couple of years, sending their chunky tap roots into the earth before allowing themselves to expand above. More than any of the other trees here, they've taught me patience – not something that I'm famous for.

Pecans need shelter and as much sun as they can get to ripen their wood, so I planted northern pecan varieties as a sunny orchard near the river, hoping the Otter would substitute well for the Mississippi, despite the lack of paddle steamers. Pecans don't ask much of you – any pruning is purely for shape or size; they can grow to 30 metres if you let them but do so very slowly.

If you see catkins in late spring (male flowers hang down, females point up) you may get clusters of nuts in autumn. As with almonds and walnuts, the outer husk splits when the nut approaches maturity.

Pecans are best dried. Their flavour, texture and appearance takes a turn for the better if left for a fortnight somewhere airy, dark and cool. To test one for readiness, bend it – it should snap.

After 5,533 kilometres, a twelve-day delay while customs decide whether the cargo infringes new EU guidelines about living matter and months of research in sourcing, a new orchard is planted with pecans, probably for the first time in this country.

—— 1 May, 2006

PECANS

Site Sunny and a soil that doesn't dry out often

Sow October–November

Harvest Carlson #3 seems to be the happiest variety here. Keep the base weed-free early in life

ELDERFLOWER

Site Relatively unfussy

Harvest May–November

Notes American elder (*Sambucus canadensis*) isn't self-fertile whereas the regular *S.nigra* is. It flowers later, so rarely fruits, giving a long season of flower-picking/champagne-making from mid-July into November

APART FROM BLACKBERRYING as a child and the odd nibble of wild samphire when I lived in Whitstable, picking elderflower was the first serious foraging I did. Candida and I had moved to Devon (back to Devon for me) and found ourselves between the moors, in a place called Black Dog.

That first spring, we explored the footpaths, a favourite loop of which took us through the neighbouring farm and along the lanes for a not particularly hard-earned pint at the pub. A large crater on the farm, where stone had long since been excavated, had become home for a few seedlings – many of them elder – as well as a playground for the free-range chickens.

The elder is something of an opportunist, turning up on disturbed ground in towns as much as country, as well as dotting roadside hedges and riverbanks. You'll find it occasionally in field boundaries too, but its lack of spines and relatively brittle trunk mean many have been grubbed out in favour of stock-proof species such as hawthorn and blackthorn.

We picked basketfuls of elderflowers three or four times that May, for cordial and champagne, and to see whether it really was good with the early gooseberries. Saccharine as it sounds to be prancing through the spring countryside picking elderflowers with your girlfriend, I love the memory of it.

I'm also attached to these first spring forages as they were the gateway into a world of free, delicious food, changing my relationship with my surroundings into a more active and rewarding one.

I still always take a partner along foraging with me, even if, as is often the case, he takes the form of a young border terrier by the name of Harris. It is the presence of this 'other' that distinguishes the forager from opportunist thief or Peeping Tom in the eyes of strangers, and allows me to explore copses, walk quiet lanes and leap into hedgerows without dark judgment.

The flowers have a heavy perfume that is something of a crowd-splitter. For me, they carry the evocative scent of spring-into-summer – it reminds me of romances in the long grass that never happened, the wicket-taking Ashes-opening over that I never bowled, that first flight in a biplane that I never flew... whereas a couple of friends can't stand it. I ought to choose my friends a little better.

The flavour that the flowers impart is universally loved, brightening everything it comes in contact with. They are at their most aromatic on a sunny day – this is the time to pick them. I pinch the heads at the first joint, using them within an hour or two to capture the fullest flavour. Leftovers are dried by laying them, flowers down, out of the sun for a day. Shaking the stems releases the flowers. Stored in an airtight container, they retain much of their early summer flavour and scent – to be used in the same way as fresh elderflowers – for the rest of the year.

Elderflowers are perhaps at their absolute best when paired with gooseberries, to make a fool, cranachan, knickerbocker glory or just a

Elderflower: Black Lace

Gooseberries (mixed varieties)

simple compote. It is, like Morecambe and Wise, and gin and tonic, one of those perfect partnerships, so much greater than the sum of its parts. The flowers are also spectacularly good teamed with strawberries, and when tempura-battered, deep-fried and dipped into either cinnamon sugar or salt, sugar and chilli.

The green parts of elder are mildly poisonous, but having come across old recipes for using the flower buds I've been tempted to give them a try pickled, and I am, at least as I write, still alive. Take your chances with my recipe if you wish.

There are a few elder trees scattered about the farm in singles – a couple a hundred yards apart in the shade by the river, dotted sparsely and randomly along the hedges and one attempting manfully to wrestle its way through the garden hedge. The most prolific of them leans into the pig pen, requiring not a little nerve to bypass playful piglets or their protective parents.

Between those foraged and picked in the field, there's certainly enough elderflowers and berries to keep us going, but I've planted a few in the garden to try something a little different from the wild harvest. Donau is a very productive Austrian variety, Viridis produces green fruit which attracts the birds less, and Black Lace, with its deep purple foliage and pink/white flowers is a particular favourite that makes beautiful pink cordial and 'champagne'.

Planting one near your house will, according to folklore, keep the devil away, although having overindulged on elderberry wine once I'm not sure that worked, given the way I felt the next morning.

Elderflower & strawberry drop scones (page 176)

Elderflower delight (page 178)

Elderflower dressing (page 165)

Gooseberry & elderflower curd (page 170)

Pickled elderflower buds (page 168)

FIRM, SHARP AND DELICIOUSLY SOUR in May and early June, then tender and sweet a month later, gooseberries are two of my favourite fruit.

As with apples, they are often separated into cookers and eaters – sharps and sweets – but in reality, most varieties will sweeten beautifully if left on the plant to enjoy more sun. Even for a sour-lover like me, the very earliest are best eaten cooked – try one raw and see how wrinkled a face can turn. The late-picked berries are a different proposition altogether: sweet, juicy and flavoursome straight from the bush.

We have four established gooseberry plants next to the veg patch, on the gamble that I would beat the birds to the fruit. Having lost out to the sparrows for the late sweet picking on one plant this year, those plants may well be making the short trip into the fruit cage this winter.

Taking an early half-harvest also helps sweeten the rest of the fruit for when you return: the plant has more energy to ripen those that remain. Sadly, like redcurrants and white currants, the early, sharp-sour fruits are becoming harder to find in the shops. We spend our lives in quiet addiction to sugar, it seems.

GOOSEBERRIES

Site Shelter, sun, well drained

Harvest May–August

Notes Berries form on short spurs from 2–3 year old wood, so prune (in winter) to snip out older wood to leave a good mix of 1–3-year-old wood. Open goblet shape is ideal to allow light and air in

For early sour berries and a later sweet harvest, I grow the old favourite Leveller, which is as good as any I've tried for this split harvest. I grow Hinnomaki Red just for sweet, late gooseberries. As well as being disease resistant and heavy yielding, its berries are large and flavoursome, and their deep pink/red colouring makes beautiful curd and fool.

Gooseberries are as hardy as their robust spikiness suggests, but they do like a good position with shelter, sun and a well-drained (though not sandy) soil.

There are two nuisances to watch out for: American mildew and sawfly. The likelihood of mildew can be minimised by open pruning and good air circulation, and by planting disease-resistant varieties and giving the plants a fortnightly high-potassium feed through summer. Although only 1–2cm long, sawfly caterpillars are spectacularly effective – a day or two is all they need to relieve plants of their leaves and very possibly their life, so pick off as soon as they are spotted. A biological control (a natural predator) works well too.

Early gooseberries and elderflower make the ultimate marriage of hedgerow and garden, and capture the essence of spring into summer. The deep muscat of the elder softens the gooseberries' edge and draws out its subtleties, while the sharpness of the gooseberry anchors the heady elderflower. They were born to be together.

Let me encourage you to embrace their sourness a little. The curd recipe uses way less sugar than most, but trust me enough to make it once this light on the sugar, to allow that glorious sharp flavour to come through, and you'll not go back.

If you have a real heap of gooseberries, they should keep for a few days in the fridge, perhaps even colouring more strongly if they're pink/red varieties. If they need dealing with quickly, get them into a large pan (there's no need for the purgatory of topping and tailing large quantities) with just enough water to cover the base and cook them slowly over a gentle heat, stirring regularly. When the berries have collapsed a little, press them through a sieve. The purée that results is a perfect sharp base for compote, ice cream, sorbet, cocktails or whatever you fancy – add sugar to suit. Freeze in containers or bags of 300g or so, to use as you like.

Today would have been my dad's 75th birthday if he hadn't gone toes up a decade ago. It's been a lovely day, apart from running over my mobile with the tractor.

I did two quiet things in his memory – I enjoyed a very fine local beer while I made and ate gooseberry and elderflower fool.
— 14 June, 2010

EVEN IN THE LEAST SPECIAL MAY, there will be a handful of evenings when the air stays warm, the light bright and the swallows swoop to take advantage of the mayfly hatch. These are evenings to be in the perennial garden.

Three or four years ago I planted a couple of musk strawberries (*Fragaria moschata*) in the perennial garden, thinking I'd source more to create part of the ground cover there – I'm glad I couldn't find any, as in just a couple of years those few have created a solid blanket across the whole garden. In May, they produce a sea of little fingernail-sized berries – some red, some white – with an intense strawberry/pineapple flavour and a hint of vanilla. Plant your foot in the perennial garden in May and you'll squash a few dozen, they're so productive.

On those warm evenings, a handful of perfectly ripe Mignonettes or musk strawberries pressed against the inside of a glass of sparkling wine makes for a fine homegrown, outdoor kir of sorts.

Mignonettes and musk strawberries are fairly unfussy about location – ours are growing in an exposed sunny spot in the perennial garden – but I suspect that if I'd planted them somewhere that mimics their woodland edge origins (sheltered, semi-shade and with a rich soil) they would be even happier.

Mignonette strawberries are the most flavoursome of the alpines and unlike musk and regular strawberries, they don't spread by throwing out mini-plants to their side (known as runners), which makes them a great choice for edging a border or bed. As with musk strawberries, these tiny, intense red sweet hearts, begin their long season of generosity around mid-May. They have a long season, fruiting whenever the weather suits them, often into October.

Mignonettes and musks are best allowed to ripen longer than my patience prefers. And tempting as it is, I try not to cram them in by the handful – they are best enjoyed one at a time, falling apart in the mouth.

Unless you have all the time in the world (or few relatives), mini strawberries are not going to provide the pudding for a family gathering – they're too small to make a straight substitution for regular strawberries – so I think of them more as a herb to complement other flavours or a sweet to dissolve on the tongue or in a glass of fizz. Their intense flavour works particularly well in muffins and drop scones too.

EARLY MINI STRAWBERRIES

Site Sunny or semi-shade

Sow Start off in modules from late winter into spring, planting out when a few centimetres tall

Harvest May–September

Notes Start with seed or young plants. Allow 30cm between plants

Elderflower & strawberry drop scones (page 176)

MINT

Site Prefers moist soil

Harvest April–October

Notes Cut back in summer for new flush of growth. Best to start with young plants

Broad bean hummus (page 142)

Cauliflower pakoras with raita (page 58)

Charlie's mojito (page 182)

Gooseberry salsa (page 166)

Herb syrups (page 266)

Grape, beetroot & mint smoothie (page 376)

Summer punch (page 183)

Vignarola (page 148)

IF YOU GROW ONLY ONE MINT, let it be Moroccan mint. It makes the finest tea, mint sauce and is an absolute essential for mojitos, which, frankly, makes it an absolute essential for the garden.

Lively, fresh and cool, Moroccan mint has just enough sweetness to offset its boldness without ever nudging into cloying, as spearmints often can. There's a carpet of it, perhaps 5 metres square, in the perennial garden – once in a while when no one is looking and the spring sun is out after a rain shower, I'll lie right in the middle of it to be suffocated in mint, terrible hippy that I am.

Chocolate mint is fast catching up Moroccan mint in our kitchen. It's great for tea and perfect for poaching pears and peaches. It smells exactly of After Eight mints, and reminds me of how my dad would put the empty envelopes back in the box so I'd think there were more left than there were. That would count as domestic abuse these days.

Berries and Cream variety marries fruitiness with mint – perfect as a lively tea and in fruit or alcoholic cocktails.

In the forest garden and under trees here and there, I want a mint to cover ground quickly. Most will unless grown in a container but apple mint is the most enthusiastic spreader. Bees and hoverflies seem to love it more than any other variety too.

Container-grown mint can become bare in the centre of the plant – Kim Hurst of the Cottage Herbery told me her remedy: take the plant out of the pot, cut it in half with a bread knife, and put back in the pot with the cut halves turned outwards towards the rim. It'll grow to cover the gaps evenly and quickly.

POTATOES

Site Good, moisture-retentive soil, manured is best

Sow February–April

Harvest May–October

Notes Plant to a trowel's depth (half that for earlies), a trowel's length apart. Salad potatoes can be a little closer – rows around two trowel lengths apart. Size of potatoes is affected if planted too closely together

I CAME TO POTATOES through love. I'd met Candida and she loved to garden, whereas I couldn't have been less interested. She had a top floor flat; I had a garden. She moved in very quickly. I did what any man would do under such circumstances: I bought some seed potatoes. I mostly listened to the football out there, being semi-helpful by moving the odd rock or heavy barrow. When she went to the loo or to put the kettle on, I pinched her trowel and sunk a few more tubers into the soil. A little watering and drawing soil up into earthy Toblerones kept me as busy as I wanted to be (i.e. not very) in the garden that spring and summer.

I grew six varieties and remember only two: International Kidney and Pink Fir Apple. The first is more famously known as Jersey Royal, an early, sweet, salad potato. Coaxing them out of the ground with a fork was a real moment – an awful, clichéd caricature of a revelatory experience: it works! Brushed free of soil, briefly boiled and eaten with only butter, salt and pepper, they were extraordinary. I was hooked.

The next four varieties matured into the summer, ready one by one. Bland, floury, some blighted and most indistinguishable in flavour from those in the shops by the same name, each was a letdown. I was unhooked.

'nt: Berries and Cream

Container potatoes: International Kidney

The late-maturing Pink Fir Apple restored my faith. Knobbly, nutty, firm and delicious, they were as good the next day pushed around a pan with a little oil and garlic as they were just boiled and buttered.

It was a lesson. My suspicion of varieties I hadn't heard of vanished and my love of early salad potatoes began. It made me start to grow things with eating – recipes even – in mind. Every February, I choose the seed potatoes according to how they'll be cooked – some for salads, others for chips or mash, and one or two for perfect roasties.

Belle de Fontenay, International Kidney (Jersey Royal) and Cherie – wonderfully waxy, delicious salad potatoes, usually ready to lift from the soil in early June – make up most of them. They are in, grown and out of the ground before the first hint of blight, vacating space for summer and autumn crops – squash, courgettes, perhaps another round of beans. Early season's potatoes cook in a few minutes, are expensive in the shops, but most importantly, the homegrown flavour and texture is worth all of the few moments of earthing up and planting time.

For chips, a short line of Yukon Gold does perfectly. This variety has a yellow flesh that's buttery in looks and texture, it boils and bakes beautifully and takes to deep-frying like no other. And in most years it matures before the arrival of blight. This year, I've also found room for a few Highland Burgundy Red – a red-fleshed, heritage potato chosen to add appropriate colour to the Duke of Burgundy's meals at the Savoy Hotel in the 1930s, and the only variety to rival Yukon Gold for chips.

For perfect mash, I grow half a row each of Kestrel and Salad Blue. Both are delicately flavoured and floury fleshed, with Salad Blue having blue flesh and skin – it makes fine roast potatoes and crisps too.

There's a row for roasties: King Edward – so much better home-grown than bought – and British Queen, a fine heritage variety. The rest changes every year. This year there's Vitelotte, a late-season salad variety that produces long purple tubers with a tremendous chestnut flavour, and Ratte, similar but earlier and less knobbly than Pink Fir Apple.

I get all mine at Potato Fairs, most of which are in February. My twenty-year-old self wouldn't believe potato fairs could replace record fairs but there we are. A Potato Fair is exactly as you'd expect: a sea of stalls, many overseen by men with luxuriant facial hair. Each of the hundreds of varieties are available as single potatoes, so even a few pots can give you a whole range of flavours and textures.

Once home, I put seed potatoes into open egg boxes to chit – where little shoots press their way out of the skin. Letting this early growth occur in the light, before planting, gets them off to a fine start.

Traditionally, with its warming temperatures and lighter days, Easter is the time for planting potatoes. They do reasonably well in most soils, but to get the most out of the smallish space I dedicate to them, I add composted manure to the bed – it holds moisture and the added nutrients speed up growth, which increases the chance of a crop before the risk of blight in late summer.

As potatoes grow, it's usual to earth them up – using a rake to draw earth into a mound high enough to cover all but the top quarter of the foliage. This keeps the developing tubers out of the light that would spoil them. I don't always remember to do this as often as I might, but a good rake up about 6 weeks after planting and once or twice when I remember is usually enough. Living in Devon, watering is not usually an issue but in particularly dry periods I'll help them along with the odd watering canful.

If I remember and have time, I sow some under cover in large pots or short tyre stacks for a super-early crop. I half-fill these with compost, sink the seed potatoes 10cm down and 15cm or so apart and water often. As the leafy stalks emerge, I add a little compost to cover all but the tops – to protect the swelling tubers from the light. A compost bag – cut along the top, emptied, turned inside out to expose the black inner, punctured here and there for drainage – works equally well. The process works for super-early carrots too – with seed sown on a 15–20cm depth of compost and just covered over with a sprinkling. Regular watering and the warmth under cover shunts growth along beautifully, with small, nutty salad potatoes and sweet, slim carrots ready around 3 months later, in May.

And from that first harvest of the year until the last Pink Fir Apple has been lifted, I know there will not be a disappointing mouthful.

Root crisps (page 60)
Sorrel potatoes (page 160)

BLUE HONEYSUCKLE

Site Unfussy about soil. Needs sun

Harvest May–June

Notes Not self-fertile, needs another variety nearby

AFTER THE WINTER, shoots and leaves are fine enough but the early homegrown fruit is welcomed like the first heat of summer. Special though it is, forced rhubarb feels like it's been ingeniously robbed from the arms of winter, whereas the early mini strawberries and blue honeysuckle fruit of May belong to the sunshine, and I love them for it.

Blue honeysuckle, aka honeyberry, is a low shrub rather than the common garden climber that shares its name. Its fluted yellow flowers come early, giving the bees a much needed playground in early spring. The flowers turn to small, oblong fruit almost before you've had time to enjoy them, ripening rapidly to be ready more years than not by the end of May.

Blue honeysuckle fruit look very much like deep-coloured, slightly stretched blueberries, and taste like blackcurrants sweetened with a little honey. I have to say I prefer them to blueberries; they have a rounded, deeper flavour and are ready to eat a couple of months earlier in the year.

Most varieties have been developed in cold climates such as Siberia, so the plant and its flowers can handle a decent chill and come out lively and bright early in spring. Their hardiness and ability to thrive in most soils makes them a fine alternative to blueberries, which can be a little temperamental in the cold and require acidic conditions to do well.

As with Mignonettes, blue honeysuckle fruits aren't going to feed the five thousand – we gather a few handfuls at a time as they ripen – but as garden sweets, punctuations in an otherwise bought fruit salad, or in pancakes, muffins or crushed in a glass of fizz, they are superb.

ue honeysuckle

June

June makes a gardener feel rich and a cook feel happy. Almost everything that's ready to harvest is short in season, expensive in the shops or is simply unbuyable. So many leaves, beans and herbs are approaching their lush peak and at last there is serious fruit.

June's peak harvest

Carrots

Garlic scapes

Globe artichokes

Lavender

Lettuces

Mexican tree spinach

Parsley

Peas

Rocket

Rose

Rhubarb

Salad burnet

Strawberries

The first of four or even five months of strawberries begins – the Honeoye is particularly good this early – and the salads are at their tenderest. The oriental leaves that have done so well through winter and spring take a little backstep for the summer, becoming punctuations to the tender, less punchy salad leaves. The peas and broad beans are at their abundant peak, with leafy herbs – parsley, chervil and sorrel especially – finding their way into almost every meal.

June is often the finest month for fly fishing on the river that draws the line around the far field. The stillest evenings late in the month, when the flies are hatching, are most likely to tempt me out there with the rod. Fly fishing is not something I was born to do. I know the techniques, I am not unfamiliar with the subtleties, yet my mind and body seem incapable of coordinating a reasonable impersonation of competence.

With fly fishing this matters little. The pleasure comes partly from the palaver and stillness of fishing – the tying of knots, the selection of flies and the choosing of the gauge and the length of line. It is mostly the standing there, apparently occupied, rather than catching which settles the soul.

A fruitless hour casting last week, the sun still hot enough to tingle the neck at 8pm, meant I saw three kingfishers and a peregrine. And being in the water of a kinking river, banked high with vegetation, gives the kingfisher little time to see you – they often turn with vertical wings within a few feet of me, trailing their high peeps and magic.

Buzzards are a daily companion, either noisily squabbling with the crows or quietly catching the warm rising currents; often more than a dozen birds glide within each spiralling tower. Sparrowhawks are fairly common and kestrels will sit on the overhead wires whenever I'm out in the tractor mowing, looking for one of the many mice and voles that furrow the soil in the vineyard, but last week's peregrine was the first I've seen here.

It's hard to mistake the noise of a bird of prey for anything else, but I knew the noise heading across the field didn't belong to a buzzard, sparrowhawk or kestrel. Being a dozen feet below soil level with my feet in the water meant it didn't see me until almost overhead. What it was shrieking about I have no idea, but it hushed the instant it saw me, like someone caught singing on the way back from the pub.

— 18 June, 2013

FOR THREE YEARS NOW I have had a very fine fruit cage standing proud. Inside, six dwarf cherry trees are getting large enough to produce well alongside six blackcurrants grown as standards. The net has yet to be strung around the frame as the plants within have been too young to produce enough to warrant protecting. That is about to change.

Birds seem to have an on/off switch. They will either leave what you grow entirely untroubled or move in – in waves of hungry beaks – to decimate your crop. Until this year, the strawberries fell into our mouths rather than theirs – this year I have eaten precious few and this is a state of affairs that cannot continue.

It's time to start again. Strawberries tend to produce well for four or five years before slowing down, and their time is approaching – the birds' feasting has just made my mind up for me.

In autumn, the raised bed that the strawberries have filled will be emptied and the plants relocated to the forest garden as part of the edible ground cover there. Inside a newly netted fruit cage, with its sunny location by the veg patch and its fertile soil, I'll plant six varieties to give me (rather than the birds) a long, sweet season of berries. Although autumn and winter planting is fine, getting new strawberries planted when summer turns to autumn gives them a chance of fruiting next year.

I want a successive harvest when it comes to strawberries, so I've chosen varieties that fruit in a slightly overlapping sequence rather than all at the same time. I love preserves, but I prefer to choose when to make them rather than be forced by the guilt of kilos of uneaten fruit starting to go over.

These are the varieties I'll be planting: Honeoye – a flavourful strawberry, to eat from the start of Wimbledon; Cambridge Favourite – an old much-loved variety that will produce from late June and through July; Mara des Bois – a steady fruiter, with a long season from August into autumn that has an incredible complexity of flavour – like fine wild strawberries but in a larger package; Royal Sovereign – it's smaller than most, less productive than some, but the flavour is extraordinary; and Florence – dark red, delicious and highly aromatic as well as being disease resistant, it provides a wonderful later summer harvest. The sixth line will be filled by single plants of a few varieties – old and new – and the one that tastes the best will replace the rest in this line.

STRAWBERRIES

Site Sunny, most soils

Harvest June–October

Notes Shallow rooting and don't like to dry out – mulch between with straw. Propagate from runners or start with young plants

Apricot & strawberry crumble (page 276)
Knickerbocker glory (page 172)
Spring into summer pudding (page 175)
Strawberry & gooseberry Eton mess (page 171)
Summer punch (page 183)

Buttercrunch lettuce

EVERY YEAR, more of the veg patch is consumed by what seems like a festival of blandness, and welcome it is too. For the summer at least, I like to eat plenty of simple one-variety salads, as well as some of mixed leaves with dashes of contrasting flavours strewn through, so I sow to suit. The majority are subtly flavoured leaves, the classic black dress as it were, with the 'louder' peppery leaves – rocket, watercress and a few oriental leaves, that I now grow in small quantities in summer – as the accessories.

Mild lettuces are often overlooked in favour of the livelier leaves and I'd like to put that right. Instead of being slapped around the tastebuds by pepper and mustard, summer deserves more of these gentle leaves, and as ever, choosing the best varieties is what makes all the difference. These are a few I grow every year.

Australian Yellow Leaf, a large, open-headed lettuce with gorgeous bright green/yellow crinkled leaves, looks fabulous, is slow to bolt and takes well to cut-and-come-again harvesting. The texture is superb – firm and crunchy – and the flavour sweet and fine. Grow it with the deep red, Really Red Deer Tongue for a fabulous visual and flavour combination.

Reine de Glaces is a superb crisphead lettuce, with gently toothed leaves and a tight crisp ball at its centre, a little like an elegantly ragged Iceberg but with much more flavour and refinement. Crisp, beautiful and reliable. A must.

Buttercrunch, along with Marvel of Four Seasons, is my favourite butterhead lettuce. While the outer leaves are soft and loose, the centre is crisp, so it's almost two lettuces in one. The flavour is gentle and buttery. It's slow to bolt and drought resistant too. Try it with just olive oil and salt, or use it as the base of a mixed salad.

Green Oak Leaf is a wavy-edged, apple-green lettuce leaf that takes as well to cut-and-come-again harvesting as any – it grows back heartily and repeatedly with no loss of succulence in the leaves. It has a good-looking, tasty red sister too.

Getting a stream of delicious and diverse summer leaves requires a little thought; careful pairing of available space with what and how you like to eat is essential. The more limited your time, space or inclination to grow, the more I'd suggest growing flavours and textures not available in the shops. Even a few unbuyable leaves grown in containers – easily done in even the smallest space – can make your salads special.

A metre or two of guttering on the windowsill or a few pots on the patio can be surprisingly productive – especially when taking a cut-and-come-again approach.

Rather than wait for all my lettuces to develop fully and lift them whole, I go in much earlier on some, pulling off individual leaves or cutting around 3–4cm above the base, leaving the plant to grow new leaves. Depending on the time of year, the weather and salad variety, I get four, five or even six cuts from each plant – which, when there are often a hundred or more seeds per packet, makes growing salads pretty appealing economically.

SUMMER SALADS

Site Relatively unfussy

Sow March–June

Harvest May–September

Notes Sow direct or start under cover in modules, planting out when a few centimetres tall

Spring into summer salad (page 162)

GARLIC

Site Sunny and free-draining; plant on a ridge if your ground is heavy

Sow Plant cloves 7cm deep (10cm for Elephant), pointed end up, 15cm apart, in October–November, or February–March. They'll all be ready in summer but autumn sowings tend to be larger

Harvest Scapes: May–June; green garlic: June–July; main crop June–August

Notes Don't sow cloves bought for eating – they're rarely hardy enough for our climate and are prone to viruses

Beef in beer (page 68)

Borlottis with mussels (page 332)

Celeriac mustard mash (page 73)

Chicken & Savoy cabbage in cider (page 64)

Courgette 'spaghetti' with fresh tomato, garlic & basil sauce (page 256)

Garlic scape mimosa (page 152)

Lamb & apricot tagine (page 247)

Ocas bravas (page 346)

Pot-roast chicken with grapes in milk (page 336)

Slow-roast five-spice pork belly (page 340)

IN MANY WAYS garlic isn't a great candidate for growing yourself – it is widely available and homegrown garlic is largely indistinguishable from shop-bought if used in the normal way. I grow more of it each year though, as it gives me five distinctive things: it's a hardworking companion plant that protects neighbouring plants from pests and, with the right blend of varieties, it opens the door to the largely unbuyable green garlic, garlic scapes and Elephant garlic, as well as giving us garlic to use in the usual way.

Elephant garlic is, as you would hope, enormous. A bulb can easily make 12cm across. Being botanically closer to a leek than garlic, Elephant garlic is gentle, with a soft sweetness alongside the familiar flavour that roasting draws out beautifully. There's also an undeniably caveman pleasure that comes with lifting something so otherwise familiar yet oversized from the soil.

Of the normal-sized garlic, I grow reasonably equal amounts of hardneck and softneck varieties. Most hardnecks come from cold climates and are well suited to wet or cold conditions and, when left to mature, tend to have a stronger and more complex flavour than softnecks although they don't store as well.

I usually grow Lautrec Wight and Carcassonne Wight as hardnecks, with the softnecks of Early Purple Wight (for a harvest as early as May), Picardy Wight and Solent Wight. I treat them differently in preparation for the kitchen.

Hardnecks throw flower stalks skywards as spring eases into summer. Through May and June, we cut the slim, often curly, stem just above the leaves, while the flower head is still small, closed and tear-shaped. A few minutes' steaming is all they need to become one of the garden treats of the year: imagine a succulent, garlicky asparagus. Harvesting the scape also allows the bulb to develop without the plant's resources being diverted to the flower that would otherwise form. A few weeks later, the bulbs are pretty much fully grown but individual cloves are not fully distinct – we pick most of the hardnecks at this stage, as green garlic. Their flavour is mild yet complex, making an understated yet distinctive backseat compared to more mature garlic. They roast wonderfully well whole and pair up perfectly with the new potatoes, broad beans and other spring-into-summer vegetables.

I let the rest of the hardnecks and most of the softnecks mature before harvesting. The leaves let you know when to harvest: hardnecks' leaves turn yellow, whereas softnecks go over and flop. We leave them to dry for a few days somewhere sunny and dry, so they can be stored. The hardnecks and Early Purple Wight store least well and are used first, with Picardy Wight and Solent Wight seeing us through winter.

Mexican tree spinach

I GROW MEXICAN TREE SPINACH for its beauty and summer leaves. With a name like that I was convinced it had to be good. I wasn't disappointed – the leaves are as delicious as they are striking. The plant is related to Good King Henry, which serves me well in spring, and fat hen, which grows wild and gets fed to the hens.

Having sown Mexican tree spinach once, it pops up where it likes: in gravel paths, in undisturbed spots in the veg patch, in the compost of potted plants and even in the much-trodden patch of grass outside the polytunnel. It can do as it likes as far as I'm concerned. Its brilliant light green leaves blush magenta as they grow, the plant reaching 2 metres high or more if left unpicked.

As its name suggests, it makes a fine (and colourful) substitute for spinach and picked small, the leaves brighten early salads. I love it wilted and creamed on toast.

As the plant ages, it becomes coarser (don't we all), so try a leaf first if picking from a plant over a couple of feet tall.

I sowed a few seeds direct and some in modules in spring in the first year and it's been with me ever since. It thrives in most soils, turning more magenta in response to the degree of sun it gets.

If you'd rather not have it from one year to the next, it's simple: don't allow any of the plants to set seed. Loving it as I do, I let the wind cast the seed where it likes and shake some intentionally where I want a splash of architectural, edible colour.

MEXICAN TREE SPINACH

Site Any

Sow March–April

Harvest May–October

Notes Mid-October seems to be when the seed is ready to shake from the plant

Stir-fried asparagus & Good King Henry (page 158)

Wild garlic risotto (page 72)

FLORENCE FENNEL IS A FUSSY little beggar – it prefers a sandy soil yet likes high fertility and plenty of water, along with steady temperatures and long daylight hours. In short, it would rather be in Italy than dealing with the vagaries of a Devonian summer. Wouldn't we all.

Closely related to the herb fennel that shares its glorious anise flavour, Florence fennel forms glassy bulbs close to the ground. Their cool, crisp texture becomes sweet and delicious when they are griddled or roasted – perfect with seafood, in salads, as a crudité, in soups and with cheese or (as is classic in Italy) with fruit.

As my garden hasn't the perfect conditions for it to grow, I've had to learn to pretend that I don't care that the plump, tight, classic bulbs of Florence fennel, which any idiot seems to be able to grow, elude me. In truth, the elongated bulbs I manage most years taste every bit as fine, but vanity won't quite let me go.

I've tried everything. Sowing fennel too early makes it open to temperature swings that encourage it to bolt (run to seed), the first stage of which is to elongate, so I religiously wait into May every year. I've tried varieties such as Finale that resist bolting, but alas, mine still stretch out a little. It may be the slightly too-heavy soil here and the fact that the veg patch tends to be a pretty full-on, busy affair, when Florence fennel

FLORENCE FENNEL

Site Sunny and warm, with a good and well-drained soil

Sow Under cover in modules April–July and plant outside from May. Sow direct May–July. Allow 25cm between plants

Harvest June–November. Cut 1–2cm above the soil, cover the cut stem with soil for a secondary crop of small shoots

Notes Sowing every 2–3 weeks will give you a good succession

would much rather have a clear, sunny, airy spot to luxuriate in. I remain undeterred, although I've changed tack a little.

I now sow a few varieties – Finale and Romanesco among them – closer than the usual 25cm spacing, and harvest plenty when they're half-developed in mid-June before they have chance to lose their shape. All the flavour is there at that stage, and growing them closer means I have no less volume in total. The rest grow on in the hope, one year, of perfectly plump full-sized bulbs.

I use Florence fennel once or twice a week perhaps, so I don't need too many at once. Sowing them in small batches every fortnight from May until the end of July gives me 4–5 months of steady picking. Perfect.

Roast trout with fennel & lemon
(page 244)

Agretti, fennel & cucumber salad
(page 260)

LAVENDER

Site Well drained

Harvest May–July

Notes Can be started from cuttings or young plants. Some plants become more wood than shoot after 4–5 years. Replace a few at a time when bad

Herb syrups (page 266)

Lavender & walnut fudge (page 179)

Loin of lamb with lavender & lemon thyme (page 146)

I INITIALLY PLANTED lavender for its scent, to give me another place to stop to rub leaves and flowers on the morning walk around the fields with the dog. Much as I love the fragrance, I can easily have too much of it – the floral equivalent of an extra sugar in the coffee – and I always came over a bit 'pot pourri face' when seeing recipes that called for lavender. No more. Nikki Duffy's fantastic lamb with lavender and lemon thyme recipe, from her *River Cottage Herb Handbook,* put paid to that once and for all.

I still use lavender sparingly but more often than ever. Pairing it with walnuts in the fudge recipe or adding it in scant pinches to the almond biscuits works beautifully.

I haven't the perfect soil to grow lavender – it prefers a light and well-drained spot – so I grow it in a couple of pots and in the garden where the soil is lighter than the veg patch. And, as with the peppers, I can't walk past them without getting some of their oil on my hands.

Lavender needs regular cutting back to keep it full of vitality – I used to snip it back in spring, midsummer and in early September, but now I'm harvesting for the kitchen regularly I find the first two cuts take care of themselves. It's best to cut back the new growth to leave some green shoots – don't cut into the old wood – and it'll grow away again healthily.

The best varieties for cooking have low levels of camphor; the angustifolia varieties, with their fragrant, soft, sweet flavour, are the ones I like best. I pick the young leaves and flowerbuds in May, June and July, before buds burst fully – lavender loses something after that to my mind.

ivender: L. angustifolia

Globe artichokes (mixed varieties)

I FIRST WENT TO FRANCE when I was eleven. It was a school trip I remember for three things: being amazed that, according to the Bayeux Tapestry, someone could aim so well as to hit King Harold in the eye with an arrow; for being shamefully caught having pinched a roommate's biscuits; and for eating my very first globe artichokes.

It may have been the biscuit shame I associated with that trip, but I didn't eat artichokes again until I went grape picking in France a decade later. We had them most lunchtimes and every evening, usually served simply with vinaigrette.

Beautiful as they are, growing here in the veg patch and perennial garden, globe artichokes can appear a little intimidating in the kitchen – they look more of a weapon than a treat. Quite what the delicious bit might be – and how to get at it – is not immediately apparent.

If ever a plant demonstrates the pleasure that comes with a minor palaver – and it is only minor – then the globe artichoke is it. Somewhere under the armour lies a sweet, succulent, fleshy heart, and how you get to it depends on the size of the artichoke and how you plan to eat it.

I love them cooked whole (for 15–45 minutes depending on size) and served with vinaigrette – I enjoy the slow demolition of tearing off each tough petal to dip in the dressing before scraping that glorious flesh free with my teeth.

When preparing the heart for a recipe, you'll need a large bowl, half-filled with cold water and the juice of a lemon or two, with the spent lemon skins added – submerge the hearts to prevent them discolouring.

To prepare small artichokes, peel the leaves off, until you reach the slender, smooth, light green/yellow centre. Slice off any remnants of hard petal from around the base, then slice the artichoke in half lengthways. There should be no fluffy choke within – if there is, remove it.

To prepare large artichokes, cut the stem to 2cm or so. Lay the artichoke on its side and using a sharp knife (I find a bread knife works well), slice through the petals about 4cm from the base. Strip off the leaves. Carve off any tough remnants. You should be left with something resembling a flat-topped spinning top. Use a teaspoon to weedle out the choke – the fluffy, inedible immature flower at the centre – and discard it. What remains is one of the finest things a garden can grow.

Artichoke hearts are fabulous in salads, vignarola, pasta sauces and numerous other dishes – I suspect they'd make a fine supper boiled alongside an old wellington, they're that good. To cook them, either poach in a little wine and/or water until tender (then submerge in oil to preserve if not using them immediately), or sauté in a pan.

I leave plenty of artichokes unharvested too. As summer passes, their once delicious buds widen, the choke develops and they morph into extraordinary late season flowers – fibre-optic platforms of purple that draw bees in large numbers, perhaps a dozen on more on each flower.

GLOBE ARTICHOKES

Site Relatively unfussy but prefers well-drained site and sun

Sow February–March under cover in modules, potting them on when large enough to handle. Plant out in May

Harvest May–September

Notes Once established, take off side shoots in winter to create new plants and revitalise the mother plant

Globe artichokes with honey & mustard or elderflower dressing (page 140)
Vignarola (page 148)

Recipes for

April, May & June

Asparagus, pea shoots & borage with elderflower dressing

Raw asparagus is a strangely under-indulged pleasure. Do give it a go. The flavour is less sweet than when cooked for sure, though it's made up for in nuttiness – there's a hint of fresh hazelnuts or peanuts about it. Elderflower and asparagus is one of those peculiar pairings that is rarely made but that makes perfect sense the instant you think of it. A fine starter or light lunch for a bright spring day.

Per person

4 asparagus spears

A handful of pea shoots

About 6 borage flowers

A few shavings of Parmesan

Elderflower dressing (page 165)

Arrange the asparagus, pea shoots, borage flowers and Parmesan on a plate however takes your fancy. Spoon the elderflower dressing over the salad and serve.

Globe artichokes with honey *&* mustard or elderflower dressing

Every time we tackle globe artichokes whole, with a dressing, I remind myself to do it more often. They are one of those convivial, sociable foods – like oysters and crab – that are best enjoyed with loved ones and slightly too much dry white wine. I love them with either a honey mustard or elderflower dressing. It takes a little time to work your way through a large globe artichoke – one each is usually plenty as a starter – which allows the main course to finish cooking or resting while you eat. Once everyone has demolished their artichoke, you'll be left with a pile of what look like dinosaur scales and happy faces.

Per person

1 globe artichoke

Honey mustard dressing (page 164)
or Elderflower dressing (page 165)

If your artichokes have spiky petals – some varieties do – snip the tips off with scissors to save your fingers numerous punctures. Slice the base from the stem, so that it will sit upright on a plate when cooked.

Add the artichokes to a pan of boiling water and simmer for 20 minutes. To test whether they are cooked, lift one out and tear off a petal – if it comes off easily it's ready; if not, allow another 5 minutes and retest. Once cooked, remove the artichokes from the pan and turn them upside down to drain.

Serve the artichokes whole, as they are, with your chosen dressing in a shallow bowl on the side. Tear the petals off, dip in the dressing and scrape them against your front teeth to release the flesh. Eventually you will end up with a green disc topped with pale petals and fibres within. This upper part is the choke, so named for perfectly appropriate reasons. Slice the choke off and discard it, leaving the delicious, pale green heart to dip and eat.

Veg patch tempura

There are a few secrets to really good tempura batter. Firstly, if at all possible, be Japanese. Otherwise, remember that the batter should be thin – no thicker than single cream. Think of it as a nightie rather than a duvet; the idea is not to completely envelop, just to cling here and there. The ingredients should be cold, and the oil hot. The batter should be mixed very briefly, with fingers or chopsticks, leaving some lumps – this helps achieve the perfect crunch. I prefer using rice flour for the batter as it is gluten-free, giving a light crisp batter, but a blend of half plain flour and half cornflour does a reasonable impersonation.

Most veg is great battered and fried in this way – I have a feeling my running shoes would taste good tempura-ed – but my favourites are mild chillies, sliced courgettes, asparagus spears and thin slices of yacon and aubergine. Edible flowers are fabulous – courgette flowers (stuffed or not), nasturtiums, elderflower heads and daylilies especially, and do try leafy herbs – the frying intensifies their flavour – shiso (aka perilla) and coriander are sensational dipped and fried very briefly.

Serves 3–4

Veg or edible flowers of your choice (see above)

Oil for deep-frying

For the tempura batter

225g rice flour

2 free-range egg yolks

375ml ice-cold water

To serve

Sweet chilli dipping sauce (page 262)

Slowly heat a 4–5cm depth of vegetable oil in a suitable heavy pan over a medium-high heat (or a deep-fat fryer) to 170°C; i.e. when a cube of bread dropped in turns golden in around a minute.

Meanwhile, make the tempura batter. Tip the flour into a bowl. Whisk the egg yolks into the water, then pour into the flour and mix together with your fingers or chopsticks in a figure-of-eight pattern. Mix for 30 seconds or so only – lumps are fine.

Dip the veg or flowers into the batter one at a time and fry in small batches – this helps ensure the oil doesn't cool too much and keeps the tempura crisp. Use a slotted spoon to flip the veg or flowers over to cook both sides. When cooked, lift out and drain on kitchen paper. Serve straight away, with sweet chilli dipping sauce.

Broad bean hummus

This is as good at the start of the year with the first rush of beans as it is at the end with the larger, tougher end-of-season beans. It works really well with half peas or even green beans thrown in. If you use very large broad beans, you may want to slip the sweet hearts out from the tough skins, but it's not usually necessary. Hard or soft goat's cheese works well here – the earthiness sets off the hummus a treat.

Serves 4 as a lunch

400g freshly podded broad beans

3 garlic cloves, finely chopped

5–6 tbsp olive oil

12 mint leaves, chopped

Juice of 1 lemon

Sea salt and freshly ground black pepper

To serve

8 slices of sourdough or other rustic bread

80g firm goat's cheese, cut into 8 slices

A splash of extra virgin olive oil (optional)

A few Greek basil, parsley or mint leaves (optional)

Put the broad beans in a pan, just cover with water and bring to the boil. Simmer for 6–10 minutes depending on their size, until tender. Drain.

Tip the beans into a food processor, add the garlic, 5 tbsp olive oil and the mint and process to a smooth purée. Add the lemon juice and process again until incorporated. Add a little more oil if you think the texture or taste would benefit from it. Season with salt and pepper to taste.

Toast the bread and spread with the hummus. Put a couple of slices on each plate and top with the goat's cheese. Splash with extra virgin olive oil and sprinkle with Greek basil, parsley or mint if you fancy.

Baked mackerel with coriander micros

Easy in the oven or over the barbecue, this simple lunch takes very little time and the coriander micros, with all their intensity, bring out the best in the mackerel.

Serves 2

2 whole mackerel, gutted and cleaned
A little olive oil
4 bay leaves
A few sprigs of thyme
3 garlic cloves, finely chopped
Sea salt and freshly ground black pepper

To serve

1 lemon, quartered
Coriander microleaves

Preheat the oven to 200°C/Gas 6 or heat up your barbecue.

Make several diagonal slashes along each side of the mackerel. Rub a little olive oil over the skin of both fish and season with salt and pepper. Lay a couple of bay leaves and a sprig or two of thyme in the cavity of each fish along with the garlic, dividing it between them.

Place on a roasting tray in the oven for about 20 minutes or barbecue on the grid or in a fish basket, turning once, until cooked.

Squeeze lemon juice over, then sprinkle generously with coriander micros. Eat immediately with a leafy salad, salsa or greens.

Loin of lamb with lavender & lemon thyme

I'm not sure I'd have risked a lovely loin of lamb by pairing it with lavender had friend and food writer Nikki Duffy not made this for me. It was a total knockout, but if you don't fancy lavender it also works very well with rosemary instead. The balance is crucial: use too much lavender and it overpowers; use too little and (as with rosemary) there's not enough floral herbiness. Nikki's been kind enough to allow me to share her recipe, unaltered, as it's unimprovable.

Serves 4

2 tbsp finely chopped lavender leaves

2 tsp finely chopped lemon thyme

Finely grated zest of 1 unwaxed lemon

1 fat garlic clove, finely chopped

A little rapeseed or olive oil

A piece of boned-out lamb loin, 500–600g

A little white wine or stock, for deglazing (optional)

Sea salt and freshly ground black pepper

Preheat the oven to 220°C/Gas 7.

Combine the lavender, lemon thyme, lemon zest and garlic in a small bowl. Add some seasoning and just enough oil to make a thick paste: 2 tbsp or so.

Lay the meat out on a board, skin side down, and smear the herb mixture all over the inside, working it into all the cracks and crevices. Fold the meat over on itself, with the eye of the meat inside, and tie securely in several places with string. Smear any escaping herby oil over the outside of the meat and season it.

Place the meat in a roasting dish, with the 'open' edge uppermost to keep the flavouring mix inside. Roast for 15 minutes, then turn the oven down to 170°C/Gas 3 and roast for a further 15 minutes (for just-pink).

Leave the meat to stand in a warm place for 15 minutes before slicing. Deglaze the pan with a little white wine or stock – or even a splash of water – to create a few spoonfuls of flavoursome gravy.

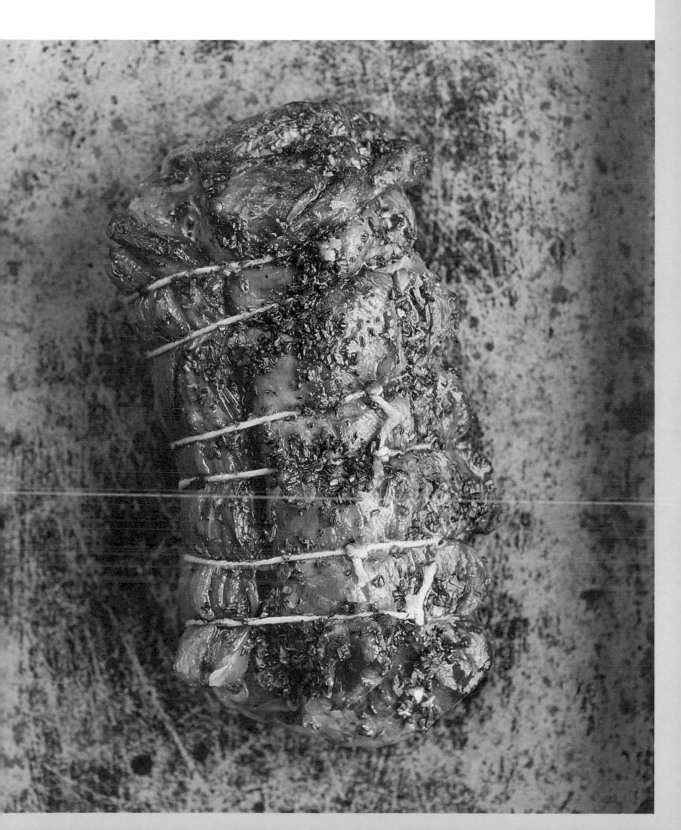

Vignarola

This fresh, light stew is a fine spring/summer recipe that is entirely adaptable to what's in season and what you have in the fridge. I've made this in April with asparagus, pea shoots and chives, then 5 months later with chard, runner beans, cherry tomatoes and lettuce. A little punchy cheese added late – instead of the pancetta – works really well, as does cider in place of the wine.

Serves 4

8 small artichokes

Finely grated zest of ½ and juice of 1 unwaxed lemon

700g broad beans in their pods

700g peas in their pods, or a couple of handfuls of frozen peas

8 spring onions

80ml olive oil

2 garlic cloves, finely chopped

80g pancetta, cut into cubes

400ml white wine, chicken stock or water (or any mixture)

A handful of green beans

A handful of mint, chopped

A handful of parsley, finely chopped

Sea salt and freshly ground black pepper

Prepare the artichokes first, pulling the leaves off to leave a small, smooth inner heart. Slice this lengthways into quarters and scoop out any hairy choke. Drop into cold water acidulated with the lemon juice, to prevent the artichokes discolouring.

Shell the broad beans and peas, and slice the spring onions. Heat 70ml of the olive oil in a pan and cook the spring onions over a moderate heat, stirring frequently, until soft. Add the garlic and cook for a couple of minutes. Add the pancetta cubes and cook until coloured, stirring often.

Add the artichoke quarters, stir and add the wine, stock/water and a pinch of salt. Stir, cover and cook for 15 minutes, stirring occasionally. Test the artichokes for tenderness – cook a little longer if needed.

Add the broad beans and cook for another couple of minutes, then add the green beans and peas, cooking for just another 2 minutes. Season with salt and pepper to taste and add the lemon zest.

Serve warm, scattered with mint and parsley and drizzled lightly with the remaining olive oil.

Asparagus & goat's cheese tart

An easy spring supper that takes only a few minutes to prepare using ready-made pastry and can be adapted to whatever is in season and in your fridge (try wilted spinach, Manchego and olives, for instance). There's no need to be prissy about putting it together – just spread the asparagus out and top quickly and don't worry if the pastry shrinks a little while cooking.

Serves 4

1 sheet of ready-rolled all-butter puff pastry, about 320g
A handful of plain flour, for dusting
550g asparagus
100g firm goat's cheese
A small handful of capers
A few anchovies
1 tbsp olive oil
3–4 tsp pesto (optional)
Sea salt and freshly ground black pepper

Preheat the oven to 200°C/Gas 6.

Roll the puff pastry on a lightly floured surface to a rectangle to fit within a 40 x 25cm baking sheet. Lay the pastry on the baking sheet and score a border 2cm from the edge on all sides, taking care not to cut completely through the pastry. Avoiding the border, pierce the pastry every 2–3cm with a fork to stop it rising too much during cooking.

Bake the pastry for 10 minutes or so, until lightly golden, then remove from the oven and let cool slightly.

Lay the asparagus across the pastry, within the border. Slice or crumble the goat's cheese and distribute over the asparagus. Scatter over the capers and anchovies, drizzle with olive oil and dot with pesto if you like. Season with salt and pepper.

Bake until the asparagus is just tender – around 20 minutes, a little longer for fat spears.

Sparga süitve

A delicious and simple, traditional Hungarian asparagus recipe that is especially good for lunch on a chilly spring day. I'd not tried paprika with asparagus before I made this and it works really well – try a light dusting on a poached or boiled egg before dipping asparagus into it for breakfast.

Serves 4 as a lunch or starter

550g asparagus

270ml natural yoghurt

1 tsp plain flour

1 large free-range egg yolk

1 tsp salt

1 tsp sugar

2 tsp paprika

50g fresh breadcrumbs (ideally from day-old bread)

30g butter, cut into cubes

A little olive oil

Freshly ground black pepper

Preheat the oven to 200°C/Gas 6.

Steam the asparagus until only just tender, 3–5 minutes depending on the thickness of the spears. Arrange the spears evenly in an ovenproof dish in which they fit quite snugly.

Stir the yoghurt, flour, egg yolk, salt, sugar and paprika together in a bowl. Pour this mixture evenly over the asparagus.

Sprinkle the breadcrumbs over the surface, dot with butter and add a trickle of olive oil and a generous grinding of pepper. Bake for around 15 minutes, until the breadcrumbs are golden.

Garlic scape mimosa

I first made this with asparagus and its simplicity and flavour make it one of those recipes I keep coming back to throughout the year – it works equally well with bamboo shoots, chard stalks or green beans. Here, garlic scapes replace the asparagus. As garlic grows, it throws up a stalk, at the end of which a flower develops – scapes are the top 15–20cm of those stalks. Harvesting them before the flower has matured directs the plant's energies to the garlic bulb rather than to creating a flower, and gives you one of my favourite spring treats into the bargain. If you aren't growing garlic, try southwestgarlicfarm.co.uk for scapes.

Serves 4 as a lunch or starter

3 medium free-range eggs

400g garlic scapes

2 tbsp capers, drained and chopped

A small handful of chives, chopped

2 or 3 chive flowers, broken into florets

A small handful of dill, chopped

Finely grated zest of ½ unwaxed lemon

A couple of good pinches of paprika

Sea salt and freshly ground black pepper

For the dressing

1 tbsp white wine vinegar

4 tsp English mustard

2 tsp honey

3 tbsp extra virgin olive oil

Place the eggs in a saucepan of cold water, bring to the boil and turn off the heat immediately. Leave the eggs in the water for 12 minutes. Drain off the water, then run cold water into the pan for a minute or so to stop the cooking process.

Steam the garlic scapes or simmer in water to cover until just tender – this can take 3–6 minutes depending on their thickness.

To make the dressing, in a small bowl, whisk the wine vinegar, mustard and honey together, add a couple of decent pinches of salt, then whisk in the extra virgin olive oil.

Peel and grate the eggs – it's a slightly messy palaver, but the texture is worth it.

Arrange the garlic scapes on a large plate and distribute the grated egg on top. Scatter over the capers, chives, chive florets, chopped dill and lemon zest. Dust with paprika, season with salt and pepper to taste and splash with the dressing.

Eggs Gordon Bennett

Now here's a prince of a breakfast, lunch or supper and there's not many recipes can say the same. When I told a friend, a cook, that I was messing with Eggs Arnold Bennett, he told me I'd better name it Eggs Gordon Bennett to warn people. Classic as Arnold Bennett may be, I just think the pea shoots make it that little bit more special. Try it and see. A leafy salad goes very well with it.

Serves 2

300ml milk

3 bay leaves

½ onion, sliced

½ unwaxed lemon, cut into 4 wedges

10 black peppercorns

250g undyed smoked pollock or haddock

6 free-range eggs

2 tbsp olive oil

20g unsalted butter

A handful of pea shoots

4 tbsp double cream

2 tbsp finely grated Parmesan

Sea salt and freshly ground black pepper

Put the milk, bay leaves, onion, lemon and peppercorns in a large shallow pan and bring to a simmer. Add the fish and poach for 4 minutes. Lift out the fish onto a plate. When it is cool enough to handle, break into flakes, removing any skin and bones.

Preheat the grill to high.

Beat the eggs in a bowl. Warm the olive oil and butter in a frying pan (suitable for use under the grill) over a medium heat, tilting the pan so that the oil coats the sides of the pan. Pour in the eggs. As the eggs begin to set, use a fork to lift little areas to allow uncooked egg to seep under and cook.

When the omelette has a cooked base but is still loose on top, scatter the pea shoots and flaked fish over the surface. Swirl the cream on top, season with salt and pepper and sprinkle with the Parmesan.

Slide the pan under the hot grill and cook for a minute or two until the omelette is lightly golden brown on top.

Spring herb omelette

The lengthening spring days mean the hens are again laying almost daily and there's a wealth of leaves and shoots to go with the eggs. I make this throughout the year and I don't suppose I've made it with the same herbs twice, but I usually include chives, parsley, garlic cress or wild garlic and a little sorrel for edge. A leaf or two of lovage works beautifully too.

Serves 1

2 free-range eggs

A knob of butter

2 tbsp chopped mixed herbs (parsley, chives, wild garlic, sorrel etc.)

Sea salt and freshly ground black pepper

Lightly beat the eggs together with a little pepper.

Place a 20cm frying pan over a medium heat and add a good knob of butter. When the butter is lightly bubbling, pour in the eggs. As the omelette begins to set, use a fork to lift little areas to allow uncooked egg to seep underneath and cook.

After a minute or so add the herbs and cook for a minute or two longer, then fold over opposite edges and slide from the pan onto a warm plate. Season with salt and eat immediately.

Broad bean falafels

I love falafels of all kinds and, with or without pollock, this is the one for spring into summer. The fish works really well – it can be smoked or unsmoked, haddock or another flaky white fish – but it is by no means integral. The falafels are as good without it, just different.

Although they are great with a leafy salad and relish or a salsa, I usually jam falafels into toasted pittas or wrap them in warm flatbreads, with something sharp, such as pickled chard stems (page 82) or a dollop of gooseberry salsa (page 166), or yoghurt with poppy seeds and mint stirred through (as for my raita on page 58).

Serves 4

400g freshly podded broad beans
½ tsp cardamom seeds
½ tsp cumin seeds
¼ tsp cayenne pepper
½ tsp coriander seeds
3 garlic cloves, crushed
½ small onion, finely chopped
30g coriander leaves, finely chopped
30g flat-leaf parsley, finely chopped
½ tsp salt
½ tsp baking powder
2½ tbsp plain flour
1 large free-range egg, lightly beaten
200g pollock, poached and flaked (optional)
Vegetable oil for shallow-frying
100g sesame seeds

Unless you're using the smallest freshest broad beans, you'll need to lightly cook the beans until just tender. Place them in a pan, just cover with water and bring to a gentle boil. Simmer for 5 minutes, then drain.

Meanwhile, lightly toast the spices in a dry pan over a medium heat to intensify their flavour. Zap to a coarse powder in a coffee grinder, or pound using a pestle and mortar.

Put the broad beans, garlic, onion and herbs in a food processor and blitz until smooth.

Add the ground spices, salt, baking powder and flour to the food processor and pulse until well combined. Add the egg and pulse until incorporated. Transfer to a bowl and stir in the pollock if using. Cover and refrigerate for an hour.

Slowly heat a 2–3cm depth of vegetable oil in a wide pan to 170°C, or until a cube of bread dropped into the oil browns all over in a minute or so. Adjust the heat if need be.

Shape the bean mixture into balls, roughly the size of golf balls, then roll each in sesame seeds to coat. Fry in small batches for 8–10 minutes, turning until evenly golden. Drain the falafels on kitchen paper.

Stir-fried asparagus *&* Good King Henry

Sir David Attenborough once told me not to name drop, but I have to mention the time when Sheila Dillon came here to record for Radio 4's Food Programme, as Martin Crawford (the forest garden expert, also here for the recording) made a delicious snack with early perennials from the garden. This is my variation, using asparagus instead of his bamboo shoots, and chervil to lend a little extra sweet, gentle aniseed. By all means use chard, spinach or Mexican tree spinach in place of the Good King Henry, sprouting broccoli instead of asparagus, or more chervil if you haven't any sweet cicely seeds.

**Serves 2 as a light lunch
or 4 as a side**

20ml olive oil

110g asparagus

100g Good King Henry leaves, shredded

12 sweet cicely seeds

A good splash of soy sauce

A handful of chervil sprigs

Sea salt and freshly ground black pepper

Warm the olive oil in a large frying pan or wok over a high heat and add the asparagus. Stir-fry for a couple of minutes, maybe a little longer if the spears are thick.

As the asparagus starts to soften and bend through cooking, add the Good King Henry. As it wilts, add the sweet cicely and a good splash of soy. Stir-fry for a minute or two, then add the chervil and cook just a minute longer.

Taste for seasoning and add a little more soy and/or salt and pepper if needed, then serve.

Sorrel potatoes

If you do only one thing with sorrel, try this: it's the best sauce for new potatoes, it takes no time at all and converts everyone to sorrel's lemon freshness. Later in the year when potatoes tend to be less waxy, try wilted sorrel stirred through mashed potato.

Serves 4 as a side dish

500g new potatoes

4 handfuls of sorrel

60g unsalted butter

Sea salt and freshly ground black pepper

Boil the potatoes until just cooked – this can be as quick as 8 minutes for small, fresh new potatoes, so check them early.

If the sorrel has a substantial central rib, strip it out. Shred the sorrel roughly.

Drain the potatoes, add the butter, replace the lid and swirl the pan around to coat the potatoes in the melting butter. Add the sorrel, season with salt and pepper, and swirl again with the lid on. The heat will wilt the sorrel in the butter as you swirl the pan.

Serve immediately, with fish, lamb or beef. Or just eat with a fork.

Spring into summer salad

If you have small-leaved lime (*Tilia cordata*) growing near you, I urge you to try its beautifully nutty early leaves. By no means powerful, they just provide the gentle flavour and fine texture for the other flavours to work against. More lettuce leaves will certainly do instead if you've no small-leaved lime to hand. Whatever you do, make the main leaves gentle – you are after a sea of subtle leaves punctuated with islands of intense flavour.

This salad is particularly good with fish and chicken, and I tend to eat it simply dressed with oil, salt and pepper.

Serves 2 as a light lunch or 4 as a side

A small lettuce

A good handful of small-leaved lime leaves

20 or so young Szechuan pepper leaves

20 or so salad burnet leaves

A dozen or so Tulbaghia or other society garlic flowers

A head or two of chive flowers, broken into florets

1–2 tbsp olive oil

Sea salt and freshly ground black pepper

Create a base of torn-up lettuce leaves and small-leaved lime. Scatter over all the small leaves and flowers, dash with olive oil, season with salt and pepper and serve.

Candida's honey mustard dressing

Dressings are, essentially, mini savoury cocktails that need to be well balanced. This one is sharp, sweet, punchy and good with virtually everything. It is our 'reach-for' dressing; there is invariably a jar or bottle of it sitting in the kitchen, always fresh as it gets used so quickly.

Makes 70ml

1 tbsp cider vinegar

1 generous tsp smooth English mustard

1 generous tsp honey

3 tbsp olive oil

Sea salt and freshly ground black pepper

Whisk the cider vinegar, mustard and honey together. Add a good pinch of salt and pepper and whisk a little more. Add the olive oil and whisk briskly until the mixture forms an emulsion. Check the seasoning.

Variation For a delicious, though distinctly different version, try red wine vinegar and grainy mustard instead.

Yoghurt dressing

A lovely, creamy dressing with a fine, gentle garlickiness that doesn't overpower. It can separate slightly – brisk whisking is the key, with one of those useful mini-whisks if you have one, otherwise a fork will do. Even if it does separate, don't worry – it will still taste very fine indeed.

Makes 110ml

1 tbsp white wine vinegar

½ garlic clove, finely chopped

1 tsp honey

3 tbsp olive oil

3 tbsp natural yoghurt

Sea salt and freshly ground black pepper

Whisk the wine vinegar, garlic and honey together. Add a good pinch of salt and pepper and whisk a little more. Add the olive oil and whisk briskly until the mixture forms an emulsion. Finally add the yoghurt and whisk again. Taste and adjust the seasoning if need be.

Variation A few chopped chives and/or a sprinkling of onion seeds add a lively oniony edge.

Elderflower dressing

If there's anything more than a hint of warmth in the air, this is the dressing for asparagus, peas, early leaves and even strawberries later in the summer.

Makes 60ml

2 tbsp elderflower cordial

1 tbsp chive flower vinegar (page 168), or white wine vinegar

1 tbsp olive oil

Sea salt and freshly ground black pepper

Whisk the elderflower cordial and vinegar together with some salt and pepper. Add the olive oil and whisk until the mixture forms an emulsion. Taste for seasoning.

Parsley pesto

Many years ago, I sat in a restaurant high up in Bellagio, Italy, looking along all three slender limbs of Lake Como. I ate pasta pesto and drank a little too much of the bottle of wine that came with it. I can truly say it remains the only time I enjoyed basil pesto. It's not that I don't like it, I just think it's a whole lot nicer with other herbs, little (or no) garlic, and almonds rather than pine nuts. Walnuts or hazelnuts work equally, if differently, well. And save the Parmesan for when you serve. I use pesto on pizzas and as a dressing (especially for beetroot) as much as a pasta sauce.

Makes about 150ml

60g parsley, tougher stalks removed

30g blanched almonds

1 garlic clove, finely chopped (optional)

Juice of ½ lemon

80ml olive oil, plus extra for storing

Sea salt and freshly ground black pepper

Put the parsley, almonds, garlic, if using, and lemon juice in a blender and blitz until fairly smooth – I like a little texture to my pesto; blitz more if you prefer. With the motor running, add the olive oil in a steady stream. Taste it when you've added 60ml or so of the oil – you may like it as it is. The intensity of flavour varies with the pungency of the parsley and oil.

Store the pesto in a sealed jar in the fridge, with a thin film of oil poured over the surface to exclude any air. Use within a month or so.

Gooseberry salsa

I'm indecently proud of this recipe. My wife is no great fan of home-smoked mackerel or very sharp/sour food, but she loves the combination of mackerel and this salsa. It works beautifully with smoked or grilled fillets and I guess it would be a fine partner to goose, duck or pork too.

Serves 4

4 tbsp caster sugar
3 tbsp white wine vinegar
150g gooseberries, topped and tailed
3 shallots, finely sliced
Finely grated zest and juice of 1 lime
A small handful of mint, finely shredded
A small handful of chives, chopped
2 lovage leaves, very finely chopped
Sea salt and freshly ground black pepper

Put the sugar, wine vinegar, a good pinch of salt and a few twists of pepper into a pan and bring slowly to a simmer.

Add the gooseberries to the pan and cook gently, stirring frequently, for a couple of minutes only – you don't want the fruit to soften. Take off the heat and allow to cool.

Stir in the shallots, lime zest and juice, and the chopped herbs. Cover and refrigerate for a couple of hours or more before serving to allow the flavours to mingle.

Gooseberry sauce

This sauce is very much in the spirit of an old-school, spicy, bottled brown sauce, with just a hint of traditional farmhouse pickle about it. Good heavens, it's fine with a sausage.

Makes about 800ml

500g gooseberries, topped and tailed
120ml white wine vinegar
600g light brown sugar
2 tsp ground allspice
2 tsp ground cloves
2 tsp ground cinnamon
1 tsp ground ginger

Put all the ingredients into a large pan, bring slowly to the boil and simmer very gently, uncovered, for an hour or so, stirring once in a while. Zap in the blender until smooth. It should be a thickish sauce but still just about pouring consistency.

Immediately pour into warm sterilised jars (see page 170) and seal once cool. It will keep in a cool, dark cupboard for at least 6 months. Keep in the fridge after opening and use within a few weeks.

Chive flower vinegar

This is less of a recipe than something to do when the chive flowers are in full bloom and you've a couple of minutes spare. It is ridiculously simple but tastes so very good. You can use cold vinegar, but I think warming it releases the flavour of the flowers a little better and encourages them to leach their beautiful colour into the liquid. Any fresh chive flowers at their best work well – I often use a combination of pink and white for looks, and garlic chives to give a subtle, mellow edge of garlic. Shake the flowers to release any bugs nestling within before you start.

Makes 1 jar or bottle

Chive flowers

White wine vinegar, to the volume of the jar/bottle(s) you are using

Fill a sterilised jar or bottle (see page 170) about 40% full of chive flowers, some broken, some whole. Warm the wine vinegar gently to a bare simmer then, using a funnel if needed, pour over the chive flowers. Seal the jar.

Allow the vinegar to mature for at least a week, preferably two, in a dark cool place, before using. As it matures, the flavour becomes more complex rather than just stronger. Strain it to remove the flowers when the flavour is how you'd like it – into another sterilised bottle. It keeps forever.

Pickled elderflower buds

Just as the first elderflowers start to open, the fattest buds are perfect for pickling – twist them off at the first joint and snip off the buds.

Makes 1 jar or bottle

Elderflower buds

White wine vinegar

Fill a sterilised jar (see page 170) with elderflower buds. Heat enough white wine vinegar to fill the jar just to the boil and then pour over the elder buds – the heat will cook them to just the right degree and the vinegar will pickle them.

Leave in a cool dark place for a couple of weeks before trying – the pickled elderflower buds will be like mini-capers, and improve with age.

Gooseberry & elderflower curd

I know it counts as heresy in some parts, but I love fruit curds even more than jams, especially when made with sharp fruit. It can be a faff with the traditional method using a bain-marie, but I don't do it that way anymore. The finest blackcurrant curd I've ever had was made by my friend Rachel Baker, who makes the wonderful preserves at withherhands.com. She was kind enough to give me her curd recipe, a faultless, easy method that works equally well with gooseberries, rhubarb, redcurrants, gooseberries or lemons. I suspect even sorrel would work well – anything with a bit of an edge to it. You'll need a cook's thermometer to check the temperature.

Makes about 6 x 225g jars

500g gooseberries

12 heads of elderflower

250g unsalted butter, diced

270g golden caster sugar

Juice of 2 small lemons

8 medium free-range eggs

Put the gooseberries in a pan with enough water to just cover the bottom of the pan. Bring to the boil, immediately lower the heat and cook, covered, for about 5 minutes until tender.

Meanwhile, strip the elderflower heads from the stems, using a fork, and set aside.

Gently heat the butter, sugar and lemon juice in a non-stick heavy-based saucepan until the butter has melted, then take the pan off the heat.

Push the fruit through a sieve into the pan and stir it into the buttery mixture. Lightly whisk the eggs in a bowl. Allow the fruity mixture to cool until no warmer than 60°C (check with a cook's thermometer) before you stir in the whisked eggs – any warmer and they will curdle.

Cook gently over a low heat without letting it boil, stirring constantly with a wooden spoon until it thickens to form a custard. This can take 5–15 minutes. At the last moment, stir in the elderflowers, then pour into sterilised jars (see below) immediately.

Cover and allow to cool; the curd will set as it cools. Store in the fridge for up to 3 months.

To sterilise jars
Wash them thoroughly, then place on a tray in an oven preheated to 170°C/Gas 3 for 15 minutes.

Strawberry *&* gooseberry Eton mess

Eton Mess couldn't be simpler – height-of-season fruit in a tumble of meringues and cream. The fruit can be whatever you fancy – mulberries, blackberries, spiced apple purée or raspberries. The strawberries and gooseberry curd in this version pair up beautifully, especially if the curd is made with elderflower; if not, you can add a tablespoonful or two of elderflower cordial to the macerating berries. Hog that I am, I've been known to finish off the remnants of a bowlful of Eton mess for breakfast the next day – the one and only time there has been any left over.

Serves 4

For the meringue

300g caster sugar

5 free-range egg whites

For the 'mess'

450g strawberries

40g caster sugar

350ml double cream

Gooseberry and elderflower curd (see left)

For the meringue, preheat the oven to 200°C/Gas 6. Line a baking sheet with baking parchment, scatter over the sugar and warm in the oven until it begins to melt at the edges but not colour; this should take 6–8 minutes.

Line a baking tray with baking parchment. Put the eggs whites in a large, clean bowl and, just as you remove the sugar from the oven, start whisking them using an electric mixer if you have one, or a handheld electric whisk. Turn the oven to its lowest setting.

Carefully tip the hot sugar onto the egg whites as you whisk. Carry on whisking until the meringue is thick, glossy and holds its shape. Spoon onto the prepared baking tray in a large round or in big dollops, leaving a little space between individual meringues to allow room for them to expand as they cook. Place in the low oven for a couple of hours.

Take the meringues out of the oven when they are crisp on the outside and can be lifted off the paper easily. Let them cool completely and store in an airtight container if not using immediately.

While the meringues are cooking, put the strawberries into a large bowl and sprinkle with the sugar. Cover and leave to macerate in the fridge.

No more than an hour before serving, lightly whip the cream. Break the meringues into pieces and fold them into the cream. Fold in the fruit and a few serving spoonfuls of the gooseberry and elderflower curd – don't incorporate everything completely, it should be a marbled 'mess'. Spoon into glasses and serve.

Knickerbocker glory

My knickerbocker glory is essentially a trifle in a tall glass that you don't have to share. How good does that sound? I make a few versions of this through the year, and I've probably not made two the same. The core components are cream, fruit, syrup or honey, something crunchy – meringue and/or caramelised nuts – and a long spoon with which to eat it. There are so many variations – peaches, raspberries, wineberries and mulberries have all found themselves glorified this summer, when in season. Here's an early summer version I make with the first strawberries.

Per person

100ml double cream

1 ripe peach, halved and stoned

1 tsp honey

75g strawberries, quartered

Lemon verbena syrup (page 266)

For the caramelised hazelnuts (enough for 3–4)

80g hazelnuts

30g caster sugar

Firstly, caramelise the hazelnuts. Put the nuts in a small saucepan over a high heat and pour in the sugar. Stir as the sugar starts to melt, coating the nuts. Once a runny caramel has formed, tip out the mixture onto a tray lined with baking parchment and allow to cool. Once cool, bash into rough pieces with a rolling pin.

Whip the cream in a bowl until just beyond soft peaks.

Blitz the peach with the honey in a blender, then push the purée through a sieve to remove the skin, if required.

Layer the strawberries, cream, peach purée, caramelised nuts and lemon verbena syrup in a tall glass and hope you've got a long enough spoon to get to the bottom.

Blackcurrant leaf sorbet

This may be my favourite sorbet of all. Blackcurrant leaves carry a little of the fruit's flavour along with a floral freshness that complements rather than overpowers it.

Blackcurrant leaves are usually plentiful enough to steal a few to make the first sorbet of the year. Rather than strip a branch bare, pinch off a couple of handfuls of leaves from across the whole bush. You can do this at any time through the summer and into autumn, but nothing quite matches the zip of the early leaves. If you have a few currant plants and forget which are blackcurrants, rub the leaves: the scent will give it away.

You can also use this recipe to make an elderflower sorbet – substitute 4 or 5 elderflower heads in full bloom – or use a handful of scented geranium leaves for a gentle floral sorbet in mid-summer.

Serves 4–6

2 large handfuls of young blackcurrant leaves (i.e. a 500ml jugful, fairly tightly packed)

270g caster sugar

700ml cold water

Juice of 3 lemons

1 free-range egg white, beaten

Crush the blackcurrant leaves to help release their aroma and flavour by either squeezing them tightly in your hand or gently pounding with the end of a rolling pin.

Put the crushed leaves, sugar and water into a stainless-steel saucepan. Slowly bring just to the boil, stirring to dissolve the sugar, and simmer for 3 minutes only.

Set aside to infuse and allow to cool completely, then add the lemon juice. Strain the sorbet syrup to remove the leaves.

If you have an ice-cream maker, churn in the usual way, adding the beaten egg white when the sorbet is almost set. Otherwise, pour the juice into a plastic tub and freeze for 3–4 hours until the sorbet is half-frozen, then whisk until smooth and return to the freezer. When almost frozen, whisk once more, fold in the beaten egg white and freeze until firm.

Spring into summer pudding

This wonderful pudding is usually made with raspberries and currants but I find whatever excuse I can to make it earlier in the year. This recipe uses the very first strawberries alongside gooseberries and rhubarb – giving it the familiar sweet-sharp combination of a traditional summer pudding. It works perfectly well with frozen fruit too, so it even makes the odd appearance in winter.

Serves 4–6

150g rhubarb, cut into 5mm slices

Finely grated zest of ½ orange

200g caster sugar

250g gooseberries

500g strawberries, quartered

10 thick slices of good white bread, crusts removed

Put the rhubarb, orange zest and sugar into a large saucepan and cook over a very gentle heat for 3 minutes or so until the sugar dissolves and the rhubarb just begins to soften. Add the gooseberries and cook for a further 2 minutes, stirring often. Add the strawberries and heat for another 30 seconds, then remove from the heat and stir.

Line a 850ml pudding basin with a double layer of cling film, leaving plenty to overhang the side. Line the base and sides of the bowl with bread, trimming the slices to fit as necessary and overlapping the pieces slightly, leaving no spaces; keep a couple of slices for the lid.

Drain 100ml of the juice from the fruit and refrigerate. Spoon the fruit and any remaining juice into the pudding basin, then top with bread and fold over the cling film to seal the pudding. Place a saucer that just fits inside the bowl on top of the pudding and add a weight (a bag of sugar works well). Refrigerate overnight.

Lift off the plate, peel back the cling film and invert a plate over the exposed pudding. Holding the plate and bowl together, turn them both over so the pudding is released onto the plate. Lift off the bowl and remove the cling film.

To serve, spoon the reserved juices over the pudding and accompany with thick double cream.

Elderflower & strawberry drop scones

Drop scones – small plump pancakes of sorts – make a fine breakfast. Even plain, without fruit, and just ribboned with honey and cream they are fabulous. Add raisins, brandy, grated apple, regular strawberries quartered – or whatever combinations come to mind – and you're unlikely to be disappointed.

This combination is the finest I have come up with. The mini strawberries just begin to break down when the scones cook, leaching some of their juice into the batter, while the florets dissolve, leaving the ghost of their scent and flavour behind. The spelt isn't critical – I like it for the nuttiness and substance but using all plain flour, wholemeal or a combination is perfectly fine.

Makes about 12

For the drop scone batter

65g plain flour

65g spelt flour

1 tsp baking powder

25g caster sugar

A pinch of salt

Up to 100ml milk

30g butter, melted

2 free-range eggs

To assemble and cook

6 heads of elderflower

2 handfuls of mini strawberries, such as Mignonettes

2–3 tsp vegetable oil for frying

Sift the flours and baking powder into a bowl and stir in the sugar and salt. Make a dip in the centre.

Add 2 tbsp of the milk and the melted butter to the eggs, and beat just enough to combine. Pour into the dip in the flour and beat in. Add the rest of the milk in a trickle, beating it into the flour until the batter drops – rather than pours – from a spoon; you may not need all of it.

Use a fork to strip the elderflower florets from their stalks and stir the florets, along with the mini strawberries, into the batter.

Put a few drops of oil into a large frying pan, wipe them around with a crumpled piece of kitchen paper, and warm over a moderate heat.

You will need to cook the drop scones in batches – cook 3 or 4 at a time. Lower dessertspoonfuls of the batter into the hot pan, leaving space in between to allow them to spread a little. When you see bubbles appearing through the batter, use a palette knife to turn the drop scones over. Cook for another minute or so, until golden. Remove and keep warm while you cook the rest.

Serve the fruity drop scones warm, with yoghurt or cream.

Elderflower delight

I first came across a brilliant elderflower variation on Turkish Delight in John Wright's *River Cottage Hedgerow Handbook*. Its flavour captures the essence of elderflower perfectly, and the melting texture is heavenly. My version is a little less sweet, a little more elderflowery and uses cream of tartar instead of gelatine. Try it with scented geraniums – especially Roses of Attar – in place of the elderflower for that familiar Turkish delight flavour.

Makes about 50 pieces

24 heads of elderflower

400ml water

650g granulated sugar

Juice of 2 lemons

140g cornflour

1½ tsp cream of tartar

40g icing sugar

Using a fork, ease the elderflower blossom from the stalks and into a muslin bag.

Put 300ml of the water, the sugar and lemon juice into a saucepan and warm gently, stirring to dissolve the sugar. Remove from the heat and allow to cool.

Put the remaining 100ml water into a small bowl and add 130g of the cornflour and the cream of tartar, stirring until smooth.

Stir the cornflour mix into the sugar syrup and bring slowly to the boil, stirring constantly. Now hang the elderflower muslin bag in the pan and simmer, stirring constantly, squeezing the bag with the back of the spoon once in a while. After 5–20 minutes (it varies seemingly randomly), the mixture will clarify and thicken. Remove from the heat and allow to cool for a few minutes.

Line the base of a 20cm square shallow baking tin with baking parchment and dust with a little icing sugar. Remove the muslin bag from the pan and then pour the molten delight into the baking tin. Leave it to cool completely, then refrigerate for a couple of hours.

Cut the elderflower delight into cubes and dust with icing sugar to serve.

Lavender & walnut fudge

I think in all my many years I've only ever met or heard of one person who didn't like fudge (yes you, Fiona KP). It is almost impossible to dislike. Make your own and I think we can drop the 'almost'.

The core recipe here works beautifully with different nuts, spices (try a few teaspoonfuls of fennel or sweet cicely), chocolate or just vanilla. One thing: invest in a cook's thermometer if you don't have one – they take the guesswork out of making fudge and preserves.

Makes 25–30 pieces

320g caster sugar

1 tbsp golden syrup

50g butter, plus extra for greasing

150ml double cream

7–8 lavender flower heads, chopped into small pieces

A generous pinch of salt

A handful of walnuts, crushed into pieces

Lightly butter a shallow baking dish, about 22 x 18cm.

Put the sugar, golden syrup, butter and cream into a large pan – the liquid will bubble up like lava, so the pan should be only one-third full at the start. Warm over a low heat, stirring frequently to dissolve the sugar.

Turn the heat up high and bring the mixture to the boil without stirring. Continue to heat until the temperature reaches 116°C (use a cook's thermometer to check), then remove from the heat and leave to rest for 10 minutes.

Add the lavender, salt and walnuts to the mixture and beat with a wooden spoon as quickly as you can – the mixture will thicken, become grainy and gradually leave the base of the pan.

Tip or spoon the mixture into the buttered baking dish and smooth with a palette knife. Leave to cool and firm up.

After an hour or so, cut the fudge into squares but don't lift the pieces out – keep your hands off for at least 3 hours longer until it has set properly. Then lift out and store any you don't eat at once in an airtight container.

Sweet cicely shortbread

Pass me a plate of shortbread and I'll make a fair dent in it, even more so when it's made with sweet cicely. That gentle aniseed lifts the traditional shortbread beautifully, sweetening it just a little too. I haven't given a weight of sweet cicely seeds as it's all about the strength of the seeds, hence making the sweet cicely sugar first – to a strength you like. I like this shortbread almost as much with fennel seeds or chopped lavender flowers instead of the sweet cicely.

Makes about 30

100g caster sugar, plus extra for dusting

10 or so sweet cicely seeds

200g unsalted butter, softened

300g plain flour, plus extra for dusting

A pinch of salt

Preheat the oven to 160°C/Gas 2–3.

Blitz 75g of the sugar with 10 sweet cicely seeds in a coffee grinder or pound in a pestle and mortar. Try the sugar for flavour – it should taste very strongly of sweet cicely. If not, add more. When it's just a little too strong in flavour, mix in the remaining sugar.

Cream the butter and sweet cicely sugar together until pale and creamy. Sift in the flour with the salt and stir to combine.

Roll out the dough on a lightly floured surface to a 5–7mm thickness and use a small scone cutter to cut out rounds, stars or other shapes.

Transfer to a baking sheet and bake in the oven for 15–20 minutes until the shortbreads are just starting to lightly brown at the edges. They will still be soft when taken from the oven.

Sprinkle with sugar and leave on the baking sheet for 10 minutes to cool slightly and firm up, then transfer to a wire rack and leave to cool completely. Store in an airtight tin.

Charlie's mojito

Eating outside calls for a drink, and the sunny evenings that often pepper May are best with something longish and cool. You can pretend summer is really here for an hour or two.

A fine cocktail needs something fruity, something edgy and something aromatic to set off the punch of the booze. A mojito answers that description perfectly – mint, sugar and lime set off the white rum, and soda water adds the fizz.

The mojito originates from Cuba and was derived from a drink called El Draque, invented in honour of Francis Drake. It is a drink that rewards (in so many ways) a little experimentation, so here is my own adaptation. In many ways, this is a gin and tonic mojito. It's the sort of thing you should get knighted for coming up with. It's most certainly the sort of drink that makes you wish for the next sunny evening.

Serves 1

Juice of 1 lime, 'spent' lime skins reserved

26 mint leaves

40ml lemon verbena syrup (page 266)

50ml gin

Crushed ice

Tonic water

The ingredients should be very cold indeed.

Put the lime juice, lime skins and mint leaves in a sturdy bowl and pound with the end of a rolling pin to extract the aroma and flavour from the mint and lime skins – this is known as 'muddling'.

Lift out the lime skins and squeeze them to extract all the juice. Add the lemon verbena syrup and gin, stir and pour into a glass. Add crushed ice and top up with tonic water to taste. Sit in the sun and enjoy.

Summer punch

This is a perfect welcome if you have people coming round and the sun is shining. I've tried this with tayberries, raspberries and a mix of fruit and it has been equally delicious. By all means play around with different fruit and herbs, but the key is to have one bottle of sparkling to one of still, as this gives the punch a little tickle, and we could all do with one of those. Whether the booze is cider, wine or perry in any combination is up to you, as long as you stick with one sparkling, one still.

Serves 12 (with a few tops-ups)

1kg strawberries, halved

About 75g caster sugar (adjust to suit the sweetness/variety of strawberries)

Finely grated zest and juice of 1 unwaxed lemon

A good handful of lemon verbena (optional)

1 bottle dry white wine, chilled

A good handful of mint (optional)

1 bottle sparkling wine, chilled

Put the halved strawberries in a bowl and sprinkle with the sugar. Add the lemon zest, lemon juice and lemon verbena if using. Pour in the still wine, stir and refrigerate for an hour or two.

Just before serving, add the mint, if using, and sparkling wine. Serve from a punch bowl.

Summer punch granita
Any leftover punch can be frozen in a plastic tub. It makes a fabulous granita and the booze ensures it has the perfect luscious granular texture.

July

A month of Test matches, mackerel and the glorious leisure of summer, when there's so much to eat and gardening seems easy. French beans are overtaking the broad beans, the tomatoes and courgettes are at least thinking of ripening and there are leaves, herbs and berries aplenty. The first currants and cherries, the early apricots and cherry plums will be ready to pick, but it is the first peaches from the polytunnel that I look forward to most.

Whether it's fruit and veg picked fresh from the plant, prepared in the kitchen or cooked out in the sun, July is for eating outdoors, and we spend as many evenings out by the veg patch as the weather allows. It might be as simple as a picnic of leftovers with a just-picked salad eaten sat on a blanket, or a quickly thrown together meal enjoyed at the outside table rather than indoors – whatever form it takes, we'll eat with the sky rather than a ceiling above whenever we can.

I love cooking outside too. It's partly the childish fun, partly the back-to-basics earthiness, and that, for some reason, it seems acceptable to uncork the bottle earlier if you're cooking outside. I've dug a hole in the ground and lined the edges with bricks for a fire pit – it works as a barbecue when the flames have died down or we hang a pot over it for stews and soups.

A hot smoker is invaluable. Inexpensive to buy and easy to make, it cooks as well as imparts food with smokiness. Essentially it's a mini barbecue in a box, with wood shavings smoking instead of charcoal or wood burning.

Wood ovens are a bit of an investment but they are very rewarding. Bread cooks beautifully and very differently at 400–500°C than it does in a domestic oven and pizzas cook in around a minute. And that's not all, as the temperature dips a shoulder of lamb or pork can be left to cook slowly for hours, overnight even, to a melting tenderness – needing only a spoon to eat it with. They are easy to make using sand and clay, though they need rebuilding from time to time.

Creating something to cook with – however homemade, however cobbled together – and somewhere to eat in your garden or allotment multiplies the pleasure of growing and eating. And in my experience, the more time spent out there not gardening, enjoying the garden and its harvests, the more it becomes part of everyday life rather than just a place you grow food.

Today Trent showed me his cock and balls.
'Run', he shouted as he re-entered the polytunnel. I ran.
'Why am I running?'
'Wasps.'
'Ok.'
80 metres away we stopped. I pretended not to breathe heavily. What happened? Trent had been tipping another barrow load of weeds onto the compost bin behind the polytunnel. He'd been doing it all day, but only now, somehow, disturbing the sizeable wasps' nest therein.
'Jeees, that was close, I was lucky to get away with thAAAAAAAHHHHH … bastard.'
A wasp had latched onto Trent's clothes and allowed him to take it for a run while (I presumed) forcing its sting through the fairly dense weave of Trent's favoured canvas work trouser.

He started to hop around (Trent, not the wasp) in obvious pain shouting, 'Get off you bastard,' loud and long. It got worse. It seemed like the wasp had actually found a way into his strides. Down came the lower garments. He carried on with the repeated 'Get off you bastards,' but was now also slapping himself amidships trying to discourage the little bugger.

I should mention that Trent had rather large boots on, so his clothes were gathered at his ankles, making staying on his feet rather problematic, especially while trying to slap the wasp senseless and at the same time not permanently damage his organs of reproduction. I flapped around behind him, not knowing quite how to help while also hoping to remain unstung.

I'd have ordinarily shouted 'It's like a cock only smaller,' but I was rather more concerned by how this scene might look from the dozen or so houses that overlook the field. The full horror dawned on me: they couldn't see the wasp. What they would see was a man with his trousers down, apparently country dancing around the field, slapping at his mid-region, genitals swinging in the breeze, shouting, 'Get off you bastard,' while being 'chased' by me with outstretched arms. I figured this may not be doing much for my standing in the local community.

I pushed him into the polytunnel with indecent haste, where I was about to turn the hose on him in any attempt to water cannon the little jasper and bring this sorry saga to a close. He colourfully requested me not to, which was fortunate as I'd forgotten that the opaque plastic side of that polytunnel was wound down, exposing the full scene to the neighbours. I'm not sure that being seen hosing down a semi-naked American with a shaven head and a goatee beard would have been any more easily explainable than the outdoor scene to those blackballing me at the village fete.

11 July, 2009

Beetroot: Burpees Golden, Barbatietola di Chioggia, Bolivar

GIVE ME A LARGE POT of cream, some herbs and a few spices and I reckon I could survive pretty happily on beetroot for at least a month, whatever the time of year.

Beetroot is the Mr Benn of the veg patch, dressing up in a variety of clothes that make it as much of a fruit as a vegetable when it reaches the kitchen. It goes with everything and every season, joining hands with savoury and sweet equally well. It seems to have the potential to be whatever you like: we use it in as many ice creams and cakes as we do salads, pizzas and fritters.

When it's cold, I'll roast beetroot with onions, thyme and cumin – especially good with lamb or beef – or make the classic River Cottage beetroot chocolate brownie. When it's sunny, breakfast may well be a smoothie of beetroot, grapes and mint, and lunch a pizza topped with beetroot, dollops of parsley pesto, blue cheese and rocket. It is pretty much impossible to dislike this root, it's so versatile. And like the potato, beetroot takes to almost all herbs – thyme, rosemary, dill, horseradish, parsley and shiso (perilla), especially.

Life throws up its mysteries though: the eternal popularity of cottage cheese; how humans managed to evolve without kitchen roll, that sort of thing. And similarly, it seems there are those who remain unconvinced about beetroot. I'm certain this is the fault of awful, shop-bought pickled beetroot forced upon young delicate palates. Even this serial offender, done properly, is a wonderful thing, I promise.

The leaves, too, are delicious. Beetroot is essentially the same plant as chard. Both are sisters selected from their botanical mother, sea beet; one chosen for its large bottom and the other for its large top. Now there's an image. The leaves are like a chardy spinach – really good when young and added raw to a leafy salad, or wilted as a side when a little larger. They make a great partner for the root itself, especially at the heart of the gratin on page 344, in place of salsify and spinach. This mirrors the northern Italian love of baking beetroot in cream or béchamel sauce, or good stock and a little horseradish.

Every year I grow the fabulous, stripy Barbatietola di Chioggia, the obviously coloured Burpees Golden and a traditional deep purple variety, such as Bolivar, for beautiful, delicious and non-woody roots from early summer through well into autumn.

BEETROOT

Site Relatively unfussy

Sow March–July

Harvest June–October

Notes Sow seed direct or start under cover – a couple of seeds per module – and thin as they grow after they've been planted out

APRICOTS

Site Well drained, sunny and sheltered

Harvest July–September

Notes Fruit mostly on last year's growth, so a tree needs a balance between new and old wood. Establish a structure of main branches, then cut new growth back in summer to 20cm long shoots, which will hopefully carry fruit next year

Apricot & strawberry crumble (page 276)
Lamb & apricot tagine (page 247)

I HAVEN'T BEEN the luckiest with apricots. Although some years I've had basketfuls of beautifully ripe, rich fruit, other years the trees stand fruitless and blank as if saying, 'Well, what do you expect, we'd prefer it somewhere hotter.'

They are fussy little devils and need a home they're really happy in. Ideally that home is somewhere closer to the Mediterranean than East Devon, but this is where I am and since the choice is giving them a go or not, I know which I'm doing.

Their apparent randomness in fruiting can make them seem a little cursed, as American Sherman tank drivers believe. Since World War Two apricots haven't been allowed in, on or near their tanks, after a supposed string of breakdowns when tins of apricots were nearby. That said, in English folklore, dreaming of apricots is supposed to bring good luck. Who to believe.

I've come to think that apricots are just very sensitive. They seem to have an invisible switch: if it is 'off' they struggle, accumulating disease and fruitlessness before finally giving up the ghost; if it is 'on' their leaves are glossy, the fruit plentiful.

Give them what they want and they've a good chance of being 'on', They need a well-drained, fertile soil, and a south-facing, sheltered spot where the sun can touch their leaves more than the wind. Every little sliver of help you give them can make the difference.

I've planted a few on the 'off' side of the line, making those that remain – a mix of old and new varieties – particularly precious. I watch them like a hawk for any hint of disease but so far they have flourished; once they are established and healthy, they seem to stay that way.

Spring is the pinch point for apricots. The blossom comes early, so shelter from the worst of the spring frosts and harsh winds is crucial. The lack of pollinating insects that early can be even more of an issue, leaving even healthy flowers unpollinated, so I use a soft, thin paintbrush to dab pollen from flower to flower.

The new apricot varieties may have superior frost tolerance and produce a little more than old cultivars such as Early Moorpark, but they can't match them for flavour, and both fruit equally reliably in a good spot.

Fresh, English apricots. Over half a kilo yesterday, 120g the day before that, 400g today. The smell is incredible – the difference in taste between the ones you buy and these is like that between juice and squash.

— 10 July, 2007

ricots: Moorpark

BLACKCURRANTS

Site Sunny, well drained and fertile

Harvest Leaves: May–September; currants July–August

Notes A few shovelfuls of well-rotted manure or compost around the base in early spring will help retain moisture and feed the plant

I SHOULD PITCH A TENT by the blackcurrants in July, as the three of us are out there so often stripping the bushes into containers, half for freezing, half for now.

Each summer, the blackcurrants surpass even my happiest memory of them. The bushes are unfailingly, branch-bendingly, heavy with fruit – even in a limp impersonation of a summer. And we get to pick them in perfect balance between sharp and sweet, which in the warmth of the early summer sun, makes them quite extraordinary. The plants remain reliably productive for years too: we reckon on plucking at least four kilos of juicy, full-flavoured fruit from each bush, which repays the cost of the plant seven or eight times over every year.

Most of our varieties have 'Ben' in their name – they can be relied on for flavour, hardiness and many of the most recent varieties have strigs (dangling bunches of fruit), which ripen together rather than randomly across the bush, making harvesting quicker. As with most fruit, a long season of harvesting is possible with the right selection of varieties. Ebony is our earliest (the first week of July here in Devon), but Titania, with its large, juicy, aromatic and deliciously sweet fruit is perhaps the favourite. Ben Lomond is noticeably later flowering than most, making it perfect for areas liable to a late frost.

Ahead of the fruit come the fresh new leaves – one of the garden's finest secondary harvests. The majority of herb or fruit teas, to me, are little short of sweet-smelling bin juice, but a few blackcurrant leaves steeped in hot water with or without honey or lemon verbena leaves is a bit special. Better still, blackcurrant leaf sorbet – make it once and you'll look forward to picking the leaves as much as the currants.

Blackcurrants make a genius of any gardener. Plant them in the sunniest, most fertile position with 1.5 metres to stretch their arms, water through dry periods and you'll be rolling in fruit by mid-summer. Care is simple: prune out the oldest third of each bush to encourage productive new growth. I sometimes do this in winter or more usually kill three birds with one stone by snipping out the oldest branches as low as I can when the currants are ripe, and place them in a vase of water, using the fruit and leaves as we need them.

Being out there in the tent would be pretty handy for discouraging the birds too. Do not imagine for one moment that they are ignoring your fruit. They will wait way beyond when the colour darkens, allowing the sweetness and fuller flavour to develop each day, until the perfect moment arrives. If your plants aren't netted, being out there is the best discouragement. Growing one of the new varieties where the fruit ripens at once also helps: birds can pick off currants as they ripen across a bush but are less likely to clear off such large numbers in one swift go.

Blackcurrant Eccles cakes (page 278)
Blackcurrant leaf sorbet (page 174)

blackcurrants

Saddleback piglets, a few weeks old

A BOAR IS AN IMPRESSIVE BEAST: a shark-sized articulated muscle on four stout legs that taper into high heels. The day he arrived on loan, a friend and I stood on the bottom rung of the field gate admiring his enormity. He came over, nestled his snout under the gate and lifted it and us a few inches up, then back down again. We were quietly impressed. And a little scared.

There is no pushing or cajoling a pig, much less a boar. You may encourage and incentivise with food, but there is no forcing. We had borrowed the boar for a couple of months, to run with our two sows. When I say 'run' I mean 'shag'. When I say 'two', I mean 'one': sow number 2 did a magnificent impersonation of a dropped flan every time he came near. Sow number 1 seemed much more amenable, but it's hard to tell how successful sty squiring is until fairly close to the day of arrival; 3 months, 3 weeks and 3 days later – a perfectly memorable pregnancy period – there may be piglets born or there may not.

> Today, piglets born. The first one tiny and dead. The second one tiny and dead. Then three and four together, bigger, moving. Like when listening to an old smoker hacking, we cleared our own throats involuntarily while clearing their nose and mouth of birth mucus. Then number five.
>   'Five' stopped moving. Fifteen minutes of clearing, washing and cajoling ended in small, sluggish movements, but she's alive at least. A few drops from a syringe of powdered milk to try and start up the suckling reflex and half an hour later she's nibbling at a teat.
>   It's hard not to think in clichés while it's happening but it is somehow miraculous and timeless, and marvellous in the way that accompanies only things in which we are irrelevant. And now it's all over I want it to happen over again, for the strangely addictive miracle to keep coming, for more to emerge.
> — 14 July, 2005

> The piglets are a week old now. For a few days it's feed, sleep, feed, sleep. And dodge being sat on by the mother. One failed, squashed dead, eaten overnight by the mother to keep the ark clean.
>   Growing quickly over the week, the piglets' individuality is apparent almost immediately – some more confident, more inquisitive than others. After six days one clambers over the lip of the ark and out, followed by the others, following the mother, copying everything.
> — 21 July, 2005

PIGLETS

Source Can only be born on site rather than sourced as piglets, as they need to be with the mother

Notes Piglets need to be with their mother to feed for at least a couple of months, ideally a little longer. The warmth of late spring and early summer is an ideal time for piglets to be born. Litters can vary considerably in size; anything up to a dozen or so is normal.

CUCUMBER, BORAGE AND SALAD BURNET

Site Sun for cucumbers. Borage unfussy. Salad burnet happy in sun/semi-shade and a little damp

Sow Cucumbers: March–May; Borage: direct in spring

Harvest Cucumbers: July–October; Borage: April–October; Salad Burnet: All year

Notes All easy to grow. Borage and salad burnet look after themselves in any reasonable soil. Cucumbers under cover or in the sunniest, sheltered spot. Start with young plants of salad burnet

IF YOU'RE A REAL BUTCH MAN, you may well have a deep suspicion of cucumbers. For all their firmness, they're insubstantial – more of a watery cosh than something likely to sustain anyone.

Cucumbers were never my favourite vegetable, but I've had a sort of conversion to them, partly as I now think of them as a spice as much as a vegetable. Homegrown cucumbers also have a finer texture and flavour, largely thanks to the varieties that can be grown.

Crystal Lemon is, as you'd hope, a pale lemon, almost round cucumber that's as gorgeous to look at as it is cool and fresh. Its flavour is superb. A few slices in a jug of water with or instead of lemon, or a handful of batons in a salad, add zing without unnecessary sweetness.

Much as I love that fine crystalline crunch, which so few vegetables possess, I think I prefer the flavour of cucumber when it is allowed to dominate without its texture. It makes a beautifully bright and refreshing ice cream, and a cucumber Martini is dangerously satisfying.

Borage, that gloriously fecund self-seeder, and salad burnet, a jagged-leaved, evergreen perennial herb, both have flowers and leaves that taste of cucumber. A plant or two of either is invaluable, as each has a longer season of harvesting than cucumber.

Borage grows from seed with minimal encouragement, into a beautiful medium-sized plant with blue or white flowers (depending on the variety) that draws bees and other beneficial insects to your garden. It is so floriferous that you'll be hard pushed to make a significant dent in its numbers even if you love them as I do. The flavour of the young leaves and flowers is gently cucumbery, so they add cool punctuation to a leafy salad or summer cocktails – Pimms especially. I use them fresh or freeze them when they are at their most abundant: half-fill ice-cube trays with water and freeze, then add a single borage flower, top up with water and freeze until solid. This keeps the flower in the centre of the ice cube.

Borage self-seeds freely, which I love – I wouldn't be without the random presence of its white or blue flowers adding a splash of colour to the spring and summer greens.

If you're after year-round cucumber flavour, salad burnet is the herb to grow. Its small green leaves, serrated like sharks teeth, are at their most succulent and flavoursome in spring and summer, but even in the depths of winter they're good. A handful in summer salads, cocktails or in a jug of water adds life and freshness.

Nasturtiums

AS WITH LEMONS, chocolate, chilli and capers, edible flowers may not keep body and soul together, but as well as being fine in their own right, they dot sweetness, colour and coolness through a leafy salad. They're on my wish list every year, and far from a cutesy afterthought.

Courgette flowers, daylilies and nasturtiums are among the most substantial – each delicious raw, or stuffed, battered and deep-fried. All have an underlying pepperiness but each has very much its own character.

The gentle mustard of the courgette petals contrasts beautifully with the fresh, sweet crunch of the base. They are especially good stuffed with either ricotta and chopped herbs or leftover risotto and deep-fried. Picking them needn't reduce your courgette harvest if you slice off the male flowers – those without a small courgette developing behind the base.

Daylilies are perennial and best grown from young plants. They were made to be eaten – beautiful as they are, the blooms last only for a day, so I enjoy their looks while the sun is high before pinching them off to eat late in the afternoon, just before they fade. They are lovely raw – the flavour is somewhere between sweet lettuce and green beans, with a peppery freshness – and delicious battered and fried. As with nasturtiums, the yellow-flowered daylilies tend to be milder than darker varieties.

Nasturtium flowers are extraordinary. The flavours unravel one at a time: initially like rocket, then honey as you get into the nectar, with a peppery shock at the end. They are the flowers to convert any sceptic.

Most of the other edible flowers offer a splash of colour and flavourful punctuation rather than dominating in themselves: they are no less lovely for it. My current favourite is *Tulbaghia violacea*, or Society garlic. Although the leaves are edible they are often all heat and little flavour, whereas the flower itself is the reverse with a fine whoosh of garlic without the harshness. Fairy Star is the finest I've tried, but most are delicious and productive, flowering from April through to early autumn. A handful cast into a leafy salad is all you need to brighten it up and dot it through with garlic. They're peculiarly good floating in cocktails, and I suspect would be similarly so crystallised on something or other I haven't thought of yet.

July is a good time to sow a tray of peas, with seeds spaced 2–3cm apart. Once they're beginning to flower, I pinch off some of the flowers and add them to salads – they give a quick return and, like pea shoots, they carry a bright, fresh version of the usual pea flavour with a succulent crisp texture. You can also pinch some from fully grown plants – it will encourage the plant to produce more too.

Viola heartsease is a favourite. Easy to grow from seed and prolific in flower, its sweetness wakes up a green salad. For fruit salads and drinks, it works well crystallised (brush with egg white and dust with caster sugar).

Many of us use saffron now and again and while it is relatively easy to grow your own, it can be tricky and time-consuming to grow a sizeable harvest. Marigold (*Calendula officinalis*) makes a fine substitute. Easy and prolific from seed, the petals of this 'poor man's saffron' can be

EDIBLE FLOWERS

Site Relatively unfussy

Sow February–July

Harvest March–October

Notes Red flowers often more peppery than paler varieties – especially nasturtiums and daylilies sprinkled over salads or made into a paste using half a handful of petals with a couple of tablespoonfuls of oil – add this to paella for the final simmer, in place of the usual saffron.

Most herb flowers are edible, carrying some of the intrinsic flavour of the herb itself. Generally speaking, flowers from soft, annual herbs are best eaten raw as cooking tends to kill their flavour, whereas those from woody perennials are usually better when their flavour is allowed to infuse. Perilla (aka shiso) flowers are my favourite – I use them to scatter a little minty cumin through salads and as a garnish with chicken and other meats. Coriander, chervil, chives and basil are the other herb flowers I use most, wherever I want a little beauty to go with the flavour.

Every garden should have borage too (see page 196).

AGRETTI

Site Relatively unfussy

Sow January–April

Harvest April–October

Notes When sowing direct, allow 12–15cm between seeds, covering with 1cm soil, then thin to 30cm apart as they grow

WHEN I LIVED IN WHITSTABLE, on the Kent coast, I ate an indecent amount of seafood. The fish, scallops and oysters are as good as any I've had, especially eaten with the glorious local marsh samphire. It looks like a succulent, mini-cactus and it thrives in a carpet of emerald in estuaries and wetlands near the sea. It is the texture as much as its fresh, faintly salty flavour that charmed me. Samphire has a short season and although I can find it occasionally in the local fishmonger's, I've taken to growing its equally delicious close relative, agretti, to give me a longer and more reliable supply. Although not identical, agretti shares samphire's minerally, succulent bite and the hint of the sea in its taste.

Agretti is another seashore inhabitant, native to the Mediterranean. It favours a well-drained soil, but even here, in the heavy-ish soils of Otter Farm, it flourishes. It is hugely popular where it grows wild, especially in Italy, where it is known as *barba di frate* or monk's beard.

I sow agretti under cover in late winter or direct in early spring as it needs cool to germinate. Germination can be a little patchy – I sow 50% more than I think I need and I'm rarely overrun with seedlings. Once growing well, it'll be 7 weeks or so until it makes full size – around 30cm across and twice that high come April. Commercially grown plants are pulled up at this stage, like lettuce, but I prefer a cut-and-come-again approach – harvesting top growth and side shoots when the plant is established. It leaves enough of a core to produce new shoots and draws the agretti season out for a few months.

Late in summer, some parts become a little tougher – this is usually the side shoots just as the plant is preparing to flower. Most of the plant will keep succulent and delicious for a while yet but by October it will probably have finished its productive life and it's time for the plants to make the short trip to the compost heap.

Agretti was made to be eaten with seafood, and its saltiness and fresh crunch works a treat with eggs too. I love it raw in salads too, or lightly steamed and dressed with a little oil and lemon juice.

Picking green walnuts

I LOVE WATCHING my daughter learning to swim. Seeing her overcome the unknown and embrace the pleasure of the water so enthusiastically has made me more than a little proud. At the end of every lesson, she feels a chocolate bar is in order; this may be commuted to a choc ice should the weather be pleasant.

In late June and July, while she eats her reward, I check the tree outside the local pool for walnuts. It's a good few months ahead of when walnuts are usually harvested, but at this stage, before the shell has formed and small as they are, they are perfect for pickling and making into a liqueur.

The trick is to let them get as large as you dare while still picking them before the shell forms. A thin needle works best – prod it into the end away from the stem to test for the presence of a shell. Late June can be the perfect time after a good spring and early summer but it is more likely to be in the first half of July, prime choc ice weather, that they're ready to pick.

Soon, rather than sneaking the odd carrier bagful from the hugely productive tree by the local pool, I hope to pick green walnuts from our trees, but they aren't producing heavily enough yet to risk an early and a late picking.

One of my first mistakes at Otter Farm was to plant a prime spot with walnut trees. Almost as soon as I sat the spade back on the two nails that keep it in place in the barn, the realisation dawned: when you are short of space, the last thing you should use your prime spot for is widely spaced trees that are slow to productivity.

The following winter I dug the walnuts up and relocated them to two new lines of hedging – 30 trees in a well-drained, sunny spot, taking up next to no room rather than an acre, almost a free harvest space-wise.

Like a lot of nut trees, walnuts throw down a tap root and they're hard to move even when young. They sulked for two years. Now, at long last, we're picking nuts by the dozens in November from each tree – hardly inundated yet, but they are slowly forgiving me my dimness.

Gloves are essential when shelling walnuts. The outer green husk is inedible and full of tannins, colouring your fingers as if you've spent your life smoking Woodbines. Cracking the shell within releases the seed kernel – what we recognise as the nut.

These familiar kernels are oilier than those in the shops, having not been dried to extend their shelf life. Known as 'wet' walnuts, they have an intense, deep flavour, yet seem brighter and fresher than bought walnuts. They are, barring the odd overseas holiday market, an unbuyable treat.

The dark brown coating holds high levels of antioxidants and helps prevent the flesh of the walnut spoiling – a rancid nut will bring on 'lemon face' as effectively as anything.

We eat most of our walnuts fresh, with cheese or in salads, and when we have an excess they'll find their way into tarts, or a sauce to serve with chicken.

GREEN WALNUTS

Site A moist, well-drained, sheltered sunny spot

Harvest Late June–July

Notes Can secrete chemicals in the soil that inhibit competing vegetation, so don't underplant with anything precious to you

Baklava (page 366)
Diaconocino (page 285)
Pickled walnuts (page 264)
Walnut tart (page 365)

August

We are spoilt for fruit in August – apples, strawberries, raspberries, wineberries, plums, peaches, nectarines and figs – with those not eaten just-picked as they are turned into cranachan, summer cocktails, Eton mess, summer pudding or ice creams. August can become a bit of a festival of cream and meringue. We are all likely to be riding a touch lower in the water at the end of the school holidays than at the beginning.

There is almost too much ready to harvest to know what to do with. The basket returns daily from the veg patch full with high summer favourites. Borlotti beans, fennel and sweetcorn, even the first of the cherry tomatoes can be ready from early in the month – a good few weeks ahead of larger varieties that need more sunlight to ripen their flesh. Conveniently, the basil and thyme that go with them so well are at their sun-warmed aromatic peak. Along with the fruit, there really is some eating to be done.

August is a month I found quite hard to adjust to when I started smallholding. The farm is pretty much freewheeling. Everything has been set up by the spring and summer sun, pollination is out of the way, and August is largely about ripening. It used to depress me a little – there was almost nothing to do compared to the rest of the year and I'm not great at idleness – but now everything is becoming increasingly productive, I've given into it as a month of rewards. I'm busy, I'm happy and I'm harvesting.

EARLY APPLES

Site Relativelt unfussy

Harvest Late July–early September

Notes Eat within a few days – most don't store

Fennel toffee apples (page 374)

Pickled apples (page 353)

AS WITH POTATOES, apples belong to mini-seasons – earlies through to lates. As a rule the earlier the apple ripens, the shorter it keeps for, which means early apples rarely make the shops.

Discovery, Devonshire Quarrenden and Beauty of Bath apples twist easily from the branch in early August. Beauty of Bath comes earliest of all and I love it as much for it signalling the start of a steady stream of apples through into winter as I do its flavour. Highly aromatic, perfectly balanced between sweet and sharp and with a fine texture, Beauty of Bath is (as are most earlies) best enjoyed fresh from the tree, keeping only for a week or so.

Early apples need a watchful eye. The fruit ripens with little notice – try them one day and they'll be sour; a couple of days later they can be dropping from the tree. Harvest time can also be a little tricky to predict: in a hot summer early varieties can be ready in July; in a cool one, perhaps as late as early September, but they are always ahead of the pack.

Once ripe, most early apples bruise easily and can leave the tree with little persuasion from the wind. I resent each one that hits the grass and is set upon by wasps, slugs and flies. I rescue those I can first thing in the morning, before wasps leave the nests: any showing serious incursions from the wildlife are thrown to the grateful pigs; the rest make juice.

For the last few days I've been looking for the moment when I could gently twist the small, almost raspberry-coloured fruits of the Devonshire Quarrenden from the tree. Each time, I've failed to notice that the caterpillar of the Eyed Hawk moth has removed all greenery between the fruit and the growing tip. It hangs upside down, looking like the early-season rolled leaves, nibbling the leaves away. I prised them off their stem and bucketed them off to the riverside willows – their other favourite lunch.

— 15 August, 2005

rly season apples

Japanese wineberries

THERE'S A LULL IN AUGUST between the peak of the summer and the autumn raspberries' productivity and, rather happily, Japanese wineberries are around to fill it.

They are particularly beautiful with their long arching, softly bristled, red-purple canes, especially in the winter when the leaves have dropped. Like blackberries, new canes are produced every year that throw out short side shoots the following year on which berries form. And what berries they are. I look forward to them as much as any of the soft fruit – they have a deeper, winier flavour than raspberries and strawberries, and balance sweet with sharp as well as a blackberry. I plant more every year.

Wineberries ripen over a long period rather than all at once, which means I eat most on the way to and from feeding the chickens. Once in a while, when I hold back and get some into the house, I use them to make cranachan, as their flavour works perfectly with the oats, whisky and honey.

If only all soft fruit learnt wineberries' trick of revealing its fruit only when it's almost ripe – the papery calyx that wraps each berry peels back a day or two before they're ready to eat, then the berries traffic-light quickly through from green to yellow to orange and into deep red. It gives the birds less time to notice the berries, so few are lost to them.

They take well to training as a fan but I prefer to let them scramble as they like. Unsupported, they form a thicket, perhaps a little over a metre high. I also have them growing through a wire fence in combination with akebia as an edible hedge, clambering through each other beautifully.

JAPANESE WINEBERRIES

Site Fertile soil, sunny/semi-shade

Harvest August–September

Notes Canes that have fruited can be pruned out or left to dry out and crumble

Knickerbocker glory (page 172)

NOTHING QUITE CAPTURES the flavour and scent of summer coming to a close as plums. There are plums, bullaces, gages and damsons scattered around the farm, with most in the orchard. Some, notably the mirabelles, come early when the sun's high in early summer, but most ripen more heavily as August slips into September. Summer salsas, fruit salads and Eton messes slide without fuss into autumnal crumbles and pies.

Bullaces and damsons tend to be the smallest, tartest 'plums' and are usually best cooked. Gages, inexplicably under-appreciated in this country, are sweeter and rounder than most plums.

Dittisham plums are my favourite, as much for their scent as their fine flavour. I left some in a bowl on the stairs last year and after a day the perfume was heady, heavy and almost alcoholic as well as fruity. The white powder bloom that coats them (and many other plums) so satisfyingly is even more beautiful close up – the marks in the bloom are a little history of each fruit rubbing against its neighbour as it ripens, the picker's hands, the basket it's dropped into, and being moved into the bowl it sits in.

Whichever plum you go for, you'll need room for two, as even self-fertile varieties fruit more heavily with a pollination partner. The exception is Victoria – a reliable, high-yielding plum equally good for eating and cooking that does perfectly well on its own.

PLUMS

Site Well drained, sunny and sheltered

Harvest July–October

Notes A plum will only pollinate another from the same or an adjacent group. So a plum of pollination group B can pollinate another from groups A, D or C

Greengage smash (page 284)

Plum & Szechuan pepper fruit leather (page 280)

Roast plums with labneh, almonds & honey (page 271)

Mulberries: King James

FEW THINGS MAKE ME HAPPIER than mulberries. There is nothing I'd rather eat, no finer drink than mulberry vodka, and the trees are charmingly lazy and irregular.

I've planted five varieties here, scattered around in no great pattern and while we pick all that the slow-growing trees produce, we also forage a little. Not far from where we live, a huge, mature mulberry sits in the grounds of a large public space (mind your own business), with literally hundreds of cidered and sandwiched sun-lovers idling nearby. The fruit is hidden by the leaves, branches arching down to the ground, and every August Nell and I slip under the tree's skirt, tubs in hand. Once under, we're in a circular room wallpapered with mulberries in various states of sweet purpleness. Twenty minutes in its leafy shade and the tubs are full and we're gone, with murderous hands and vampire chins to give us away.

It has become something of a summer tradition. I've never seen anyone else picking them, despite the crowds a few yards away. Every year, a few people who see us picking try a few and the reaction is always astonishment that something so delicious is just there, unnoticed, waiting to be picked. As with all foraging, we leave plenty for others and the wildlife, but in this case most of the fruit falls to the floor, turning the grass purple, so there's little danger of over-picking.

Mulberries are long-lived trees, and many of those planted in the stately homes and public parks centuries ago remain. If you haven't enough space to plant one, keep your eyes out for one – it may be right next to somewhere you walk every day.

Mulberries release their sweet juice under the slightest pressure. When they're ready to pick, it's best to wear old (preferably purple) clothes or go naked (unless you're picking in public). They are best enjoyed on the day, or at least dealt with on the day, as they dissolve quickly, seemingly incapable of bearing the weight of their own juice. They make the most incredible ice cream, and mulberry vodka was made for enjoying after a day out in the worst that winter has to offer.

Mulberry trees like shelter and sun but they can take time to get their hefty roots established. Choice of variety is important with this fruit – King James and Chelsea are widely available and very fine of flavour but go for a tree that's a few years old if you don't want to wait for a harvest. Illinois Everbearing and Carmen are among the cultivars that produce early in life, but they are tricky to lay your hands on.

MULBERRIES

Site Sheltered and sunny

Harvest August–September

Notes Trees hate competition – keep 1 metre around the trunk free of weeds/grass for a few years

Mulberry bakewell tart (page 277)
Mulberry vodka (page 286)

SHEEP

Source As adults to breed, or start off with lambs, usually in spring

Feed Grass and more grass. Feeding them a little compound feed once a day helps keep them happy with contact, useful for when they need treating

Notes Need their feet checking regularly, shearing in summer and keep an eye out for fly strike. Any animals going to the abattoir tend to go in late summer/autumn, before the grass passes its peak and the ground gets too wet

Lamb & apricot tagine (page 247)

Lamb chops with chicory & Jerusalem artichoke purée (page 66)

Loin of lamb with lavender & lemon thyme (page 146)

SHEEP ARE A LOVABLE PAIN in the arse. As anyone who's kept them will tell you, they are born looking for a way to die. Despite roaming harsh uplands and marshes for centuries, evolution seems to have given sheep sandals rather than clogs, so their feet need regular checks for rot, even on the driest ground.

Not content with tracing their tedious parallelograms in my kitchen, flies are drawn to sheep, laying eggs in their fleece which hatch into maggots that begin to feed on the nearest thing to hand – the sheep. As voracious as it is unpleasant, flystrike can kill a healthy adult sheep in little over a day. It means a daily check, looking for any behaviour that is out of the ordinary – a head twitching round trying to nibble at their rump, sluggishness or just keeping away from the main flock. They are high maintenance.

In their favour, sheep eat grass, an essentially free resource, and in so doing stop you having to get the mower out. They turn grass into possibly my favourite meat. Compared to pigs, they're also relatively easy to handle, although catching one against the clock is very much like getting a grip on a giant, oiled ice cube.

As with all our animals, I like them to enjoy a longer life than is usual. All our sheep have over a year to graze, sit in the shade and develop whichever range of ailments suits them best. Most live for between one and two years (when they are known as hoggets) before going to slaughter. Hogget meat has, to my mind, the perfect balance of tenderness with depth of flavour – far superior to younger lamb or older mutton.

Despite the attention they need, I get attached to the sheep, especially if they've been born here.

At ease making arrangements, calling the abattoir to organise times over the last week, I'm now nervous, business-like, focusing on making sure the sheep are relaxed. As usual the Longwool male, my favourite, lets me separate him from the rest. I'm annoyed at his cooperation, feeling guilty at what feels like deception. Another chosen, both in the trailer, and the short journey starts.

Everything at the abattoir is efficient, impersonal but not unfriendly, and I'm grateful for it. This happens all day, every day. Perhaps it's different elsewhere, but at our small, local abattoir there's a sense of process that stops short of conveyor-belting, which takes away hesitation; it stops me prevaricating or retracting.

Only if you wait for the offal or skin do you fully appreciate how quick, organised and how oddly caring this efficiency is. The skins go to salting and tanning to return as sheepskins, and we head home with the offal.

Once home, I walk to the polytunnel as I do every day to catch butterflies, moths and dragonflies trapped against the plastic and release them from the prospect of a desiccated death.

— 23 August, 2005

Devon Longwool lamb with mother

Uncapping honeycomb

LIKE THE TOUR DE FRANCE, John le Carré novels, The Wire and Steely Dan, I had unconsciously parked 'bees and honey' somewhere in the Waiting Room of Interests for Later in Life. I recognised that this was something I might be hooked by if I started investigating, but I'm already swimming in a sea of semi-understood fascinations and borderline incompetencies. Any more could wait.

My hand was rather forced when my wife, who had spent months randomly delivering apian facts from behind a stream of bee-related books, acquired a colony of bees.

Most colonies have a single fertile female, the queen, who lays all the eggs. The males, known as drones, have a bit of a rum-do of things. Their single role in life is to mate with the queen (or indeed any other queen), at perhaps 80 metres up in the air, often some distance from the hive. So far so good. Although a queen bee is likely to mate with only a handful of the many drones, they, sadly, are the unlucky ones. The male's intimate apparatus is barbed and as drone and queen part, it, along with a good part of its internal organs, is ripped off and he dies.

Infertile females are known as workers, and it is these we see most of. They are quietly incredible. As well as cleaning and repairing any damage to the hive, workers fly out in search of pollen to bring back to the hive and turn into honey.

It is this simple activity upon which the whole of human existence depends. As the bees forage from flower to flower, a little pollen from one plant rubs onto the reproductive organs of another, in this way pollinating almost every crop on which we rely.

The workers also build honeycomb to store nectar and pollen (for food) and as a home for larvae to develop. Some of the nectar will eventually be turned into honey by the workers partially digesting, regurgitating and fanning with their wings to evaporate most of the water. That the cells of honeycomb are created as interlocking hexagons is beyond my comprehension. Bees building something perfectly hexagonal; that's like a giraffe doing a crossword, or a tapir using the cashpoint.

Beekeeping is the process of us taking advantage of what bees do naturally. We provide a home (known as a brood box) onto which we add tiers (known as supers) that contain hanging rectangles (known as frames) in which the honeycomb is formed. As the hexagons fill with honey, they are sealed with wax by the workers and as one super's frames become full another is added.

As they build up, you can consider harvesting some of the honey. We took three of the four full supers for honey this summer, leaving time for the fourth to be filled for winter food.

Each of the frames (in our set-up, there are ten to each super) is heavy, typically a little over 2kg each, three-quarters of which is honey. You have to uncap the honeycomb, cutting their tops off with a bread knife, and place supers on either side of a centrifugal spinner. Turn the handle and the frames are spun, the honey is cast out, glistening onto the

HONEY

Harvest August–September

Notes Leave plenty of honey for the bees

inner walls of the cylinder and falling to the bottom. When sufficient accumulates, a tap releases the honey to pour though a filter into a separate settling tank (a wine fermenting barrel in our case). A couple of days settling and it can be decanted into jars.

How much can you get? A poor spring and a glorious half-summer has given us 72 jars, leaving plenty of honey unharvested for the colony. It is very different in flavour, aroma and invisible properties to most commercial honey.

Supermarket honey has been filtered and heated, which changes it fundamentally. Filtering sieves out many of the beneficial elements, including propolis (a resin the bees use to repair and seal) alongside the nuggets of wax, while heating destroys valuable enzymes and removes the possibility of useful bacteria surviving. It renders most commercial honey nutritionally inferior to what's produced on a small scale.

It tastes like honey you'd dream about after a long evening on the strong cheese. Sweet yes, but there's no hint of cloying. You can keep eating and eating it. This first batch is bright, pineapple-y and minty – quite glorious.

One thing the bees do love is the Szechuan pepper. The flowers seem too small to attract their attention, but at a time of year when nectar and pollen sources are usually few, the peppers give them what they need. I'm sure I can pick up a little zingy trace of pepper in the honey but I may be imagining things.

Candida's honey mustard dressing (page 164)

Kiwi cranachan (page 362)

Plum & Szechuan pepper fruit leather (page 280)

Poached & roasted quince (page 356)

Roast plums with labneh, almonds & honey (page 271)

CHERRIES

Site As sunny and sheltered as possible, not wet

Harvest July–September

Notes With its white cherries, Vega sidesteps the birds' attentions

'BIRD FOOD, CHERRIES'. Two neighbours told me the same, when I planted a couple of trees and the miserable buggers were right too. Obviously, the trees have romped away fruitfully and the birds are looking very happy about it.

Lesson learnt, I've planted six dwarf Maynard cherries, growing no higher than 2.5 metres tall, that I can prune to keep just below the fruit cage's roof. As with most true dwarf trees, they seem disproportionately productive. Each branch is showered with blossom in spring, looking like metre-long candy floss, turning heavy with cherries a few months later.

Dwarf trees and plants, trained as fans against a wall, are really the only way to grow cherries I think. They can be left uncovered for most of the year, as my fruit cage is, then netted as the flowers turn to fruit.

Unsurprisingly, this year I've become quietly obsessed with these newly found homegrown cherries, eating them fresh, in the usual puddings – especially the classic clafoutis – and increasingly in salads and main courses. In the same way that beetroot extends a generous hand from being a vegetable to tasting like a fruit, cherry lends its deep colour, acid-sweetness and texture to the savoury beautifully. Pair them with saltiness and a little pepper or chilli heat and you'll be most of the way to a lovely salad or a fine pizza topping.

Warm salad of Padron peppers, sugar snaps, cherries & halloumi (page 255)

erries: Stella

PEACHES AND NECTARINES

Site Full sun, well drained

Harvest July–September

Notes Prune in summer, to minimise the chances of disease

THERE'S A HOLY GRAIL when it comes to peaches and nectarines – to catch a fruit as it falls from the tree. I've almost managed this once. Sitting in the shade of a tree, a peach fell into the long grass at my feet. It smelt like heaven and tasted even better. It is at this moment of falling that the fruit has reached its peak and, having had chance to mature on the tree, they are unutterably finer than even the finest peach you can buy.

A peach or nectarine that's loosening its grip on the tree welcomes you from a few metres away with its scent, and with nectarines the colour will often deepen as the moment to pick them approaches. Once every few days, I cup each ripening fruit in the palm of my hand and turn it with as little grip as I can. If it stays attached, good: it will keep improving in taste, texture and aroma. The fruit mustn't be squeezed – any pressure damages the flesh, causing little pools of juice to form behind the skin, spoiling the texture and accelerating decay. It needs gentleness and patience: it can be a week or so from when the scent comes until the perfect moment arrives.

Eating a perfectly ripe peach is quite an experience. I eat most bent over to avoid the juice covering my chin, shirt and boots.

Peaches and nectarines may not deliver every year, so it's best to learn to love them when they do. I grow a few in the polytunnel for an early and more reliable crop, as well as small groups in sheltered, outdoor spots here and there where I hope their blossom will dodge the worst of the late frosts. Some years they do; some years they don't.

Spring often decides whether there are peaches and nectarines in midsummer. Late frosts, especially after a warm spell, can see off the flowers and with it any hope of fruit. Even if the blossom sidesteps the cold, spring rains often bring leaf curl, which, while rarely fatal, can weaken a tree enough to cause it to drop its baby fruit. Growing the tree against a wall and/or covering it to keep the rains off the leaves, while allowing pollinators in under it is the best way to dodge the disease. A few minutes dabbing a soft brush from flower to flower helps pollination if there are few insects about, and the more blossom that's pollinated, the more fruit results. Get your tree to late April unscathed and with luck and a little sun, you should be in fruit by midsummer.

The much missed actor and writer Spalding Gray talked in one of his monologues about perfect moments, when everything lined up in a sweet second to create the sense that all was right and whole. I thought of him as I drove around the field, admiring both my new skills as a tractor driver and the peach tree that I'd saved from leaf curl by removing every blighted leaf on first sight. With the sun blazing, a cool wind blowing, the beautiful peach tree rejuvenated, the chickens pecking and the sight of my pregnant wife planting in the garden, a perfect moment beckoned. Distracted by the moment, I mismanoeuvred the tractor's mower across the peach tree, turning it into a thousand pieces of sweet-smelling mulch.
— 20 August, 2005

warf nectarines

September

If there is one reliable baton change of the seasons it is in September. Autumn arrives without fail. Early in the month, summer feels like it's making its mind up about exactly when to leave and everything on the smallholding seems to sense a change coming. The animals become less active, the trees look less upright and lively, and the chickens lay less frequently. The vigour and chirpiness of spring and summer seem to be becoming loose and tatty, like favourite jeans aging.

September's peak harvest

Aubergines

Carolina allspice

Chillies

Courgettes

Lemon verbena

Szechuan pepper

Tomatoes

Blackberries

Elderberries

Melons

Plums, damsons, gages

Raspberries (autumn)

As September progresses, my mind is increasingly distracted by the wood store and by seed and plant catalogues. The beer comes out of the fridge, I drink less wine and more whisky, and I start looking forward to the nights when the fire is set.

Before the soft slip into autumn, the sun-loving summer veg is at its absolute peak. Although we've been harvesting some in August, the September tomatoes, aubergines, sweet and chilli peppers are gathered in abundance. You can smell and taste the weeks of warmth that have seeped into them. Most of the Szechuan and sansho peppercorns are picked now – a delicate thorn-dodging operation, best tackled confidently.

Even late on in September, days can be still warm enough to impersonate summer for a few hours, but the mornings and evenings bear the shadow of autumn. It sharpens the senses into appreciating every hour of sunshine.

As well as eating sun-warmed fruit outside, there's also a flurry of kitchen activity – jams, fruit leathers, gins and vodkas, oils, syrups and the drying of herbs – trying to capture the essence of that high harvest, for anything we can't or don't want to eat immediately.

LEMON VERBENA

Site Well drained, sunny, sheltered

Harvest April–October

Notes Tricky from cuttings or seed so best to buy a plant

IF YOU'RE NOT GROWING lemon verbena, stop what you're doing and go and buy a plant immediately. Bright, aromatic and refreshing, it has a scent and flavour like lemons, only better. There's no sourness to this herb and it carries a strange sherbettiness – to the smell as well as the flavour. It is my Desert Island herb.

I keep a couple of plants in pots by the back door, as it's one of those flavours I turn to all the time. As with bay, lemon verbena is mostly used to infuse its flavour rather than be eaten itself. From April until mid-October, I use it in ice creams, cocktails (fruit and boozy), cakes and tea. I'm no fan of herb teas – too many promise to be warm Ribena but taste of tepid Tippex – but on its own or combined with Moroccan mint, lemon verbena is genuinely, deliciously refreshing.

By September, the warm days are running out and when they go lemon verbena hibernates. I make syrups of a few of the herbs that don't produce over winter, and lemon verbena is top of that list. I use it more as a syrup than I do in any other form, and in every way that I would use the herb fresh.

The leaves dry well, too, so a few handfuls taken now and left to dry for a few days and jarred keep the flavour going in the kitchen until the plant is growing again. Try a few zapped with sugar – in a coffee grinder or with a pestle and mortar – on desserts or in cocktails.

Lemon verbena is easy to grow and there are no varieties to confuse things. All it needs is sun, shelter and a well-drained soil. It is vulnerable to extreme cold, so be prepared to mulch around the roots and/or cover it. As mine are in pots, I bring them under cover over winter.

Charlie's mojito (page 182)

Herb syrups (page 266)

Peach & raspberry galette (page 274)

Summer punch (page 183)

non verbena

Szechuan pepper

THE SZECHUAN PEPPER give me more pleasure than anything else at Otter Farm. Their leaves come early in spring and make the walk to the polytunnels longer – every day I stop to rub a few and get that pepper scent on my fingers. It's a heavy aroma, lightened to varying degrees, depending on variety, by a citrusy brightness. Once the leaves start to uncurl, growth accelerates and flowers begin to form.

Around late June and early July they draw the bees from the hive at a time when there may otherwise be a shortage of nectar. A few weeks later, the bees suddenly stop coming, as if the drawbridge has come down across all the plants, and slowly the flowers form the tiny bobbles that will turn into peppercorns.

Even this tiny, they carry something of that intense pepperiness and citrus. While you can pick them at any stage, they are usually harvested when they've turned from their deep green through purple-brown into a gloriously vibrant pink-red. We pick some in August, when they've reached full size (5mm or so across) and the colour just starts to take on a hint of purple-brown – they have a freshness that while not better is certainly different to those picked pink-red. They're wonderful sparingly crushed into dressings or as a marinade for meat, especially steak.

When they're pink-red and the outer casing is starting to split open on the first few, it is time to harvest. I twist the peppercorns off in clusters and lay them somewhere out of the rain – usually the polytunnel – to dry for a couple of days, or place them in the dehydrator. This allows enough moisture to evaporate for them to pass easily through a pepper mill.

If ripened long enough to allow the seed casing to split, the black seed within will fall to the ground in an attempt to spread the pepper population – it carries little flavour as most is in the colourful outer shell, but I usually pick them intact because they go through the grinder more easily than just the seed casing.

Szechuan pepper has more to it than beauty, flavour and aroma. Nibble half a peppercorn at the front of your mouth and your tastebuds turn on full beam. Your mouth fills with saliva. Slowly a tingle develops on your lips and the tip of your tongue, a gentle anaesthetising that is known as '*ma*' is Chinese cooking. This is believed by some to give you a spiritual lift. It certainly brings on the smiles.

A few types of pepper have a little of this *ma* but with Szechuan the *ma* outweighs the usual spicy heat (known as '*la*') that dominates in most peppers. It is peculiarly addictive and unlike anything I've ever eaten.

You can find Szechuan pepper in some shops; it is expensive and while some is pretty good, it lacks the zing and brightness of freshly picked pepper. Its *ma* is diminished and some of its heart is lost as a result.

Grow your own and you can keep yourself, your family and very possibly your neighbours in pepper from a single plant. Szechuan pepper grows as a spiky bush that can be kept small enough for a big pot or left to get much larger in the ground. They need no pruning, but they'll happily submit to shaping if you want to tame them a little. They can be grown

SZECHUAN PEPPER

Site Well drained, sunny

Harvest July–November

Notes A few *Zanthoxylum* varieties come under the umbrella of Szechuan pepper – *Z. schinifolium* is my favourite, though all are very good. Start from a plant as starting from seed can be tricky and germination erratic

pretty much anywhere in Britain, other than in the gardens of the few who live on the highest, most exposed moors and mountains. Here, in a windy field, they flourish, even withstanding down to −18°C a few winters ago.

The leaves of the Szechuan pepper plant are also lovely to eat. I pinch a few off as they emerge to brighten up early salads, and take some larger leaves through the summer for flavouring mayonnaise or adding a zip to spice mixes and marinades.

Right here, right now, I may have the most beautifully aromatic pockets in the world. I've been picking pepper.

Of the few pepper varieties that are collectively known as Szechuan, all of which belong to the Zanthoxylum family, I've had many handfuls from the young Z. schinifolium and Z. simulans. The Z. simulans is pretty pokey. The corns are a livid red, like the worst eczema. Rub them or the leaves and the lively scent takes over your fingers for an hour or two. A few in your pocket refresh your fingers with the scent every time your hand reaches in.

Today, along with some of both Szechuans, a pot of Nepalese pepper (Z. alatum) and Japanese pepper (Z. piperitum). I've had bagfuls of Japanese pepper leaves (aka sansho) over the last few years and a few peppercorns, but this year the dozen or so plants seem to have agreed to produce a little more heavily.

— 30 September, 2013

TOMATOES

Site	Sunny and sheltered
Sow	February–March under cover
Harvest	July–November
Notes	Plant out late May–June. Grow well in 7-litre plus containers if fed regularly to maintain fertility

HOMEGROWN TOMATOES may be the single most effective drug for intoxicating non-gardeners into picking up a trowel. Even after years of growing them, that first Sungold tomato of every summer, picked at its perfect moment and warm from the sun, drives a double decker bus through my memory of how good they are. Along with Peacevine Cherry and Gardener's Delight, they take up over half the space I set aside for tomatoes in the polytunnel – each as reliable as they are delicious.

I always advise newcomers to grow at least four tomato varieties. In the first year, the law of averages means you'll find a couple of good ones, one that's reasonable and a real duffer. Eat the best, cook and preserve with the reasonable one, and give the fruit of the duffer to someone you don't care to impress. In subsequent years, grow the two favourites and try two new varieties, keeping your two favourites (even if they change) each time. It means you get at least two delicious varieties while keeping the door open to new flavours and textures.

As well as the cherry varieties, I usually grow two large fruiting tomato varieties, including Costoluto Fiorentino, and the rest of the tomato patch is made up of three or four medium-sized varieties – Black Krim (pick it when purple-red), Japanese Black Trifle, San Marzano and a couple of new varieties each year.

...natoes: Nectar

Even in Devon, a polytunnel is the only way to be sure of a good crop of fully ripe fruit. Once in a while, if I've a few too many plants for the polytunnel, I'll plant a few cherry tomatoes (the small fruit need less sun to ripen) and perhaps a few Black Krim and Japanese Black Trifle outside. Often as not they do well, but generally it's not a gamble I'm happy to take.

Tomatoes are one of those plants that repay care and attention to detail. I start them off early, under cover, sowing most in modules on Valentine's Day and a second batch in mid-March in a heated propagator, but a sunny windowsill, especially if it's near a radiator, will do.

The first pair of leaves (known as seed leaves) is followed by true leaves. When they have developed a little, I move each seedling into a 9cm pot, planting them a couple of millimetres beneath the seed leaves – this encourages the development of more roots from the stem.

I plant seedlings in the ground from early June, when they're about 20cm tall, with flowers starting to open on the lowest branch (known as a truss). Again, they can be planted a little deeper than they were in their pot, to encourage more roots to develop from the stem. In a very sheltered, mild location they can be chanced a little earlier but large day-night temperature swings can rapidly take the vigour out of tomato plants.

Tomatoes need food, water, light and heat. Short-change them on any of these essentials and they will under-perform. Maintaining soil (or compost) fertility is vital: I add well-rotted manure or compost before I plant and feed them with comfrey tea or another high-potassium feed every fortnight from flowering. Water the soil/compost, rather than the plant, as more water reaches the roots and wet leaves can encourage fungal diseases and scorch.

Whether tall cordon varieties or short bush cultivars, tomato plants need a little support: canes or dangling string for tying the taller cordons to; netting or a few shorter sticks for the bush varieties.

As with grape vines, a balance has to be struck between vigorous green growth and fruit. The shoots that develop between the stems and the main leaves should be pinched out – they're stealing valuable nutrients as well as creating shade and reducing air circulation. I also pinch or cut off the top of outdoor plants when six trusses have set fruit, in the hope that it gives these trusses the resources to develop well.

When plants reach 1.5 metres tall it's worth taking off lower leaves – certainly up to the first truss – to promote air and light access, and so reduce the chance of disease.

Companion planting works beautifully and very effectively with tomatoes. Garlic, nasturtiums and marigolds (*Tagetes spp*) planted nearby are particularly effective at repelling green and blackfly with their smell, whereas basil draws the aphids to it from the tomato where you can deal with them more easily.

The indoor harvest can start in July and run into early November, whereas outside it tends to squeeze into late August and September.

A FEW OF THE HEDGES near the river have wild blackberries scrambling through them, and their berries are as beautifully sat on the tart side of sweet as the ones I remember as a kid.

If you consider yourself British, then you should be keen to scrabble about in hedges, braving the stingers and the last of the wasps, to exercise your right to free fruit. Every September we head out with plastic tubs, arguing over whether it'll be pie or crumble for tea. I love it for the fruit and that those dark berries usher in the autumnal foraging season, with haws, hips, sloes, crab apples and wild damsons to look forward to.

Plentiful as they are in the hedgerows, I still grow blackberries near the house. Cultivated varieties have been bred for sweetness, size and to yield heavily, and are in many ways different fruit to their wild relatives. I certainly wouldn't choose cultivated varieties above wild blackberries – I love the tart edge and the mess-about that comes with foraged berries – but homegrown blackberries give another flavour to enjoy, and as most grow naturally upright, they lend themselves well to training.

If your fingers have had enough of being pricked by the brambles, there are good thornless varieties, such as Adrienne, Waldo and Oregon Thornless. Not overly vigorous, Waldo is a good choice for container growing or for a small space. For a more traditional flavour, the heavy cropping Ashton Cross is the closest to the hedgerow berries I've tried.

As their hedgerow presence suggests, blackberries are unfussy about their site, but if given a good fertile soil and compost or manure each year, they'll thrive. Early autumn is a good time to plant them. Cut the strongest stems back to 30cm or so and remove thin shoots to encourage strong shoots to grow. As well as watering them in thoroughly, I find watering them during dry patches in the first summer helps them establish.

Each year, blackberries grow long shoots (known as canes) that in the following year develop fruiting side shoots (known as laterals). Each autumn, I prune old canes back to the base after they've fruited, leaving this year's canes to replace them. I mulch around the base every spring with well-rotted manure or compost and give them a comfrey or seaweed feed once or twice in summer to up the harvest a little.

Depending on the quality of the summer, variety and location, blackberries can be ready to harvest from August through until the end of October. They usually ripen gradually across the plant rather than all at once, which gives plenty of opportunity to pick and avoids huge gluts. It also makes blackberrying one of the most sustainable forages, as even if you clear a plant of ripe berries, others are waiting to mature. We try to pick on a dry day, as I've found that wet berries spoil rapidly.

Although blackberries are generally disease-free, birds can be a nuisance. I dislike netting but after seeing what the birds did to other fruit in midsummer, I covered the blackberries as they began to ripen.

There are a number of blackberry hybrids available, some of which are hardly worth the space. Loganberries and tayberries certainly are, and I wouldn't be without the juiciness and depth of flavour of boysenberries.

BLACKBERRIES

Site Relatively unfussy

Harvest July–September

Notes Self-fertile, so just one is fine. Expect 5kg per plant from most productive varieties once established

Blackberry whisky (page 286)

COURGETTES

Site Sunny

Sow April–June under cover, in small pots

Harvest July–October

Notes Sow in spring and another in early summer to keep long harvest period. Plant 60cm apart, May–July. Water through dry spells

I AM A MAN. I open a packet of seeds and am compelled by my Y chromosome to sow all of the seeds therein. I pause a moment to consider: there's my wife, my daughter and me, we'd like some courgettes in the summer, so allowing for one not to germinate, one to be eaten by the slugs, four should be plenty. I then sow all twelve seeds in the packet. Weeks later, I consider how many of the dozen or so thriving seedlings to offer friends and quickly conclude zero, planting out all twelve. A month or two down the line I complain to anyone who'll listen about how terribly over-productive courgettes are.

I have a few suggestions if you want to get the best from your courgettes. Firstly, leave the sowing to someone sensible. Over-sowing is often down to confidence – we doubt they'll germinate or, if they do, the slugs will get them, so we wildly overcompensate. A plant per person plus one for the slugs is usually enough to ensure you have a good harvest.

I always sow three varieties – a classic green 'cigar' courgette such as Alberello di Sarzarna, a round green variety like Rondo di Nizza and a yellow courgette, almost always Soleil. Each has a distinctive flavour and texture, so there's immediate variety to the harvest.

I pick them small too, never bigger than a slim 15cm, often much smaller. If they get bigger, I cut them off the plant and add them to the compost heap. This isn't a waste of food; it's an affirmation of life. Think of a courgette as a bottle of squash – adding more water increases the size but dilutes the flavour, so while there may be more to eat you'll have less enthusiasm for doing so. While you wrestle that oversized courgette into a flavourless meal or two, other perfectly sized, beautifully flavoursome courgettes are growing – these are the ones you should be eating.

It's important to remember that the plant hasn't decided to thank you, its 'creator', with bountiful fruit – it is simply trying to reproduce. It's clever enough to wrap up its seeds in an edible coating to bribe you into distributing them elsewhere. As the courgette grows the seed develops, sending a telegram to the plant that its primary task – to replicate itself – has been achieved and it slows production. Cutting off any large courgettes, before they reach clown's shoe proportions, ensures that the telegram is never sent, so the plant keeps on producing – you get more food by composting the large ones – and you keep eating delicious courgettes for longer.

I also manage thriving plants by indulging in a couple of feasts of courgette flowers. It's especially effective if I target the flowers with a small courgette developing behind them. I get one of the treats of the summer garden – the tiny courgettes are superb raw or battered and deep-fried with the flower intact – while keeping the numbers in check.

Once runners cross the garden path, encroach too far into the neighbouring crops or (in the case of squash) start producing fruit that is way behind the rest on the plant, I'll snip the shoots short. Most head for the compost bin, but some, along with a handful of leaves, make it to the kitchen to be stir-fried in olive oil with garlic and chilli, or used in soups.

Courgettes: Alberello di Sarzana

CHILLIES

Site Sunny, best under cover

Sow February–April, under cover in modules or Jiffy 7s

Harvest July–November

Notes Plant out in June. Feed every fortnight. Perennial, so can overwinter but not often so productive in their second year

GIVEN THAT HE IS NO LONGER with us and is therefore incapable of mounting a spirited rebuttal, I will blame my father for putting me off chillies. Born in Sri Lanka, he seemed to think that 'curry' was the third meal after breakfast and lunch. And he liked it hot. The daily dose left me if not exactly ambivalent about chillies, then certainly not an enthusiast.

Until a few years ago, I was as uninterested in chillies as I was (am) in where Jeremy Clarkson buys his clothes. That has now changed (the chillies, not Clarkson's clothes) thanks to the weakest chilli I've ever eaten.

Visiting friends and chilli experts Joy and Michael Michaud at their smallholding in Dorset, I was offered a chilli to eat whole and, despite protesting that chillies weren't my thing, I did as I was told. My father may have put me off chillies, but he brought me up to be polite.

Boom: not the expected blast of heat but an explosion of fruitiness – apricot and melon – and a noseful of aromatic loveliness. It was a revelation, the culinary equivalent of hearing Miles Davis' Kind of Blue and realising that jazz isn't all bad jackets and busy fingers.

Once sensitised to those chilli flavours, textures and aromas that can often be hidden by the heat, it is easier to pick them up in many of the hotter chillies.

Chilli heat is measured in Scoville Heat Units (SHU). Most of those we buy in the shops sit somewhere in the 5–10k SHU range. The Apricot chilli that converted me is one of the weakest at around 500 SHU (think Charles Hawtry in the Carry On films), whereas the world's hottest chilli, the Dorset Naga, is seriously mean at around 1 million SHU (think Robert Mitchum in *Cape Fear*). As you'd imagine, they make very different salsas.

Choice of variety is everything in determining the flavours, aromas and spiciness of the harvest, but heat is only part of the story. There are four main types of chilli, each with their own character. They are worth getting to know.

Vegetable chillies are thick fleshed, large fruited and usually fairly mild. Most belong to the *Capsicum annuum* species, are early to mature and the easiest, most reliable to grow. Hungarian Hot Wax (6k SHU) is the best known and much better grown at home than bought. Pimiento de Padron (12k SHU) is one of my favourites – picked young and tender, it is usually very mild and delicious, warming up as it matures.

Spice chillies are thin fleshed, small fruited and usually fairly to very hot. Spike (97k SHU) is fiery and grows well in containers. Super Chile (36k SHU) is early, lively and happy grown in a pot. It dries well and looks a treat, but most pleasingly it is prolific – it's perfectly possible to pick 300 chillies from each plant. NuMex Twilight (30k SHU) is one of the most beautiful chillies. The fruit start purple and move through greens and oranges to red, but as fruit are produced continually the plant is usually multicoloured. Superb fresh or dried.

Habaneros are a subgroup of the spice chillies, belonging to the species *Capsicum chinense*. Their defining characteristic is their incredible fruitiness and while they tend to be very hot, some, such as Apricot, are very mild. For a medium-hot habanero with all the fruitiness you'd expect, try Trinity (40k SHU).

The Superhots are the hottest of the habaneros and largely for the man with a certain inferiority complex but without the money to indulge in a Ferrari. These are all seriously hot, measuring over 500k SHU, with the Dorset Naga often well over 1 million SHU. They need respecting as serious discomfort can result. I wouldn't even look at them too long if I were you.

Vegetable chillies or early ripening spice chillies are a must as they are unlikely to run out of summer heat before being ready to pick. The Super Chillies I sow in February are usually ready to start picking in July.

Most chillies can be grown on a sunny windowsill. Stumpy is a hottish (20k SHU) chilli that stays naturally small in stature, growing only to 12cm or so in height. For something livelier but still small, I grow Prairie Fire, which lives up to its name at a throat-warming 108k SHU. In truth, pretty much any chilli can be grown indoors in a sunny spot – keeping them in small pots (3 litre is ideal) has the effect of bonsaiing the plant.

Chillies are pretty easy to grow, but they are particular. They are tropical plants so they need light and heat at every stage of growth. They germinate best at around 27°C – a heated propagator is perfect, a warm windowsill will do.

Timing is crucial: I sow a batch in mid-February and another a month later – the first batch might perish with the cold and low light levels but in a good year they'll get away well and fruit will be early and plentiful. Sowing later than the end of March is a punt on a long, hot summer.

I sow chilli seeds into modules using a fine seed compost, covering the seed by 6mm or so, or Jiffy 7s – small discs of coconut husk that expand when wet.

I used to put them into the warmth of the airing cupboard as chillies will germinate in the dark, taking the seedlings out into the light at the first sign of germination to avoid spindly growth. But using the heated propagator means less compost on the pillow cases, as well as greater success rates.

Germination can take a while – perhaps a month – but even from the day of sowing, I never let the compost dry out completely until the plants have finished producing.

Once germinated, chilli seedlings grow best at around 21°C during the day and around 17°C at night – the propagator allows me to set this automatically; the warmest, sunniest windowsill with a radiator beneath it did a reasonable impersonation of those conditions before we owned a propagator.

When the roots begin to fill the Jiffy 7s or modules, I pot the seedlings on into 10cm pots using a peat-free multipurpose compost, planting to a depth just below the initial seed leaves. I usually tear off the Jiffy 7s' outer netting to allow the roots to grow unimpeded.

Chillies: Spike

Chillies are as hungry as they are thirsty. I use a liquid plant feed (at room temperature to avoid shocking the plant) fortnightly, to promote healthy growth and fruiting.

When the roots start to take up the pot, I transplant the seedlings to their final location. This is around 2 months or so after sowing. Leggy plants (yes, I get them too once in a while) are sunk deeper into the soil – up to the first seed leaves – when planting out. A handful of pelleted chicken manure usually goes into the hole with the plant to slowly feed it.

In the finest summer, in the sunniest of sheltered outdoor spots in southern England I have coaxed an outdoor harvest out of the earliest fruiting chilli varieties but it's a gamble I rarely take. Normally I grow my chillies under cover in the heat of the polytunnel, closing the doors on the dog's early evening walk to trap still-warm air, giving the plants a gentler transition into the cool of night.

Aphids can be a nuisance. At their height in June and July, these tiresome sapsuckers can seriously weaken a plant. They are messy eaters too, spilling sap onto the leaves below. This causes fungal growth that stresses the plant and reduces photosynthesis, impairing the plant's ability to recover.

I grow flowering plants that attract ladybirds, natural predators that snaffle their way through the aphids remarkably quickly. Thankfully, an infestation is easy to deal with provided action is quick, as aphids are born pregnant. The polytunnel's hose aimed at the undersides of the leaves, repeating every day until they're eradicated, is safe, free, immediate and effective. Once in a while if they're a little stubborn, I use a biological control or an organic, non-harmful spray (such as Savona).

Other than that, the plants need little care: I just quietly say, 'heat, light, food and water,' to myself every time I pass them to remind me of what they need if I want chillies when the weather finally turns hot again.

The gamble of early sowing should be paying off handsomely in September. Many of the smallest fruiting varieties will have started producing chillies in July and continue through August so by September we are usually inundated with chillies of all kinds. Fortunately, they are easy to preserve.

Most varieties freeze well, retaining their flavour and heat once defrosted. To avoid them freezing together in a clump, I spread the fruit out on a tray to freeze, then bag them up. Scotch Bonnets, Apricot and other habaneros, being fleshy, take to freezing the best.

Preserving in oil is common but I find it needs a little attention. I start with 500ml of olive oil to every half-dozen medium-strength chillies, split lengthways. I usually warm the oil before pouring it over the chillies – it seems to draw the flavour out quickly. After 3 weeks I test the oil, adding a little more if it turns out to be napalm or replacing the original chillies with a second batch if the oil is too mild. Don't leave chillies in the oil for longer than 3 weeks – they won't add much more after that time and can go mouldy.

Chillies take to drying wonderfully well, intensifying in flavour and colour. They need warmth and good ventilation to dry thoroughly and minimise the risk of mould. Depending on available space, I spread them out, untouching, on a tray in a greenhouse, polytunnel or sunny windowsill for a fortnight or so, or use the dehydrator.

Chillies can be oven-dried too – I slice them lengthways in half, lay them on a baking tray and leave them to dry in the oven on its lowest setting – nothing over 100°C – as the gentler the heat, the better the results. It can take as little as half an hour for thin-skinned varieties to dry, or hours for fleshy chillies. Once in a while, I make a string of dried chillies – known as a ristra – by sowing them through the stem (not the fruit) and tying them up to dry somewhere well ventilated, warm and dry.

Pickling is criminally overlooked; chillies take beautifully to a little vinegar and sugar.

ELDERBERRIES

Site Relatively unfussy

Harvest September–October

Notes Berries can suddenly vanish in late October – the birds wait until they are perfect

THE PIG PENS separate a few elder shrubs and the Szechuan pepper hedge that runs down to the polytunnel. On the face of it, they couldn't be more different – elder being a soft, traditional part of our countryside, and Szechuan pepper a spiky incomer from the other side of the world – but their annual arc is uncannily similar.

Both form wide, flat flowerheads that face the spring sun; helipads for the many insects they attract. Once the sun and the pollinators have done their work, berries form, causing the heads to flip under their weight as they grow.

The berries of both ripen as summer turns to autumn. Elderberries turn deep purple, are high in vitamin C and look a treat, but I don't find them wildly adaptable in the kitchen. That said, there are two really fine recipes that I make with them every year.

Firstly, elderberry juice. Cook a kilo of berries in a little water until they break down, pass them through a sieve and add sugar until the liquor reaches a sweetness you like. It should taste akin to, but much better than, cranberry juice.

Secondly, Pontack sauce.

Elderberries

Recipes for

July, August & September

Courgette shoots & leaves soup

A gloriously bright and lively soup that takes the shoots, tips, leaves, fruit and flowers of the courgette and puts them to use. It is a very adaptable recipe – you can make this with just the shoots in early season, shoots and flowers mid-season to keep courgette production under control, or all parts later in the summer and into autumn. Squash shoots and tips work equally well.

Mild habanero chillies are perfect here – they are all big aromas and fruitiness with just a tickle of heat. If you haven't any, use a third of a regular-heat chilli instead.

You can add a potato if you're looking for more heartiness – it's good, but I prefer it fresh and bright as it is.

Serves 3

2 tbsp olive oil

2 mild habanero chillies, such as Apricot or Bellaforma, deseeded and thinly sliced

3 garlic cloves, chopped

2 courgettes, cut into 5mm dice

A bowlful of youngish, tender courgette leaves, shredded

2 celery sticks or 3 lovage leaves, shredded

1 large tomato, skinned and roughly chopped

A splash of Marsala or sherry

A few slices of bread

3 courgette flowers

A splash of extra virgin olive oil

A handful of Greek basil or oregano

Sea salt and freshly ground black pepper

Heat the olive oil in a large pan over a medium heat. Add the chillies and cook, stirring occasionally, for a couple of minutes. Add the garlic, stir and cook for 2 minutes more, stirring often.

Add the courgettes and cook for 3–4 minutes, stirring frequently. Add all the shredded shoots and leaves with half the tomato and cook for another 3–4 minutes, stirring often.

Add a splash of Marsala and stir well, scraping up any nuggets sticking to the base of the pan.

Pour in enough water to just cover and bring to a simmer. Let simmer, uncovered, for 10–15 minutes, depending on the tenderness of the leaves and shoots, adding the rest of the tomato after 5 minutes.

While the soup is simmering, griddle the bread.

Remove the soup from the heat and season with salt and pepper to taste. Tear the bread into pieces and partially stir into the soup.

Add the courgette flowers, splash with olive oil and scatter Greek basil or oregano over the top to serve.

Salt & pepper Padron peppers

This very fine tapas is almost not a recipe, it is so simple. It is best accompanied by a very cold beer. There's a touch of Russian roulette about it – Padrons are mild and fruity when young, becoming hotter as they mature. You can eat a dozen that are gentle, then bam, a rogue with some heat. Delicious and plenty of fun.

Per person

A little vegetable oil

12 Padron peppers

Sea salt and freshly ground black pepper

Heat a slick of oil in a wok or large saucepan over a very high heat until the oil begins to smoke, then add the peppers. Fry, flipping them as they begin to blister, and add salt and pepper as they cook. They should be ready in only a minute or two – blistered on all sides here and there.

Serve hot, well salted and peppered, with a cold beer.

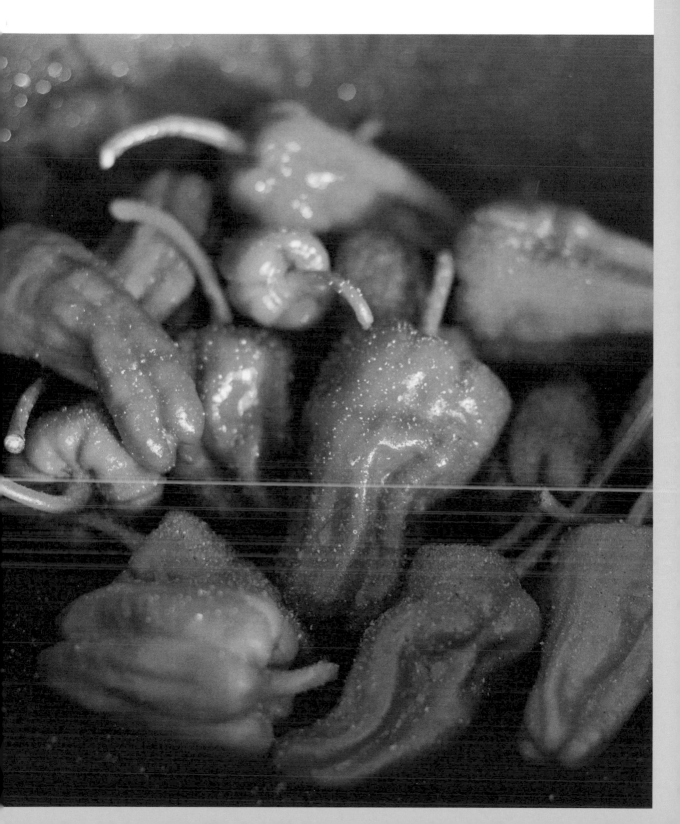

Roast trout with fennel *&* lemon

I don't eat a whole lot of trout – partly because I am to fly fishing what Oliver Reed was to quiet nights in – but when I do, I like it baked. This is quick, easy and goes perfectly with a green salad, tomato salsa and/or agretti, fennel and cucumber salad (page 260).

Serves 2

2 medium trout, gutted and cleaned
1 unwaxed lemon, cut into 8 wedges
2 bay leaves
1 red onion, thinly sliced
½ fennel bulb, thinly sliced
A good splash of olive oil
Sea salt and freshly ground black pepper

Preheat the oven to 200°C/Gas 6.

Lay the trout in a roasting tin. Fill the cavity of each fish with 3 lemon wedges, a bay leaf and some onion and fennel slices. Season well with salt and pepper. Any remaining onion or fennel can be scattered around.

Splash with olive oil and bake for 30 minutes. Serve with the remaining lemon wedges.

Agretti with scallops

Having become quietly addicted to samphire, I love growing agretti – it shares many of its qualities and can be picked over a long season. If only I could grow my own scallops…

Serves 2

A handful of agretti

2–3 tbsp olive oil

½ chilli, deseeded and finely sliced

4 spring onions, sliced into rings

1 garlic clove, finely chopped

A large handful of spinach or young chard, central ribs removed

6 scallops, shelled and cleaned

Juice of ½ lime

Sea salt and freshly ground black pepper

Blanch the agretti in boiling water for 1 minute, drain and allow to cool.

Heat 2 tbsp olive oil in a large frying pan. Add the sliced chilli and spring onions and cook gently for a few minutes to soften, stirring occasionally to prevent browning. Add the garlic and cook for another minute or two, stirring often.

Add the spinach and cook until just wilted. Add the agretti and toss to warm through. Transfer a warm plate and cover with foil to keep warm.

Turn the heat under the pan up high and add a little more oil if need be. Season the scallops with salt and pepper on one side. Add them seasoned side down to the hot pan and cook for 1 minute, seasoning the tops as they cook. Turn them over – they should be golden on the cooked side – and cook the other side for a minute.

Squeeze the lime juice over and lift the scallops from the pan. Place them on top of the agretti and spicy spinach and serve.

Lamb & apricot tagine

Taking its name from the earthenware pot in which it is traditionally cooked, a tagine is a rich, spicy, slow-cooked Moroccan stew that marries savoury and sweet, with apricots typically providing the balance to meat or vegetables.

Once in a while, when we have more than enough apricots for eating fresh or turning into ice cream, a tagine is inevitably where they end up. This year the cold spring meant few apricots, but the hot summer gave us plenty of figs, which I used instead on a cool, end-of-summer day. They worked a treat.

Serves 4–6

1kg lamb shoulder, diced
10cm cinnamon stick, finely ground, or 2 tsp ground cinnamon
2 tsp ground cumin
1 tsp sweet paprika
1 tsp hot paprika
1 tsp ground coriander
1 tsp ground turmeric
4 cardamom pods, lightly crushed
400g tin chopped tomatoes
2 onions, finely sliced
25g fresh ginger, peeled and grated
1 tsp saffron threads
2 tbsp tomato purée
2 tbsp olive oil
8 garlic cloves, finely chopped
500g fresh apricots
Beurre manié (knob of soft butter mixed with 2 tsp plain flour), if needed
Juice of 1 lemon
4–6 tbsp honey
A handful of coriander leaves, finely chopped
A small handful of mint leaves, finely chopped
Sea salt and freshly ground black pepper

Put the lamb in a bowl, add all the dry spices and toss well together, then leave to stand for at least 3 hours.

Put the spiced lamb, tomatoes and onions into a large cooking pot and add enough water to just cover. Bring to a simmer, then add the ginger, saffron, tomato purée, olive oil and garlic. Stir well, return to a simmer, then lower the heat and cook very gently, with the lid partially on, for 2½ hours.

In the meantime, preheat the oven to 150°C/Gas 2. Halve the apricots and place them cut side up in a baking dish. Bake until they are soft and yielding but still hold their shape, about 20 minutes, depending on the ripeness of the fruit.

If the tagine is in danger of drying out at any time during cooking, add a little water. If the liquor seems too thin at the end of cooking, you can thicken it with a little buerre manié. Lift the meat out with a slotted spoon and add buerre manié to the sauce in little pieces every minute or so, whisking constantly, until the sauce is the thickness you want. Cook the sauce for a few minutes to cook out the flour, then return the meat to the pan.

Add the apricots, lemon juice and 4 tbsp honey to the tagine and stir well, simmering for a few minutes only. Taste and season, adding a little more honey, too, if you fancy. Scatter over the chopped coriander and mint and serve with rice.

Garden pizza

If you have a wood oven, you'll be firing it up at every opportunity. If, on the other hand, you fancy making one, check out Dan Steven's step-by-step guide in his *River Cottage Bread Handbook*. Once in place, you'll be cooking pizzas and bread any weekend it's sunny.

This pizza dough recipe is easy and reliable, it freezes well and will keep in the fridge for a week or more, so you can make a batch well ahead. As for the dressing, olive oil, a tin or two of tomatoes reduced to a paste and a pot of pesto are the basics to add to whatever you have doing well in the garden. Try the following combinations: cooked beetroot, blue cheese, cherry tomatoes and pesto; tomato sauce, the first cherry tomatoes, mozzarella, capers, basil and sweet peppers; courgette slices, onions, dill and Manchego. And you really must make pizza topped with nectarine slices, Parma ham, blue cheese and parsley pesto – it's phenomenal.

Put out the topping ingredients and let everyone make up their own pizza – better still, especially with children, let them pick one or two things from the garden for it.

Makes 6–8 small pizzas

For the pizza dough

500g strong white bread flour

10g active dried yeast

10g salt

320ml warm water

1 tbsp olive oil

A handful of plain flour, for dusting

For the topping

1–2 x 400g tins chopped tomatoes

A pot of pesto

Your choice of vegetables, cheese, ham, salami, fish, fruit etc.

Capers, olives, anchovies and/or other flavourings

Olive oil

Basil or other herbs

Sea salt and freshly ground black pepper

To make the dough, sift the flour into a bowl and mix in the yeast and salt. Add the warm water and olive oil and mix to form a dough. Lightly flour a work surface and knead the dough on it until silky and smooth.

Transfer the dough in a large, clean bowl and cover with cling film or a damp cloth. Leave somewhere draught-free and warm to rise until doubled in size.

Whether it's outdoors or in, get the oven as hot as it can be – ideally to 250°C/Gas 9.

Pinch off satsuma-sized pieces of dough and allow them to rest on your work surface for 15 minutes or more – this will make rolling them easier.

When ready, roll the balls into thin, circular bases, about 5mm thick, and lay on a lightly floured baking sheet or baker's peel. Add your chosen toppings. Bake until cooked – 7–10 minutes in a standard domestic oven, 1–2 minutes in an outdoor wood oven.

Agretti frittata

If you keep chickens, you'll be familiar with that occasional build up of eggs when the hens are being productive. This is what to do with those excess eggs. If you don't keep hens, this is a fine excuse to buy some extra free-range eggs.

The core recipe works with many other ingredients – potatoes, chorizo, wild garlic and asparagus among my favourites. A great deal of pepper is compulsory. A crisp Little Gem or two, dressed only in olive oil and salt, is recommended.

Serves 2

3 tbsp olive oil

20g butter

2 onions, finely sliced

2 garlic cloves, finely chopped

6 free-range eggs

A splash of milk

A good handful of agretti

Sea salt and freshly ground black pepper

Warm the olive oil and butter in an 18–20cm frying pan (suitable for use under the grill) over a medium heat. Add the onions and cook until soft, stirring once in a while to prevent them browning; be patient – this can take 15 minutes or more. Add the garlic and cook for another 5 minutes.

Preheat the grill to medium-high.

Whisk the eggs together with a splash of milk to loosen them. Add the agretti to the pan and stir with the garlicky onions. Add plenty of pepper and a little salt, pour in the eggs and cook over a moderate heat. Use a fork to lift the egg as it starts to cook, pulling it away from the sides and base, allowing egg to run beneath to cook. Cook until the underside is set and golden.

Grind more pepper over the surface and add a little more salt, then place the pan under the grill and cook for a few minutes until the frittata is just set on top and golden.

Allow to rest for a couple of minutes before serving, as the frittata will set a little better and come free from the pan more easily.

Beetroot rosti, agretti & Manchego

A quick and easy lunch or light supper that can be adapted to other veg (salsify and parsnip are two well worth trying), other leaves (rocket or samphire especially) or different cheese.

The rosti are good with plain flour but gram flour/chickpea flour works really well with the cumin and beetroot.

Makes 6–8 rosti

2 tbsp cumin seeds

4 large raw beetroots, coarsely grated

6 tbsp gram flour, plus a little extra for shaping

2 garlic cloves, finely chopped

4 tbsp sunflower oil

Sea salt and freshly ground black pepper

To serve

A good handful of agretti, rocket or watercress

A little Manchego, Parmesan or hard goat's cheese

Yoghurt dressing (page 164)

Toast the cumin seeds in a dry pan, shaking the pan frequently to prevent burning, until the seeds release their aroma.

Combine the grated beetroot with the flour, garlic, cumin seeds, a good pinch of salt and a dozen or more turns of the pepper mill.

Allow the mixture to rest for a few minutes, then squeeze out the moisture between your hands – this will help the rosti hold together. With a little flour on your hands, form small handfuls of the beetroot mixture into discs, 2cm or so thick.

Heat the sunflower oil in a frying pan over a moderate heat. Fry the rosti, in batches as necessary, turning them as they brown and crisp underneath. When cooked, lift out on to kitchen paper to drain.

Serve the rosti with agretti, Manchego and plenty of yoghurt dressing.

Courgettes & Manchego on toast

A lunch or supper that takes 5 minutes to prepare and shows off courgettes at their best. Any basil will be good here, but Greek basil sets everything off perfectly to my taste.

Serves 2

4 small-medium courgettes

3 tbsp olive oil

4 slices of bread, ideally sourdough

10g Manchego or other hard cheese

A small handful of Greek basil

Sea salt and freshly ground black pepper

Cut the courgettes into 5–10mm slices. Warm the olive oil in a frying pan over a medium-high heat. Add the courgettes and cook until well coloured on the flat sides, stirring to prevent burning.

In the meantime, toast the bread.

Pile the courgettes onto the toast slices and season with salt and pepper as you like. Shave the Manchego over using a vegetable peeler and sprinkle with the basil.

Panzanella

We might eat a version of this three times a week in summer. It's a real what's-in-the-fridge favourite, sweeping up the odd courgette, half-onion or aubergine that might otherwise go unused. The recipe is really just a core around which to improvise – a little leftover chicken can replace the sardines, last night's potatoes can be sliced, fried and thrown in instead of the bread, and parsley or chervil work well in place of the basil.

Serves 3 as a light lunch

1 aubergine, sliced into 1cm thick rounds

Olive oil for brushing

A few slices of bread (preferably not too fresh)

½ cucumber, peeled and diced

1 or 2 courgettes, thinly sliced

10 or so cherry tomatoes, halved

1 smallish red onion, thinly sliced

1 garlic clove, finely chopped

2 tbsp capers, drained and roughly chopped

1 tin sardines (about 120g), drained (optional)

A splash of extra virgin olive oil

A handful of basil leaves

Sea salt and freshly ground black pepper

Heat a ridged griddle pan over a high heat. You will probably need to cook the aubergine slices in batches. Brush them with olive oil and place oiled side down on the griddle pan. Cook for a couple of minutes or so until charred on the underside, then brush the tops with oil, turn the slices over and cook the other side. Set aside.

Repeat to cook the rest of the aubergine, then oil and griddle the bread in the same way.

While the aubergine and bread are cooking, put the cucumber, courgettes, tomatoes, onion and garlic in a serving bowl and toss to mix. Tear the bread into rough pieces and add to the salad with the charred aubergine slices, capers and sardines, if using.

Splash with a little extra virgin olive oil, season with salt and pepper to taste and tear the basil roughly over. Toss well and serve.

Warm salad of Padron peppers, sugar snaps, cherries & halloumi

An unlikely blend of contrasting flavours and textures as it may seem, this is a belter. Salt, sweet, crunch and the Russian roulette of the peppers. If you're new to Padron peppers, embrace them with open arms. Fruity and mild enough to eat like apples when young, the odd one matures with a brilliant 'wham' of a slap in the mouth.

Serves 4 for lunch

3 tbsp olive oil

125g halloumi, sliced

200g Padron peppers

1 tsp smoked paprika

300g sugar snap peas

Finely grated zest of 1 unwaxed lemon and juice of ½ lemon

200g cherries, halved and stoned

A small handful of oregano

Sea salt and freshly ground black pepper

Warm the olive oil in a wok over a medium heat and fry the halloumi slices in batches for a few minutes, turning each slice as it turns golden underneath. Drain on kitchen paper.

Turn the heat up a little and add the peppers to the pan. Sprinkle with the smoked paprika, salt and pepper and cook over a high heat for 5–10 minutes, tossing the peppers, until they blister, colour here and there and just begin to collapse a little. Lift out with a slotted spoon into a bowl.

Add the sugar snaps to the pan and cook for a couple of minutes. Add the lemon juice, toss and cook for another 4 minutes or so.

Tip the sugar snaps and juices into the bowl with the peppers, add the halloumi and cherries and toss them together. Turn into a shallow dish and sprinkle with the oregano, lemon zest and a little salt and pepper.

Courgette 'spaghetti' with fresh tomato, garlic & basil sauce

In contrast to most tomato sauces, this is light, bright and fresh, as it isn't cooked. An old friend, the lovely Laura, introduced me to it a couple of decades ago and I've been making it every summer since. The ingredients half dissolve into each other in a bowl overnight, resulting in a fabulously pungent sauce. It's fantastic with pasta, but I have it mostly with courgette 'spaghetti', making a lovely, low-carb ratatouille of sorts.

Serves 4

10 courgettes

For the fresh tomato sauce

700g large, ripe tomatoes

8 garlic cloves, finely chopped

120ml extra virgin olive oil

50g basil leaves, torn into pieces

Sea salt and freshly ground black pepper

For the sauce, lower the tomatoes into a large bowl or pan of boiling water and leave them for a couple of minutes, then lift out onto a board. Cut a cross in the end of each one and peel away the skin. Chop the tomatoes roughly, discarding the tough stalk.

Put the chopped tomatoes in a large bowl with the garlic, extra virgin olive oil and basil. Cover and leave to marinate in the fridge for a few hours, at least – overnight if possible.

If you have one, pass the courgettes through a spiraliser – a handy gadget that results in spaghetti-like twists of courgette. If not, cut the courgettes lengthways into thin slices, about 4mm thick, and then slice each of the strips lengthways again to create 'spaghetti'.

Lower the courgette spaghetti into a pan of salted boiling water and cook for 1 minute only. Drain and return the courgette spaghetti to the pan.

Spoon on the sauce and heat just long enough to warm the sauce through, stirring frequently; you don't want to cook it. Season well with salt and pepper and serve immediately.

Beetroot with labneh, hazelnuts, parsley & elderflower dressing

This is almost a pudding, yet the sourness of the labneh and the fresh earthiness of the parsley stop the sweetness of the roasted beetroot, hazelnuts and elderflower running away with things. A simple, delicious light lunch or starter.

Serves 4

8 small beetroots

1–2 tbsp olive oil

40g hazelnuts

160g labneh, mascarpone or other curd cheese

A handful of flat-leaf parsley, leaves only

Elderflower dressing (page 165)

Sea salt and freshly ground black pepper

Leaving a couple of centimetres or so of stalk and the root still intact, lay the beetroots on a baking tray. Trickle olive oil over them and roast until tender but still firm – around 40 minutes, depending on size.

Meanwhile, toast the hazelnuts in a dry pan over a medium-high heat, shaking the pan frequently, until they just begin to colour. Tip onto a board and smash the hazelnuts up a little.

Halve the beetroots lengthways, or quarter if large. Spoon the labneh onto serving plates and add the beetroot halves. Scatter over the parsley and hazelnuts and season with salt and pepper to taste. Serve with the elderflower dressing.

Agretti, fennel & cucumber salad

A fresh cool salad that goes with just about anything – ham and other cold meats, smoked mackerel and especially with baked trout. Dill works well in place of fennel too.

Serves 2

¼ small-medium cucumber

A handful of agretti

A few pinches of fennel tops

20 capers

16 cherry tomatoes on-the-vine

Honey mustard dressing (page 164)

Peel the cucumber, and then use the peeler to cut the pale flesh into strips. If the agretti is less than succulent, blanch it in boiling water for a minute or so, then plunge it into cold water and drain it when cool.

Mix the cucumber strips, agretti and fennel tops together and sprinkle over the capers. Place the cherry tomatoes on top and dress with honey mustard dressing.

Sweet chilli dipping sauce

If I'm having tempura then this is often what I make to go with it. If I'm out of gooseberry sauce and sausages are cooking, I'll often turn to this sauce instead. Full of zing and bite, it's for dipping your finger into as much as anything.

Serves 4

4 tbsp sorb jelly (page 83), or redcurrant or other fruit jelly

1 tbsp cider vinegar

1 tbsp soy sauce

1½ garlic cloves, finely chopped

1 red chilli, ideally a habanero, finely chopped

1 tbsp lime juice

Sea salt

In a small saucepan, warm the fruit jelly, cider vinegar and soy, stirring until the jelly has dissolved. Add the garlic and chilli, stirring well, and allow to bubble gently for a minute or two. Add the lime juice and a good pinch of salt, and serve.

Pontack sauce

A fine, centuries-old dark, pungent spicy sauce for game and slow-roasted pork, and for adding depth to stews. It's very good with sausages too. It also works really well, if differently and more brightly in colour, with autumn olive berries instead of elderberries.

Makes about 350ml

500g elderberries (stripped of their stalks with a fork)

200g caster sugar

350ml cider vinegar or red wine vinegar

250g shallots, finely chopped

5 allspice berries

8 cloves

A good grating of fresh nutmeg

3cm piece of ginger, grated

A good pinch of salt

1 tbsp black peppercorns

Warm the elderberries, sugar and cider vinegar in a pan until the sugar dissolves. Add the remaining ingredients and simmer until the mixture forms a glossy syrup and has reduced a little.

Blitz in a blender, then pass through a sieve and pour into sterilised bottles or jars (see page 170). Seal and keep in a cool, dark cupboard. The sauce will keep and improve for years. Refrigerate once opened.

Pickled chillies

Chillies freeze and dry well, but pickling preserves their shape, colour and flavour best. It takes only a few minutes to do too. The shape and size of the chillies will determine the number and weight you need – many more smaller ones will pack upright in a jar.

Makes about 250g

100g caster sugar

A pinch of salt

500ml white wine vinegar

12 Szechuan (or black) peppercorns

3 bay leaves

About 250g chillies

Dissolve the sugar and salt in the wine vinegar in a pan over a medium heat. Add the peppercorns and bay leaves, increase the heat and simmer for 10 minutes. Remove from the heat.

Put the chillies in a sterilised jar (see page 170), pour the hot spicy vinegar over them and seal. Store in a cool, dark cupboard for up to a year. Keep in the fridge once opened.

Pickled walnuts

I prepare these in July (see page 203) and let them mature until autumn arrives. They're delicious with cheese, cured meats and cold roast beef.

Makes about 1kg

1kg green walnuts

100g salt

1 litre water

250g unrefined granulated sugar

500ml distilled malt vinegar

½ tsp black peppercorns

½ tsp grated ginger

½ tsp allspice

½ tsp cloves

½ tsp ground cinnamon

Prick each walnut a few times with a fork. Dissolve the salt in the water over a low heat to make a brine. Add the walnuts and bring slowly to the boil, then take off the heat and leave to stand for a day or two.

Drain the walnuts, discarding the brine. Spread them out on a tray and leave in a well-ventilated dry place. The nuts will turn black in 2 or 3 days.

Now, to make the pickling liquid, dissolve the sugar in the vinegar over a low heat, add the spices and bring to the boil slowly. Add the nuts and simmer for 15 minutes. Remove from the heat and leave to cool.

Lift the walnuts out with a slotted spoon into sterilised jars (see page 170) and cover with the pickling liquid. Store in a cool, dark cupboard. Leave for a few weeks, ideally a month or more, before using.

Herb syrups

I make these syrups through the year but especially as summer fades and the flavours will otherwise be out of reach until spring and beyond. Many herbs carry their best into a syrup – lavender, mint, lemon verbena, sage, rosemary and orange thyme are my favourites. Do try scented pelargoniums too. Although inedible in themselves, they easily release their aromatic loveliness into sweet syrup.

There's a bit of experimentation in finding the 'right' amount of each herb that works – their potency varies with the time of year, the intensity of the sun and the variety itself – so try a teaspoonful to test the strength as it simmers, and adjust if needs be. The core method – whatever the herb – is the same.

Makes about 200ml

200g caster sugar

200g water

Your chosen herb (such as a dozen lemon verbena leaves, or a few good stems of mint or 2–3 tbsp lavender buds)

Put the sugar and water in a pan and warm, stirring constantly, until the sugar is dissolved. Bring the sugar syrup up to a simmer, add your chosen herb and simmer for 5–10 minutes to infuse. Remove from the heat and allow to cool.

Strain the cooled herb syrup into a bottle. It will keep for a week or two at least in a cool, dark cupboard, longer if refrigerated. I usually make larger quantities and freeze them in small batches in plastic containers or freezer bags.

Chinese five-spice powder

I know there are jars of this in most supermarkets but if you can bear to free up the few minutes it takes to make your own every few months, you'll be very glad you did. Homemade, it has a zing and intensity that lifts whatever you cook with it – especially if that something is goose skin or pork. Five-spice works really well with squash too, calming down that occasional too-sweet edge it has, and with seafood – squid especially. It even brings out the loveliness in plums. Come to think of it, perhaps it just goes with everything and I'm finding out one combination at a time.

Makes 3–4 tbsp

2 star anise

2 tsp fennel seeds

5cm piece of cinnamon stick

2 tsp Szechuan peppercorns

7 cloves

Put a frying pan over a medium-high heat and add all the spices. Toast them, without oil, until they release their aromas a little. Keep shaking the pan to avoid burning them.

Blitz the toasted spices together in a coffee grinder or pound using a pestle and mortar until the spices are reduced to a fine powder.

Store in an airtight jar. It will keep for 3 months or more in a sealed container out of the light.

Butterscotch nectarines

I first made this while staying at a friend's campsite near Lewes. Despite the glorious weather, the peaches we'd bought wouldn't soften, so I threw them in a pan with semi-random quantities of butter and sugar in a slightly tipsy attempt to force them into becoming edible. It worked.

The less ripe the fruit, the slower you should cook the uncut side of the nectarine, before turning them over to cook them cut side down – you may even want to quarter large, firm fruit before cooking.

Serves 2

2 large nectarines or peaches

20g butter

1 tsp ground cloves (optional)

80g caster sugar

Halve and stone the nectarines. Melt the butter in a large frying pan over a medium-low heat. Place the nectarine halves cut side up in the pan and cook slowly until they begin to soften – this can take 2–15 minutes depending on the ripeness of the fruit.

Sprinkle the cut side of the peaches with ground cloves, if using, and flip the nectarine halves over. Cook slowly until softened.

Add the sugar and increase the heat to medium-high. Shake the pan now and again to help incorporate the sugar into the butter. As it cooks, the sugar/butter mix will begin to colour and turn to butterscotch; keep shaking the pan frequently.

When the butterscotch thickens to a loose fudginess, remove from the heat. Serve immediately, with double cream or vanilla ice cream.

Poached peaches

This is a good recipe for dealing with a glut of peaches and nectarines or coaxing all the flavour from under-ripe fruit, but I make it every year even if we only have a small crop, as it's so fine. The recipe is very flexible – you can use all water or more wine (try it with cider too) and any mint works well, though chocolate mint is perfect if you have some.

Serves 4–6

1kg peaches (about 6 large or 10–12 small fruit)

About 800ml water

400ml white wine

500g sugar

1 vanilla pod, split lengthways

Zest of 1 unwaxed lemon, in strips

A couple of large sprigs of mint

6–12 cloves (1 per peach)

Cut a shallow cross in the base of each peach and push a clove into the skin of each one. Put the water, wine and sugar in a large pan and bring slowly to a simmer, stirring to dissolve the sugar. Add the vanilla, lemon zest and mint. Lower the peaches into the pan and add a little extra water if necessary, to ensure they are just covered.

To help keep the peaches submerged, lay a cartouche over the surface (a piece of baking parchment a little larger than the diameter of the pan with a small hole cut in the centre to allow steam to escape). Bring slowly to a simmer and cook at a gentle simmer for 7–15 minutes, depending on the ripeness of the peaches.

Lift the peaches out with a slotted spoon and allow them to cool a little. Peel each fruit (the cross in the base of each makes this easy), discard the cloves and return the peaches to the liquor.

Serve the peaches warm or cold with a little of the poaching liquor.

Peach sorbet

Refrigerate the peeled peaches in their poaching liquor overnight. The next day, drain, halve and stone the peaches, then blitz to a purée in a food processor. Pass the purée through a sieve to remove any bits of skin and mint stalk (unless you don't mind them). Churn the purée in an ice-cream maker until thick, then spoon into a plastic tub and freeze. Alternatively, if you don't have an ice-cream maker, freeze until almost solid, then whisk to break down the ice crystals. Repeat once more, then allow to freeze solid.

Roast plums with labneh, almonds & honey

There's just enough of a nod of autumn in this to bring out the best of the plums, while keeping things light and feeling like the end of summer. The five-spice and plums marry delightfully, though cinnamon, ginger or mixed spice are very good if you fancy a change.

Serves 4

16 plums, halved and stoned

1 tbsp Chinese five-spice powder (page 267)

A few sprigs of thyme

40g blanched almonds

160g labneh, mascarpone or other curd cheese

2 tbsp runny honey

Preheat the oven to 150°C/Gas 2.

Place the plum halves cut side up on a baking tray, sprinkle with five-spice powder and lay the thyme sprigs across them. Roast for 40 minutes until soft but still holding their shape. If the plums are very unripe they may need another 15–20 minutes.

While the plums are in the oven, toast the almonds in a dry frying pan over a medium-high heat, shaking the pan frequently, until they just begin to colour.

Arrange the plums, labneh and almonds on a plate, swirl the honey over and serve.

Cucumber ice cream

Along with the Martini on page 282, I can think of no better cause for the cucumber to surrender itself to than this ice cream. It is just so refreshing. The mint doesn't dominate, it just adds a little extra layer of cool to the cucumber. Add more if you like (and/or a little salt, lovage seed or lime) and it will be good, but I prefer it simple, as it is.

Serves 4–6

1 large cucumber
24 mint leaves
170g granulated sugar
300ml whole milk
200ml double cream
1 vanilla pod, split lengthways
4 free-range egg yolks

Juice the cucumber, skin and all, or blitz it in a food processor and squeeze the pulp through a piece of muslin – you'll need 300ml cucumber juice.

Zap the mint and sugar in a food processor until it resembles green sugar.

Warm the milk, cream and vanilla pod in a heavy-based saucepan over a moderate heat, stirring occasionally, not allowing it to reach a simmer.

Meanwhile, whisk the egg yolks briefly, then add the minty sugar and whisk until incorporated. Take the warm, creamy milk off the heat. Stir a ladleful into the minty eggs to loosen them, then tip this mixture into the creamy milk, stirring as you do.

Return to a medium heat and cook the custard, stirring constantly. It will slowly thicken. When it is thick enough to just coat the back of a wooden spoon, remove from the heat, take out the vanilla pod and lower the pan into a sinkful of cold water to cool the custard down quickly.

When cooled, pour the custard into an ice-cream maker and churn until thickened. Spoon into a plastic tub and freeze.

Peach *&* raspberry galette

One of those fabulously adaptable, rough-and-ready puddings that allows the fruit's natural sweetness to dominate rather than the sugar. I can also recommend the following combinations: nectarine and wineberry; plum and apple; strawberry and blueberry. The pastry freezes brilliantly too.

Serves 6

For the pastry

200g plain flour, plus extra for dusting

100g spelt flour

1 tsp sea salt

45g caster sugar

250g cold unsalted butter, cut into small cubes

75ml cold water

For the filling

6 lemon verbena leaves (optional but very good)

20g caster sugar

400g peaches, stoned and cut into wedges

300g raspberries

1 tsp ground cinnamon

½ tsp ground cloves

80g ground almonds

To finish

Egg wash (1 lightly beaten egg, loosened with a little milk)

10g demerara sugar

For the pastry, put the flours, salt and sugar in a food processor and pulse for a moment. Add the butter and whiz briefly until the mixture resembles breadcrumbs. With the motor running, add the water, processing until the dough just holds together; you may not need all of it. Take out and flatten slightly into a disc. Wrap in cling film and refrigerate for at least an hour.

For the filling, zap the lemon verbena leaves, if using, with 10g of the caster sugar in a coffee grinder to a fine powder.

Gently combine the peaches and raspberries with the ground spices and verbena sugar or 10g plain sugar. Warm the remaining 10g sugar with 2 tsp water until dissolved to make a syrup.

Line a baking sheet with baking parchment. Roll the pastry out on a lightly floured surface to a rough circle, 5mm thick, and lay on the baking sheet.

Sprinkle the ground almonds over the pastry, leaving a 6–7cm clear border. Lay the peaches on top and dot with half the raspberries. Fold the edges of the dough in over the edge of the fruit, roughly pleating them as you go.

Rest in the fridge for an hour or so before cooking if possible, to help the galette retain its shape during cooking. Preheat the oven to 170°C/Gas 3.

Brush the pastry with the egg wash and sprinkle with the demerara sugar. Brush the fruit with half of the syrup. Bake in the centre of the oven for 20 minutes. Take the galette out and scatter over the remaining raspberries. Brush the fruit with the rest of the syrup and bake for a further 15 minutes or until the fruit is cooked and the pastry is lightly coloured.

Allow the galette to stand for 15 minutes – the fruity flavours and spices will be much improved. Serve with yoghurt or double cream.

Apricot & strawberry crumble

If, or rather when, the temperature dips dramatically in midsummer, this is the recipe that satisfies my crumble craving. It has a fairly light topping, more of a crisp than a crumble, and it works well with raspberries and dried apricots too. Don't be surprised if the strawberries partly dissolve – the sauce this creates is heavenly and runs nicely into whatever dairy you choose to pair it with.

Serves 6

For the crumble

75g plain flour

65g light brown sugar

65g caster sugar

1 tsp ground ginger

1 tsp ground cinnamon

A good pinch of salt

80g cold butter, cut into small cubes

100g oats

100g nuts (Brazils, walnuts, hazels, almonds or a mix), chopped

For the filling

300g strawberries

400g apricots, pitted and halved

80g caster sugar

Finely grated zest and juice of ½ unwaxed lemon

5 cardamom pods, seeds crushed, skins discarded

1 vanilla pod, seeds extracted

For the crumble, combine the flour, sugars, ginger, cinnamon and salt in a food processor (or a bowl). Add the butter and pulse (or work it in with your fingers) until it resembles coarse breadcrumbs. Stir in the oats and nuts, cover and refrigerate.

Preheat the oven to 190°C/Gas 5.

For the filling, combine the fruit in a bowl. Add the sugar, lemon zest and juice, crushed cardamom and vanilla seeds and stir to combine.

Spoon the filling into a baking dish and cover with the chilled crumble topping. Bake for 30–40 minutes, until the crumble is golden.

Serve warm, with cream, yoghurt or crème fraîche.

Mulberry bakewell tart

I'm not given to risking mulberries' wonderful flavour in baking, but this tart, with the frangipane filling, brings out their best. It works well with blackberries and raspberries too. If you are dozy enough to upend your tart on the work surface, as I did when last I made it, get a plate under it quickly and flip it right side up, scoop the filling in and press it down. While it may look a little rustic, it glues together remarkably well.

Serves 6

For the pastry

170g plain flour, plus extra for dusting

A pinch of sea salt

100g cold unsalted butter, cut into small cubes

25g caster sugar

1 free-range egg yolk

For the filling

90g butter, softened

125g caster sugar

125g blanched whole almonds, coarsely ground

Finely grated zest of 1 unwaxed lemon

3 free-range eggs

240g mulberries

A handful of flaked almonds

For the pastry, put the flour and salt in a food processor, add the butter and whiz briefly until the mixture resembles breadcrumbs. Add the sugar and pulse briefly. Now add the egg yolk and process until the dough just holds together; add a few drops of water if necessary.

Take out the dough and flatten slightly into a disc. Wrap in cling film and refrigerate for an hour.

Preheat the oven to 180°C/Gas 4. Lightly butter and flour a 25cm tart tin.

Roll the pastry out thinly on a lightly floured surface and use to line the tart tin. Prick the base all over with a fork and line the case with baking parchment and baking beans. Bake for 15 minutes, then remove from the oven and take out the parchment and beans. Bake for a further 5 minutes, then set aside to cool while you make the filling.

For the filling, beat the butter and sugar together until pale and fluffy. Stir in the ground almonds and lemon zest, then add the eggs one at a time, beating well.

Scatter the mulberries evenly in the pastry case and spoon the almond mixture on top. Scatter flaked almonds over the surface and bake for 35–45 minutes until golden brown. Serve with double cream or ice cream.

Blackcurrant Eccles cakes

The very lovely food writer Xanthe Clay told me she'd heard Eccles cakes were originally made with blackcurrants. I beat her to trying them out – and I think I prefer them this way to the more usual currants. I owe her huge thanks and lunch at the Ethicurean. These Eccles cakes are best served with far too much double cream or crème fraîche.

Serves 6

1 sheet of ready-rolled all-butter puff pastry, about 320g

For the filling

20g unsalted butter

70g soft dark brown sugar

½ tsp ground allspice

½ tsp ground fennel seeds

80g blackcurrants

For the glaze

3 free-range egg whites, lightly beaten

70g or so of caster sugar

Preheat the oven to 180°C/Gas 4.

For the filling, melt the butter and mix with the sugar and spices. Allow to cool, then stir in the blackcurrants.

Lay the pastry on a very lightly floured surface and cut out 12cm circles, using a scone cutter. Spoon the filling into the centre of the pastry rounds. Pull up the sides over the filling and pinch them together with your fingers to seal and enclose the filling.

Turn each pastry over, brush with egg white and roll in the caster sugar. Place the pastries seam side down on a baking sheet. Makes three slashes in the top of each – be careful not to make the slashes too wide unless you want the filling to spill out a little. Bake for 15–20 minutes until golden.

Plum & Szechuan pepper fruit leather

This reminds me of the stretchy chews I ate on far too many journeys into school. Leathers are good with pretty much any fruit – raspberries, blackberries and blackcurrants are the most common versions we make, although I'm not sure why we don't make apricot leather more – it's equally fine. Fruit leathers freeze very well in a sealed container and keep for around a year.

Makes 2 sheets, about 20 x 30cm

700g plums, halved and stoned

600g peeled, cored and chopped cooking apples

Juice of 1 lemon

About 160g runny honey

10–20g Szechuan peppercorns, roughly crushed

Preheat the oven to 70°C/Gas very low.

Line two baking sheets, each approximately 24 x 30cm, with good-quality greaseproof paper.

Put the plums, apples and lemon juice in a large pan. Bring to a simmer, partially cover the pan and cook gently for about 20 minutes, stirring once in a while. Transfer to a food processor and blitz to a smooth pulp.

Add one-fifth of the weight of the purée in honey, along with the crushed pepper, and stir in well.

Spoon the fruit mixture onto the baking sheets, tipping the sheets a little to spread the mixture to the edges.

Place in the oven and allow them to dry in the gentle heat for 8–10 hours. The leathers should be a little tacky but not sticky, and easy to peel from the paper. Allow them to cool completely.

Once cooled, cut the leathers into strips, roll them in baking parchment or cling film and store in an airtight container. Keep in a cool place and use within 3 months.

282

Cucumber Martini

I make this every summer. It really hits the nail on the head at the end of a hot day working (or idling, for that matter) in the sun. The lovage might sound an odd addition, but I promise, it pairs with cucumber perfectly.

All the ingredients should be completely cold – keep the vodka in the freezer and chill everything else well before making the cocktail. To get your cucumber juice, push a cucumber through a juicer, or if you don't have one, blitz it in a blender, then strain through muslin.

Serves 1

5 tbsp cucumber juice

5 tbsp vodka

3 tbsp sugar syrup (see right)

Juice of ½ lime

A good pinch of lovage seeds, ground (optional, but fabulous)

A few borage flowers (optional)

Shake all the ingredients together, with a little crushed ice if you like, and serve. And get ready to make another, because you'll want one.

A few borage flowers floating add beauty and a little extra nibble of cucumber.

Sugar syrup
Dissolve 150g caster sugar in 150ml water in a pan over a low heat, stirring constantly, then simmer for 1 minute. Allow to cool, then chill. Use as required.

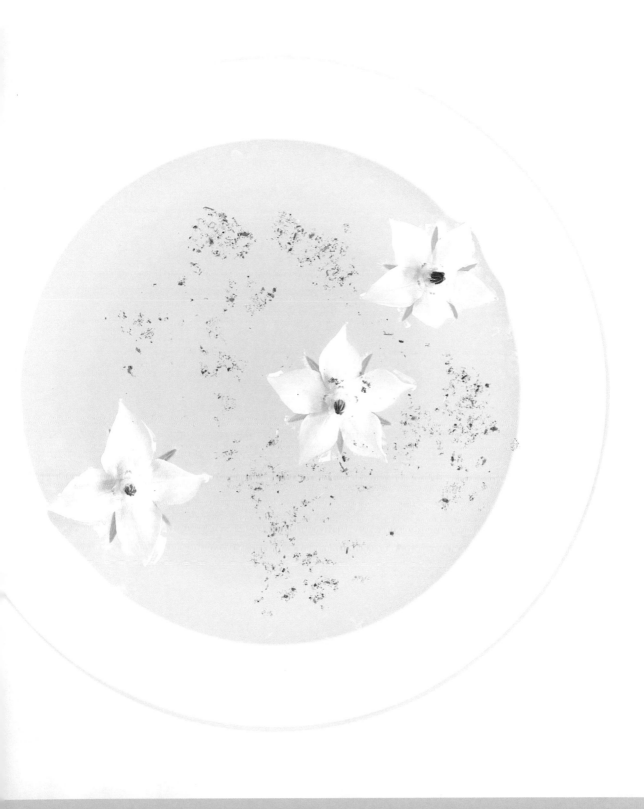

Greengage smash

There are several pertinent rules when it comes to drinking: one is one, two is ten; always ascend the alcoholic ladder (never drink a weaker brew next); never mix the grape and the grain. Only this latter rule may be bent a little from time to time, and this cocktail is one of those occasions. That said, the greengage smash is not one to overindulge in.

Use a wine with a degree of sweetness to it – a Gewurztraminer or Riesling, maybe. I last made this with the Somerset Cider Company's fabulous Somerset Pomona (a blend of their own brandy and apple juice) in place of the wine and it was just as good.

Serves 1

3–4 greengages, stoned and quartered

12 mint leaves

Juice of ½ lime

35ml vodka

45ml medium white wine

2 tbsp honey

6 ice cubes

Place everything except the ice cubes in a blender and zap until smooth. Pass through a medium sieve to remove any bits of skin and stalk if they're not entirely incorporated.

Return the juice to the blender, add the ice cubes and blitz until they're well smashed but still coarse and granular. Serve to happy faces.

Diaconocino

In Emilia-Romagna, the slice of Italy that runs from Piacenza in the northwest to San Marino in the southeast, green walnuts are used to make a liqueur called Nocino. As you'd hope, families and localities have their own versions of what is essentially a Mediterranean sloe gin, and I have my own which I've been unable to prevent myself christening Diaconocino.

Tradition demands that the nearest not-necessarily-legally-produced neat alcohol forms the basis of the brew, along with an uneven number of nuts: I'm not about to stray from the latter but my version substitutes vodka for hootch.

You need to make this in late June or early July when the walnuts are just right (see page 203). After 5 months (i.e. in time for Christmas) the liqueur will be pretty much as good as it gets. It changes after another year, becoming mellower, a little smoother perhaps – different but not necessarily better.

Makes about 1 litre

29 (or 31) green walnuts

500g unrefined granulated sugar

1 litre vodka

20cm cinnamon stick

12 cloves

1 vanilla pod, split lengthways

Zest of 1 unwaxed lemon, in strips

Wash, dry and quarter the walnuts. Stir the sugar into the vodka until it dissolves, then add the cinnamon, cloves, vanilla and lemon zest.

Fill a large sterilised jar (see page 170) with the walnut quarters and cover them with the spicy vodka.

As with sloe gin, a few weeks of giving it a daily turn helps the flavours mingle and keeps the sugar dissolved – I have mine on my desk so I'll not forget it. After that, let it rest for a month, then strain the liquid into a clean bottle.

By Christmas, it will have turned into a syrupy, dark, sweet-bitter liqueur. It is best served ice-cold at the end of a meal, or trickled over (or indeed mixed into) ice cream.

Mulberry vodka

Frankly, homemade booze doesn't get any better than this. The first time you make it, make two lots – you'll drink one before it's really at its best as it will taste so good and because you don't yet know that it will be even better after a year.

Mulberries
Caster sugar
Vodka

Quarter-fill a sterilised jar (see page 170) with caster sugar, then tip it out into a bowl. Half-fill the jar with mulberries, tip on the sugar, then top up with vodka.

Now sit on your hands until next autumn if you can.

Blackberry whisky

There is the equivalent of a secret handshake that goes on between those who have made blackberry whisky. If you're in the clan and see someone picking blackberries, you are compelled to ask whether they've tried this recipe and to pass it on if they haven't. If they have, you are forever bonded. Sad but true. It is a pairing as peculiar as it is delicious – everyone loves it, but once it's matured you'd never know it has either blackberry or whisky in it.

Makes about 1 litre
1.5kg blackberries
250g caster sugar
1 litre whisky (40% or higher)

Put the berries and sugar into a large sterilised jar or two (see page 170), pour on the whisky to cover and seal. Invert the bottle as many days as you remember – to keep the sugar dissolved and encourage the flavours to mingle.

After 3 months, strain the fruity whisky into a sterilised bottle or jar and leave in a cool dark place to mature.

Like sloe gin, a year is a good length to leave it to develop, although it will continue to improve with time if you can bear to leave it.

October

Time, said Woody Allen, is nature's way of keeping everything from happening at once. Frankly, nature doesn't do such a fine job of that in the first half of October. A lot needs taking care of and putting away until spring. The veg patch is cleared, compost and manure start to be added to the beds and around the trees – but there are still some harvests to come, including the grapes.

October's peak harvest

Borlotti beans

Mushrooms

Rosemary

Squash & pumpkins

Almonds

Apples (late)

Autumn olive

Grapes

Hazelnuts

Sweet chestnuts

Walnuts

The vines are grateful for what little sunshine there is, which can make all the difference in taking the ripening grapes to a sweeter place. Once they are picked, usually halfway through the month, everything eases off. A huge exhale comes with no more having to hope for sun. The heat is all but gone, and although a trace remains in the soil and there's the odd hour where an optimist feels a ghost of summertime, it is more light than heat in October.

The days shorten and it becomes the season for warming food and warming drinks, Nick Drake, crumbles, pies, whisky, men with beards singing in pubs, baked apples, and the anticipation of quince and medlars almost, but not quite, ready to pick. It's on with the wood burner and the whisky tide line falls quicker than usual. In a few weeks it will be mulled cider, bonfire night and (seemingly) the day after that will be Christmas.

This is how an old man wishes away the year, by anticipating away the weeks and months. Although that's how I feel when it's so sodding hard to get up in these cold, dark mornings.

Trent will be off back to the States in 6 weeks. It's a shame but even my tedious powers of persuasion have failed. I'd hoped to bore him into submission, making his life a misery with endless reminders of exciting things happening over the next year, but Trent has a heart of stone: he's bought his plane ticket.

Six weeks is a long time though and we have much to do. Starting with the planting of an orchard of Japanese plums. And I have to keep Trent's mind away from being on the other side of the Atlantic, which may not be easy. The Elaeagnus ebbingei is in flower and the scent is incredible. Five or six feet tall, right at the edge of the forest garden by the pig pen, the Elaeagnus lets out invisible clouds of fragrance that's not a million miles away from the scent of broad bean flowers – which may well be my most happy-making smell. I told Trent about it. He pushed his face in smiling, like a man having a waterfall shower. He couldn't place the smell at first. Like Robert Duvall in Apocalypse Now, he felt for it: 'It smells like… like… Hawaii'.

— 13 October, 2010

GRAPES

Site Sun, well drained

Harvest August–November

Notes Prune in December–January. Fruits from last year's wood

IN A RARE OUTBREAK of activity in my early twenties, I went grape picking in France and Switzerland. Despite the backbreaking work I'd never felt so good – the work, summer views down to Lake Geneva, alpine air, company (from Basildon to Brazil), food and wine had me feeling properly alive.

It was glorious. I loved the French way of dedicating courses to a single pleasure: soup, then fish, meat and so on. Even work in the vines was punctuated with chocolate and wine every couple of hours from

apes: Pinot Noir

dawn till dusk. Cutting bunches, crating them to trailers, eating and drinking, laughter and conversation: this was the punch line to the year, the last waltz of the annual vineyard dance. Everyone was happy.

The sense of celebration stayed with me, and having planted nearly 4 acres of vines here in 2008, I now understand the smiles a little better.

A vineyard is a gamble. On this scale, it's hard to make an argument for it unless you allow your mind to linger on the romantic side. It takes patience to get vines established, to develop an understanding of each variety – Pinot Noir, Gerwurtztraminer, Solaris, Sauvignon Blanc and Seyval Blanc here – and to work with them in the hope of a harvest. In the hope of wine.

Even then, you can do everything perfectly and still be hijacked by a miserable midsummer or end of season. If the rain prevents the tiny flower caps from being blown from the flowers then pollen can't leave or enter the flowers, and however good the weather for the rest of the summer, there will be few grapes. A wet, overcast September and October encourages disease and keeps the sugars (and thence the alcohol levels) low. It is an unreliable business: one year you are plucking luscious grapes from bunches almost too large to hold, making endless bottles of wine and eating basketfuls under the pergola; the next there's nothing to send to the winery.

Remembering sunny days looking down at Lake Geneva can be enough to get the thing planted but it is recalling those horizontal hours eating grapes in the half-shade and the memory of the first glass of your own fizz – and the promise of more – that gets you out of a warm bed and into a cold dark January morning to prune them all.

They say a vine likes nothing better than hearing the footsteps of the grower, and it makes complete sense: you build up a depth of understanding almost accidentally, incidentally, while walking the dog around the vineyard as much as when actively caring for the plants.

In the first year I got to know each variety and how it behaves – the Pinot wants to make dark bunches of grapes even when the wood isn't yet up to it, while the Gerwurtz is all leaf and no fruit early on – and so on. Over a few years, the character of different rows (there are 56) began to stick in my mind; and now I'm starting to mentally locate and anticipate individual vines as I walk through the vineyard. I could take you to The Beast blindfolded. Since that first summer, it has grown at least three times faster than the others – a rogue of unknown variety.

With luck, we harvest grapes some time in October. After a year of pruning, training, feeding and caring, there will be a day this month when the guess is made – when we judge that the balance of the weather, sugars and potential for disease makes today the day.

It is such a big deal as, more than anything else we grow, the vines have so much invested in them. Start-up costs are considerable, then it's three or four years until the first small harvest with all the work and input that requires.

Once harvested in autumn, the grapes are pressed immediately and the process of wine making begins. Still wine usually comes back to you, bottled, corked, labelled and ready to drink the following summer; the process of making sparkling wine takes a year longer. During that time, you've pruned the vines twice, nursed the plants and fruit as best you can and picked more yet grapes and had them made into sparkling wine, with all the costs that involves.

With luck and good summers you may break even in year eight or so. This is why it's hard to take anyone seriously when they suggest that what I'm up to in this 17 acres of smallholding is hobby farming. I may have some daft ideas, I may have some pretty good ones, some may have failed already, it may be entirely enjoyable and far better than a real job, I may not know too much about some of the things I'm trying to do, it may take all the time I can throw at it, but just a hobby it ain't.

Grape, beetroot & mint smoothie
(page 376)
Pot-roast chicken with grapes in milk
(page 336)

Next week, probably on Monday, we'll be picking the first grapes. A month or two ago I was trying to find a way of having this year's first, small grape harvest turned into wine without it being mixed with somebody else's grapes. It's no problem to have it made into wine but this first harvest is too small for most wineries to want to make into its own separate batch.

A friend suggested I try a small, young winery near him, in Sussex. I rang. 'No way, quarter of a ton? Forget it. I'd love to, but no…needs to be 2 tons at least…shame though, it would be fun.'

We chatted some more, mostly about the varieties I was growing and where he'd learnt to do what he does. He liked the mix of fairly reliable grapes with more adventurous ones. I smelt a change in the air. We kept talking. He, Ulrich, started talking about maybe there is a small tank he could borrow…

So a deal has been done, more expensive per bottle than it would be for a larger load, but for that I get wine made only from grapes grown here at Otter Farm and Ulrich gets what's fair for the mess-about of dealing with such a small quantity. It has its compromise – 350 miles added to the carbon footprint of the wine isn't ideal but on the upside that will be spread between (we hope) 300 bottles.

We now have to watch the grapes very closely. The balance between development of the sugars and the onset and spread of rot is critical. The warm wet patch last week kicked off a little light rot but the cold wind is keeping it from spreading too quickly. Next Monday looks like the day.

— 13 October, 2010

BORLOTTI BEANS

Site Sunny and sheltered, ideally a moisture-retentive soil

Sow April–July in root trainers, planting out when roots are established

Harvest August–October

Notes Allow 20cm between plants. A comfrey tea (or other high-potassium) feed every fortnight will help increase your crop

THE SPRING AFTER I'D GROWN my first potatoes, I sowed the seeds for a few flavours that were new to me – borlotti beans was one of them, and they've been a constant presence in the veg patch ever since.

Scrambling energetically to 2 metres or more, borlottis dangle vivid, red-spattered, finger-thick pods that Jackson Pollock the garden with splashes of Italy through late summer and into autumn. They are undo-without-able.

Their red colouring is a curious thing. Both pods and the beans within are speckled red on cream, though each pod seems blessed with only so much red 'paint': the redder the pod, the paler the beans and vice versa. In any event, cooking renders them a chestnut brown, with only the occasional dark remnant of the once-generous speckling.

Despite their Italian provenance, borlottis are easy to grow in our relatively cool climate. I start them off from mid-April in root trainers or loo-roll inners, planting them out from the second half of May, two to each cane in a line of crossing canes. They are enthusiastic climbers and generous providers, though once in a while – for no apparent reason – they give a low return. The plants tend to grow more slowly than peas and other beans, but give them a sunny, sheltered spot and don't let them dry out and most years they'll reach their productive best towards the end of the school holidays.

Genuinely one of those vegetables worthy of their place in the garden for their looks alone, borlottis are similarly indispensable in the kitchen. Their nutty flavour and creamy texture is equally at home with meat, fish and vegetables, and stands up well to big flavours – especially chilli, garlic and woody herbs such as rosemary, soaking them up while retaining their own identity.

Once picked, there is no rush to eat the beans as freezing or drying captures the best of their qualities – thank heavens too, as their meaty texture and nutty creaminess is as welcome in summer as it is in winter. Picked early and soft in August and early September, borlottis are superb in late-summer salads, hummus and sunny weather soups such as ribollita.

We pick some early, but we harvest most of our borlotti beans demi-sec (half-dry) from late September into October when the pods are twisted and splitting. I think their flavour and texture is right at its peak then and by that time the green beans are usually on the wane and the cooling air suits the hearty soups and stews that borlottis lend themselves to so well. They make perfect partners for pork (especially chorizo and bacon) and seafood – I particularly love them with mussels, which tend to be at their best during the cold months.

Any unlikely to be eaten soon after picking can be frozen or dried. The whole plant can be lifted and hung somewhere covered – a porch or polytunnel – until the pods and their beans are completely desiccated. Overnight soaking reconstitutes the dried beans, ready to be cooked for hearty winter stews or for adding substance to spring dishes. And if you've any left over, they can be sown in spring to provide next year's harvest.

Borlottis with mussels (page 332)
Chicken, pork & borlotti stew (page 338)
Chorizo, borlotti & cabbage soup (page 62)

borlotti beans

SQUASH

Site Full sun in a rich moisture-retentive soil

Sow In April, in 9cm pots. Plant out when they have four leaves showing late May–end July

Harvest In autumn, timing depends on the variety, but before the first frosts

Notes A spadeful of well-rotted manure or compost will get them off to a great start

AT A FOOD FESTIVAL in Ireland last year, I overheard a beginner, concerned that he'd bitten off more than he could chew, asking a respected grower what he should grow on his allotment. 'Sure as shite, y'should give up half of it to squash, so y'should. They'll grow for any clown.'

This is as good a piece of gardening advice as any I've heard. Half a dozen squash plants will triffid across your patch, lacing through other plants, smothering out weeds and helping to retain soil moisture, while pretty much taking care of themselves. And the early autumn harvest is undeniably impressive – the vivid colours, often ludicrous shapes ('Yes, it's just like an orange willy, dear'), and sheer weight of the things. Even better: choose the right varieties and they'll give you great options in the kitchen.

I won't go into the complex botanics of the squash family, beyond saying that gourds are largely ornamental, pumpkins typically large and best hollowed out with a candle inside and squash are by far the best to eat.

More than straight, unmitigated sweetness, I like a little earthiness in squash, so Uchi Kuri is ever-present, with its bulb-shaped fruits lighting up the veg patch as they ripen from yellow to deep orange. Easy, reliable and with a sweet yet complex flavour, they are a must. Crown Prince too, with its light blue skin, honeyed sweet, gold flesh and full flavour, roasts and mashes beautifully. It can, however, be hard to source the seeds some years, in which case I'll happily grow the similar Queensland Blue instead.

Acorn Table has a gorgeous shape, its leaves not unlike rhubarb, and deep green fruit. The flavour steers a path between squash and swede beautifully – perfect for a not-too-sweet gratin, or a squash mash.

Butternuts are a little unreliable here – they like a better summer than even Devon is inclined to offer most years, but Early Butternut needs a little less heat than most varieties, and produces most years.

What little effort is required to grow squash is all at the early stage. Watered well and protected from the attentions of slugs and snails until they're established, things are usually plain sailing.

Squash are ready to pick as autumn draws in. They should be left until hollow sounding, which here in the rainy Southwest means I often have to slide a slate under each fruit to keep them from sitting in the damp while they ripen. If the weather looks bad for an extended period, we'll pick the lot and store them covered, outside, with their undersides facing upwards to continue ripening a little longer.

Whatever the weather, they need picking and bringing indoors before the frosts hit. We cut them from the plant, leaving a short stalk on each squash as they seem to store for longer into winter that way.

Most squash are a palaver to peel, so I halve them and spoon out the seeds and fibrous core, then chop them into large chunks and either steam or roast, after which the skin separates from the flesh with ease. There's little point in saving the seed to sow next year – squash cross-pollinate readily, so unpredictable results are likely – and besides, they're delicious. Wash and dry the seeds, scatter on a roasting tray, sprinkle with sea salt and roast at 200°C for a few minutes to intensify their flavour.

Curried squash & mussel soup (page 334)

Squash, shallot & mushroom tart (page 342)

Spiced fudgy squash cake (page 360)

Squash: Crown Prince

Almonds: Ingrid

ALMONDS ARE ALMOST PEACHES. The trees and leaves are hard to tell apart and when young, the fleshy, furry hull that surrounds the shell in which the almond sits is almost indistinguishable from a peach. They can pollinate each other too, which isn't good – bitter almonds can result, so they need planting as far apart as possible. With our peach trees in the near field, the almonds had to cross the river, and take the most well-drained spot furthest from the house.

They have done well in their first years, growing strongly in the spring and summer after planting and giving us an unexpectedly early crop – basketfuls in their second year. I was convinced the young branches would loosen their grip on the nuts every time the wind picked up in summer, but they clung on.

Nell and I collected them on a sunny October afternoon when the splitting husks and withering stalks told us they were ready. We split the hulls from the centres and cracked a few: not a hint of bitterness, just gentle, creamy fresh almond flavour.

Almonds, like most nut trees, are often long-lived, so choosing good varieties is crucial: you are reminded of the quality of your selection for decades to come. That said, they will give up the ghost if planted in too inhospitable a site. Sun, good drainage and shelter are essentials. I've found Ingrid and Robijn – almond-peach crosses that produce delicious nuts – to be more reliable and hardy in our climate than any of the new or traditional varieties.

ALMONDS

Site Sun, well drained, sheltered

Harvest October

Notes Wait to harvest beyond when the hull splits, until the stalk joining it to the branch weakens – often 6 weeks – to allow the nut to mature

Almond biscuits (page 372)

Mulberry bakewell tart (page 277)

Parsley pesto (page 165)

Roast plums with labneh, almonds & honey (page 271)

Spiced almonds (page 352)

Spiced fudgy squash cake (page 360)

AFTER THE SUMMER FLUSH of bright, early apples, comes the bulk of the orchard's harvest. Veitch's Perfection is a particular favourite. It was bred a couple of centuries ago nearby in Exeter. The skin of its large fruit is green and deep mauve with a light brown russeting. Sweet and sharp in perfect balance, with a texture not unlike an Egremont Russet and a slight nuttiness to the flavour, it is beautiful to eat from the tree but also keeps its shape when baked.

The tree likes it here, growing more strongly and productively than any other variety. And why wouldn't it, having originated so close by. But all of the apples are doing well – eaters, cookers and cider varieties alike. If only we named cars or places with the poetry we do apples: Old Somerset Russet and Luccombe's Pine, for example, and how could you not plant a tree called Fair Maid of Devon or Slack Ma Girdle?

The Old Somerset Russet may not be the most vigorous tree, it may produce small fruit, but it's a very late variety, often ready to pick in November when there are few others fruiting, and I love its refreshing pineapple flavour.

Unlike the earlies, many of the late-ripening apples store well into winter and beyond but, once in a while, the harvest is too big to store so we make juice. Last year, we made no fewer than 505 bottles of lovely juice.

LATE APPLES

Site Relatively unfussy

Harvest September–November

Notes Plant more Veitches – the best

Caraway sprout tops with bacon & apple (page 345)

Fennel toffee apples (page 374)

Pickled apples (page 353)

Plum & Szechuan pepper fruit leather (page 280)

Romanesco, apple & hazelnut salad with blue cheese dressing (page 348)

SWEET CHESTNUTS

Site Well drained, loamy

Harvest October

Notes Will suddenly drop all chestnuts from the tree in late October

FOR A FEW YEARS sweet chestnuts act like a girlfriend you're not sure is keen on you – giving you the odd, but delightful encouragement (half a dozen nuts or so), so you don't give up on them. What you can't see is the plant acting like the proverbial swan, with all the action going on unseen, long roots driving into the lower layers of the soil in search of nutrients and water, unconcerned with looking lively above ground. Eventually they come good.

Sweet chestnuts are under-appreciated, partly because you can't eat them raw, so there's no instant pleasure when picking, but also because in some parts of Europe they are synonymous with hard times, having seen communities through in times of poverty. We often reject 'poor' food when prosperity returns, but eventually flavour wins people around again.

The small harvests we've had from our three-year-old trees have largely been roasted in the wood burner – a small cut in the end of each stops them exploding when roasted for 25 minutes or so on a fire shovel. They do almost as well in a hot oven. When cooled a little, they're fit to be torn into – the shell comes easily away, revealing the sweet, earthy centre. A hoppy ale, smokey whisky or dark chocolate is the ideal complement.

Sweet chestnuts are rich in carbohydrates and, being a perennial plant, have the wherewithal to produce year after year without much help. Wheat, one of our major carbs, is an annual that typically takes huge energy and chemical inputs to get to harvest, so I reckon there might just be a gap in the market for a low-input, flour-producing high-carbohydrate food like sweet chestnuts. I have selflessly planted 59 trees as my small contribution to the nation's future energy needs – the produce from which we shall roast over an autumnal fire and turn into sweet chestnut jam and as many cakes as I can dream up. Tackling climate change by eating my weight in marrons glacés... Now there's an idea.

MUSHROOMS

Site Damp, shade/semi-shade

Harvest Foraged mushrooms: September–November; homegrown mushrooms: all year round

IT RAINED SOLIDLY the day we moved here. By the time boxes and bags had been dumped and the kettle found, it was dark. There was no chance to go outside. I woke early and headed out to the fields. The land looked vast.

I could make something out about halfway down the field: I knew what I hoped it was. I skirted around the field; it didn't feel right walking through the middle so soon after arriving. The closer I got, the more certain I became: it was a dozen puffball mushrooms. They are mightily impressive up close: 30cm across, spherical and white, looking very much like a huge over-proved loaf. Their flavour is gentle, the texture gloriously meaty and particularly fine fried. Although not uncommon, they're a rare enough sight. The puffballs were a little over the top and saggy. I hoofed them about, taking imaginary free kicks, to spread the spores in the hope that there would be more in years to come. Every year since, nothing, not a single puffball. So much for my free kicks.

sweet chestnuts

Oyster mushrooms growing on an old book

I've since discovered that mushrooms are perennial organisms that can live for decades. They have two distinct parts. The mycelium, a web of thread-like hyphae, spreads underground often covering a huge area, absorbing nutrients and producing energy. The visible fruit above ground is the reproductive organs that I'd hoofed around so enthusiastically. The good news is that as most of their 'body' exists underground for years, puffballs could return here at any time.

Our wet autumns are usually good for mushrooms, so a woodland or countryside forage can be fruitful as the days shorten. I search only for a few mushroom varieties I know to be delicious and safe, rather than try to positively identify every species I find. Mostly, that means ceps, parasols, the odd morel (they seem to like the mulch mat in the polytunnel) and, once in a blue moon, a puffball to mock the lack of them in the field.

As with hedgerow fruits, harvesting wild mushrooms has inspired me to grow some of my own. It's ridiculously easy and gives you safe, delicious mushrooms that might be tricky to acquire otherwise.

Oyster mushrooms are among my favourites. Delicately flavoured and quick to grow, these native mushrooms produce most readily in spring and autumn. They come in pink, yellow, white and blue varieties. I also grow Lion's Mane, a weirdly shaggy, pale mushroom, and morels, which are mildly flavoured and beautiful. Poisonous when raw, morels are perfectly safe once cooked. Garden Giants have deep burgundy caps and white stems. They can grow as large as puffballs but are best picked small for eating. Shiitake mushrooms are easy to grow and richly flavoured, adding depth and character to soups, risottos and stews.

There are various methods for growing mushrooms, each of which introduces mushroom spawn to a growing medium – such as a book, straw or hardwood log – that will encourage mycelium to develop and in turn produce mushrooms. Below are a few I have tried.

Grain spawn is sprinkled between the soaked pages of a book that is kept warm and moist in a plastic bag. After a few weeks, the white fur of the mycelium begins to cover the book. A couple of days in the fridge shocks the mycelium into production and within a week baby mushrooms appear, growing rapidly across the book for picking a few days later.

Replicating the principle on a larger scale, soaked straw in a bin bag provides a fine growing medium for mycelium. Mushrooms grow through slits and are often larger than those produced by the book method.

We grow *Stropharia* around the base of a coppiced eucalyptus in the garden but they'll grow well around any tree or bush. They will also grow on soaked hardwood chips, garden shreddings or clean straw. Wooden dowels inoculated with spawn are pushed through the mulch into the soil and mushrooms follow 3 months to a year later, depending on the conditions. An under-tree site can remain productive for three years or so, and if you keep re-mulching they can keep producing indefinitely.

Fresh hardwood logs are a fine medium for growing shiitake and Lion's mane, especially. The logs should be around 40cm long and 10–20cm in diameter, clean and free of branches. Wooden dowels inoculated with spawn are tapped into holes drilled along each log, which is then wrapped in a plastic bag to retain moisture and kept somewhere cool, out of the sun and wind. Mycelium usually develop 6 months to a year later.

Mushrooms often start to form during a warm patch following cold rain. Once mycelium have formed, it's feasible to replicate these conditions by soaking the log in cold water for 48 hours during warm weather. Once set up, there's little to do other than be patient for a few days or months.

Squash, shallot & mushroom tart (page 342)

AUTUMN OLIVE

Site Relatively unfussy

Harvest October–November

Notes Early fruit good for fruit leather (see page 280); the sharpness stands out perfectly

I LIKE A GENEROUS plant: hazel for poles and nuts; nasturtiums for covering the soil, mulching as they grow, and their delicious leaves and flowers; Jerusalem artichokes possibly top the lot with their earthy tubers and sunflowers, attracting beneficial insects and giving you loads of compostable material. Autumn olive is right up there too.

Although not related, its leaves resemble those of the olive. The fruit ripens late, moving from early October sharpness into sweetness as Halloween approaches. Only 6–8mm across, the silver-speckled pink berries have a blueberry-like flavour that fills out as the days shorten.

Autumn olive makes a fast-growing, fruitful and beautiful hedge that retains leaves late and regrows at the first sign of winter's end. So while deciduous, the trees are bare for a short time only, nurturing plants in their lee as well as providing fruit. This can make a difference to other harvests – perhaps protecting delicate peach blossom from late, cold spring winds, or ensuring that outdoor tomatoes aren't buffeted while trying to ripen.

Autumn olive also takes nitrogen from the air and makes it available to its roots, effectively feeding itself and neighbouring plants. This means it can thrive in less than favourable locations and that when its leaves drop they are high in nitrogen, naturally fertilising wherever they blow.

Spring flowers are plentiful and tiny, with a sweet, light fragrance that, as with quince, is hard to chase – it arrives on your nose randomly rather than repaying a deep sniff of the blossom. Over the summer, small fruit form that turn a lively pink-purple. They shouldn't be picked too early: allowing autumn to settle in changes their appearance little, but under the skin sweetness develops.

As with grapes, autumn olive fruit can be ready to pick a month earlier or later than the previous year, depending on the strength and spread of the summer's sun. I quite like a few picked a little early and tart, for making a sharp jam or indeed a tart tart, which is usually in October.

The rest normally ripen fully in early November, when I half-fill a bottle with the berries, add a few centimetres of sugar and top with vodka. A length of fennel top is perfect if you have some to hand. Invert the bottle as many days as you remember and strain the liquor into another container after 3 months. It will be delicious immediately but leave it at least a year and it'll be incredible.

Autumn into winter fruit tart (page 364)

autumn olive

November

I'm sat at the end of the garden drinking coffee, looking out over the vineyard. The pigs are fed, the chickens let out and the mists are lifting enough for me to make out the buzzard whose screech has accompanied me for the last ten minutes. After the madness of September and October, where everything has to be harvested at a particular moment, November shifts down a gear.

With this year's grapes pressed and fermenting in the winery, it's the first time the vineyard has 'stopped' all year. For a short time, the farm and its owner are slowing down. The ease in intensity is delicious. There's time to appreciate what's happening, to enjoy the first frosts and the beginnings of the slow slip of autumn into winter.

It is a month of forgotten fruit: quince, medlars and Chilean guava. They'll all be picked but it isn't quite 'today' that it has to happen. Once gathered, there's no rush to use quince – left in a bowl to ripen, they'll fill the house into December with their perfume. Even the late pears – Louise Bonne of Jersey and Josephine de Maline, our first planted and most productive – allow us a month or two from picking before they're ready.

Sometime before the frosts properly kick in, the last of the squash can be cut and stored to enjoy through winter. The first of the winter's roots and leaves should be ready too. There are dozens of pheasants scuttling down the field away from me every morning; hopefully one or two will find their way back courtesy of a friend's gun. The pigs make their short final trip and any spring-born cockerel that has grown into an aggressive nuisance finds its neck extended beyond its elastic limit.

QUINCE

Site Happy in most soils, even damp (though not waterlogged). Sunny

Harvest October–November

Notes Plunge the fruit into acidulated water (juice of ½ lemon in a large bowl is enough) to prevent exposed flesh discolouring

IF I WAS LESS GORMLESS and a little more romantic, I'd have given my wife a quince as a wedding present. It is the fruit of love: the 'apple' that supposedly tempted Adam, that Paris gave to Aphrodite, the Goddess of Love, that for centuries was served at Roman weddings, and that in Ancient Greece was thrown into the wedding carriage for the bride to eat to sweeten her breath before her wedding night.

I did, however, buy her a beautiful young quince tree when we first had space to plant it. One is perfect – a single tree will pollinate its own flowers, flourish in one of the many damp (but not waterlogged) spots we had, perfume the garden with its flowers and the house with its ripening fruit. It will also give enough fruit to eat in cold-weather pies, stews and crumbles, as well as for preserves that will last until the next harvest.

The tree is as beautiful as its fruit, and at home in the smallest garden space. Rarely getting larger than a small apple tree (1.5 metres in height and spread if you plant a true dwarf), a quince grows in a lazy randomness that needs pruning only by those keenest with the secateurs. I snip back rubbing or crowded branches on one of those rare sunny winter afternoons. Essentially you plant a quince in a sunny and sheltered place and come back to admire it when the mood takes, before picking the fruit as autumn moves towards winter. They couldn't be less trouble.

Mid-spring they flower in soft white twists blushed with pink along the length of their branches, which open into lazy loose saucers. Their elusive perfume, genuinely enchanting, is drawn out by the sun.

Superficially, the fruit lies somewhere between the pears and apples it is closely related to, but quince are more 'Sophia Loren' than either –

quince

Medlars

all generous curves and elegant luminescence. With the light covering of downy fur that sometimes still clings to the skin rubbed off, the fruits look almost too perfect, enough to be alabaster. You would think they must be sweet, succulent and aromatic – and they are, but not yet: you have to patiently charm their loveliness out.

As I do with all the fruit trees, I brought my wife the first quince that the first tree produced. For a fortnight, it sat in her clothes drawer, releasing its perfume as it ripened, before being poached in a sweet, spiced syrup and then roasted. It seems a big to-do for a single fruit, but a single fruit is all the tree gave that first year, and we weren't about to waste it.

Thankfully, the quince orchard is now more generous. The fruit hang bright like lanterns along their leafless branches in late October and November. We pick them before anything more than icing-sugar frosts arrive – when they are ready, they part from the tree with just a light twist.

A week or two in the warmth of the house is enough to take them from light green to yellow, and to release their glorious perfume. Like the blossom's scent, this can't be chased. A deep inhale, nose against the fruit or the flower, will give a hint of its fragrance but the heady, sweet scent of both prefers to arrive on the air, more strongly, in its own time.

Even in this aromatic state, the fruits are hard and sour; they need sweetness and alcohol to bring them out of their shell. Don't we all. Marsala, honey, cider, red wine or white – they aren't fussy.

Poached whole in a spicy sugar/wine syrup they can take three-quarters of an hour or more to surrender to the point of a sharp knife; put them to bake in the oven and they will take around twice as long. Quince are meltingly delicious either way, often turning a rosy red as they cook, so do try them like that, but as often as not I use quince as a spice, a condiment, punctuating and brightening in sweet or savoury recipes.

Quince is a fruit made for dipping temperatures, happily taking on warming flavours such as cloves and cinnamon. Sweetening develops rather than masks its subtlety in ice creams, sorbets and many other puddings, but be sure not to overload them with flavours or sugar, unless making preserves, as that subtle flavour and sharp edge can be lost.

Take care when peeling, chopping or coring quince – it is like doing the same with a cricket ball.

Poached & roasted quince (page 356)
Quince cheese (page 354)
Quince doughnuts (page 368)

FROM A LOSING POSITION, and with the last go of the game, I once won Scrabble by placing the first four and the last three letters of 'bletting' on either side of an inviting, dangling 'T'. For this petty glory alone, I owe the medlar.

Bletting is the process of gentle decay that takes some fruit, including medlars and sorbs, from hard and unappetising to a sweet creamy delight. It comes from the French *blettir* – to make soft. Hard as conkers, even when the leaves have passed through their autumn colours

MEDLARS

Site Happy in most soils, even damp (though not waterlogged)

Harvest October–November

Notes Wait for the frosts to soften at least some of the fruit

and fallen, medlars need a good hard frost or two for the cell walls to buckle and softening to begin. The firm, pale flesh gives way to a deep brown pulp thanks to bletting. It is a fine word to sneak into a game of Scrabble, but not perhaps that handy when trying to market the fruit: there are few things that sell well when labelled 'allow to rot'. Hence, they are rarely found in shops or markets.

Like quince, the flavour of medlars is somehow very autumnal – the bletted flesh is sweet (but not too much so), deep and winey, and one of the reasons I look forward to this time of year. They make a jelly and jam as good as any, and are spectacularly good roasted with a little honey and eaten with cream or yoghurt. There's no enjoying the fruit in the dappled shade of their canopy though, nor the sunny delirium of half-drinking, half-eating a perfectly ripe peach: medlars aren't appetising until you get to know them a little.

When making jam, cakes or other puddings, it's best to use well-bletted medlars with brown, soft flesh. Either skin and deseed them – fiddly but not too onerous – before gently simmering and stirring to a smooth pulp, or chop them up and push through a sieve after cooking.

I planted an orchard of medlars in the far field, between the long curve of the unkempt hazel hedge and the ancient oak in the centre of the field. I pick more of the fruit from the ground, tangled in a carpet of their crisp leaves, than I do from the otherwise bare limps of the tree. Medlars need treating with care: once the apple-like flesh begins to break down and turn brown, even a slight tear in the skin will cause the inside to ooze out and spoil. A wide, shallow basket is favourite when harvesting to spread the weight of the delicate fruit. Don't leave it too long before you pick bletting medlars – if they soften too much they seem to ferment a little, causing the flesh to swell. This turns their indented end from an innie to an outie, and adds a sickly syrupiness to their flavour that I'm not keen on.

Never the fastest growing tree – the five-year-old ones in the far field are perhaps 2 metres tall – medlars are at least very low maintenance. When you have a vineyard or a veg patch to look after, with all that entails, you're mighty grateful for the medlars of this world. They are easy to love – just getting on with things, whether or not you pay them any attention. They are frost-dodgingly late into leaf, self-fertile (so growing just one is fine), and long lived. You can prune them a little if there's a shape you have in mind, or leave them, as I do, untroubled by the secateurs to do their charmingly irregular thing. They don't seem to attract a pest or disease, and they fruit late, away from the panic of late summer and early autumn. They're even happy in a damp (though not waterlogged) spot.

Medlar sticky toffee pudding
(page 358)

The few dozen medlars whose flowers dodged the late frosts have been hanging in the bare trees like Christmas baubles. At last, the frosts have turned them softer and I've picked them for jam – my favourite at this time of year.
— 28 November, 2008

LIKE MOST PEOPLE who take the step, adding livestock to our veg patch came in spring with a few hens. We increase the flock once in a while with friends' surplus chicks, fertile eggs bought for hatching or a hen from a local supplier. It keeps numbers vaguely in balance. The fox has taken the odd one (or the odd three, in the case of the seemingly rather too white White Sussex) but for the most part our hens have been able to free range as they like.

In winter, we tend to fence the smallest birds into the veg patch – this year, four chicks from a late June batch of hatching eggs. They spent their first month in my office, under a lamp, in a cardboard box. Now they're doing what I'm either incapable of doing because of the weather or reluctant to do because of idleness – clearing and improving the ground where we'll be growing much of the food we eat next year. They pluck out weeds, snaffle up the tatty leafy remnants of summer and fertilise as they go.

It seems like a fair exchange – lovely conditions in which to live, for eggs and maybe a meaty meal or two in return.

For their first months, it's hard to be sure of the ratio of cockerels to hens, but at around 18 weeks old they'll either lay or squawk, and that's the time for some difficult decisions to be made.

When I was very young and immeasurably more pleasant, I had a very soft spot for Lauren Hutton. That smile, those dimples and most importantly the marvellous gap between her front teeth got me all giddy. She had a look of someone who was up to something, or at least wanted you to think that she was. I imagined that she'd had both parts of a Bounty Bar without having to save one half for after tea, or something. I suspect the same of one of my chickens.

Squeaky has a sideways look that, like Lauren Hutton, makes me think he's been up to something he perhaps oughtn't to have been – that 'something' being trying to get across one of the hens he's with, his sister.

After a few months of wondering if he was a she or vice versa, I think the newly acquired, ludicrous crow has given him away. That and his amorous intentions.

It occurred to me that had either he or his sister been a meat bird destined for the supermarkets, they would have been long dead. They could even have been born today and found their way to the oven for the twelfth day of Christmas. Forty days, from the cradle to the gravy.

Not for these two though: she'll be a fine layer, and the flock needs a cockerel. Time to move him in with the other two hens in the Egloo.

— 27 November, 2012

CHICKENS

Notes Move the chickens onto any unproductive parts of the veg patch in winter – they'll take care of plenty of pests and weeds for the following year, fertilising the soil as they go

Chicken & Savoy cabbage in cider (page 64)
Chicken, celeriac & leek pie (page 65)
Chicken, pork & borlotti stew (page 338)
Pot-roast chicken with grapes in milk (page 336)
Eggs Gordon Bennet (page 154)
Spring herb omelette (page 155)

CHILEAN GUAVA

Site Well drained, sheltered, sunny

Harvest October–November

Notes Leave the fruit as long as possible to sweeten

IN THE 1840S, Queen Victoria was shot at on at least four different occasions by an assortment of would-be assassins. In 1850, she took a hearty bash on the forehead from a man named, appropriately, Robert Pate. It wouldn't have done much for her famously dour demeanour, but around this time botanist and plant collector William Lobb was busy doing something that would improve her mood: introducing a medium-sized perennial shrub from Chile that was to become her favourite fruit.

Having developed a taste for them, Queen Victoria had them grown in Cornwall and sent by train to her table. They've never become common in Britain, though they are popular in Australia and New Zealand, where they are known as tazziberries. Perhaps it's our obsession with yield – you'll not get fat on your Chilean guava harvest, but the same could be said of ubiquitous blueberries, which, to my mind, have less flavour.

Chilean guava is a small evergreen shrub, similar to common myrtle, and grows up to a metre high and wide. The leaves are deep green, small and waxy, with the odd dapple of red-pink. The variegated Flambeau has cream and lime colours to the leaves and is slightly hardier than the common variety. In sunny years, pale pink and white bell-shaped flowers dot the branches from late spring. As the summer passes, the flowers turn into fruit that ripen into dark berries late in autumn and into winter.

Chilean guava are hardy only to −10°C or so – they often get that cold here and shrink back to the ground in protest, but so far, crossed fingers, they come back each spring. A clump of straw over the heart of the plant keeps it protected during serious cold.

They naturally colonise the edge of woodlands or clearings where the mix of light and shelter suits them well. Bear that in mind if you intend to grow them: the more shelter and sun they get, the more fruit you'll enjoy.

The fruit are lovely straight off the plant, but if it's chilly most find their way into pancakes, muffins, cakes and Murtado, the Chilean version of sloe gin: gin, fruit, sugar in a 3:2:1 ratio, in a jar and disturbed only to invert the jar once in a while. Sit on your hands – it takes a year to reach its best. Quince and Chilean guava is an inspired pairing that makes a gorgeous variation too. Poached, they partner each other beautifully as a fruity breakfast or dessert, with blueberries making a good substitute if you've snaffled all the Chilean guava straight from the plant.

Today, after looking after a few Chilean guava plants for a couple of years, it's time to pick the first fruit. I've had the odd one that's yielded fruit, but today it's slightly more warranting the term 'harvest'. You've got to try a few of whatever you're picking as you pick, obviously. That's one of the downsides of picking pears, all that promise, so little reward on the day – they ripen later, off the tree, perhaps months after being picked. So you have to wait.

Not so with Chilean guava. Pop them in and you'll probably say 'strawberry', maybe 'kiwi'. But then you'd not have what my wife thinks is my rather worrying ability to identify a taste-alike.

Chilean guava

Oca

Flavours and smells can take a little time to reveal themselves and with tastes it's often as much to do with the nose as anything. So it is with Chilean guava. Yes, a little strawberry, a touch of kiwi, something bubblegummy about them. But I knew I hadn't cracked it. Until this morning. I popped one in and got it without thinking: Strawberry Space Dust.

— 13 November, 2009

OCA, YACON AND potatoes are South American tubers. Each has been grown for centuries. The first tastes of lemon and sorrel, the second of pears, and neither of these are available in the shops. The third tastes of, well, potatoes, and is available in almost every supermarket and greengrocer's. That most gardeners grow only the third of the three strikes me as bizarre. This is the horticultural equivalent of us all being handed a guitar and joining a tribute band rather than making music of our own.

A patch of the perennial garden is dedicated to oca and yacon, and I grow far more than I need, largely as I give them away in the hope of convincing others to grow them too. They have much going for them. Unlike potatoes, neither oca or yacon get blight, you can't buy them in the shops and you only have to buy them once.

Oca looks like a new potato with a little lipstick on, about to hit the town. It tastes lightly lemony raw when just dug up, a little like sorrel. I love oca at this stage – oxalic acid gives it its sharp edge. Leave them in the sun and they don't turn green and spoil like potatoes, they sweeten gradually. They're fine raw and cooked too – roasting or steaming is best.

Where oca grows a low mat of leaves, like a succulent clover, yacon throws up beautiful green shoots a metre or two tall, with furry pointed leaves. As with oca, you have to let winter arrive before nosing under the soil for the tubers. Fresh out of the ground they're very much like baking potatoes to look at, with a texture like water chestnuts. Their flavour is gentle when first harvested – like mild green apples with a very faint hint of celery – but left in the sun for a few days their sweetness develops and they taste like crisp, refreshing pears.

Both oca and yacon are replant perennials, with some tubers saved from one year to grow again and multiply the next.

Oca tubers are sown as for potatoes (see page 116) once the frosts have passed. Any tubers harvested now and kept to re-sow should be stored unwatered in compost over winter and taken into the light in spring, watering occasionally. Once the frosts have passed, the growing plants can be planted 60cm or so apart.

Yacon has two sets of tubers – the largest set is eaten, the smallest should be potted up with a little of the growing tip and stored in a dark, cool room before being brought into the light in spring and planted out around 60cm from its neighbour when the danger of frosts has passed.

OCA AND YACON

Site Moist

Sow Sow oca mid-spring and plant out yucon after the last frosts

Harvest October–November

Notes Overwinter both in dry compost, somewhere cool and away from mice

Ocas bravas (page 346)
Veg patch tempura (page 141)

PIGS

Feed Change to finisher feed for the last weeks

Notes Get them used to the trailer ahead of taking them to the abattoir – it reduces their and your stress on the day

Chicken, pork & borlotti stew (page 338)
Slow-roast five-spice pork belly (page 340)

THE YOUNG PIGS that arrive or are born in spring are instantly lovable. All summer long they eat everything that the veg patch offers that's no good to us – tough stalks, bolted lettuces, peelings, slug-ravaged potatoes. They grow at an alarming rate: in a few short months a piglet you can easily hold in one hand becomes five feet long and unmoved by any coercing push you might give it.

This speed of growth means that a typical commercial pig may live for only 4 months, having reached the point at which the cost of rearing it isn't matched by a return in meat. Our pigs live considerably longer – certainly twice that, often more. We choose slow-growing breeds, such as Saddlebacks, and give them plenty of space to run around in, so they mature less quickly. But 'The Day' still comes, and it's often in November.

Today was an early start – our two pigs, both boys but named Daisy and Alice by Nell, were due at the abattoir. It was just getting light when Trent and I opened the gate of their pen so they could walk up the lowered back of the trailer. Getting them to go in is all about acting like you don't mind if they get in or not. No tension, a bucket with a little food in: all carrot and no stick. It can take minutes or an hour or so. Eventually they ambled into the trailer in their own time. We shut the door and drove.

Driving to the abattoir is a nervous business. With the end in sight, I'm always certain something bad will happen, even if it never has. Today, almost there, I felt a lurch and stopped sharply: the trailer roof had lifted up. The bolt on one corner of the roof had sheared off and the combined strength of the pigs warped it enough for Alice to clamber out, just as we stopped.

Alice was lying in the road – a busy main road at rush hour. By some fluke there was a red apple where she was lying and it seemed to have grabbed her attention. Trent went to her; I wrestled with the roof, trying to stop Daisy escaping. Trent stopped the traffic his way, I mine. We looked at each other. What could we do now? Open the door to the trailer to try and get Alice back in and Daisy would try to bolt for it, but with traffic heading back both ways for hundreds of yards there wasn't much time for pondering.

A man hurried towards us through the stationary traffic. I guessed a commuter, pissed off at being held up. Miraculously he'd just left the abattoir and he had a trailer. Alice helpfully waltzed into the new trailer and off to the abattoir, leaving me to drive the Land Rover and Trent to run along behind, trying to keep the roof on and the ever lively Daisy from escaping. We made it. They trotted out of their trailers as if nothing had happened.

Driving back is always the same – the conversation starts, the radio can go on, but by the time I get back to the farm I've always forgotten that they're not here anymore.

— 5 November, 2010

...gs, enjoying windfall apples

December

I couldn't be less interested in being outside in December. It's the run up to Christmas and if I'm not by the fire I'm in the kitchen. If I have to be outside, it's largely to harvest. The veg patch may look unspectacular but it is full with the unglamorous heart and heft of the roots and greens – to my mind, as good as anything that comes from the summer garden.

December's peak harvest

Brussels sprouts

Endive

Herb fennel

Horseradish

Parsnips

Romanesco

Salsify & scorzonera

Kiwi fruit

December is reliably damp, all mists and drizzle rather than downpours, but it pools in the core of the brassicas and turns the soil heavy and slick. There is a tendency to worship the Mediterranean exotic over our wintry abundance and this is the month when your tastebuds tell you otherwise. There's a different beautiful brassica for each day of the week – Romanesco, Red Bor kale, Brussels sprouts, early sprouting broccoli, calabrese, cabbage and the last cuttings of cime di rapa – as varied and delicious as a sunny basket of Mediterranean favourites. And the parsnips, salsify and Jerusalem artichokes are all at their best too. It might well be my favourite month when it comes to flavours.

I'm very fond of December. It's the month in which I got my first bike, saw my first football match and met my first girlfriend. It's open season on mince pies, and It's A Wonderful Life is on TV. And I love Christmas. What's not to like? The weather, that's what.

I have hands like monkey's paws. You'd swear they belong to someone with great-great-grandchildren, to an emu, or to a man whose job it is to remove the paintwork from hot Cadillacs in Death Valley using white spirit, wearing no gloves, after eating salt and vinegar crisps and squeezing the juice out of three dozen lemons with his bare hands. They need all the keeping out of the wind they can get. Early last week I risked a few more hand wrinkles and got the fork in the ground for a few minutes – I'm glad I did, it's been frozen ever since. My reward: a large armful of salsify roots. Their underground sideshoots make them a slight nuisance to dig up – you have to lift them carefully with a fork – but it's worth a little trouble and the wrinkly fingers.

— 21 December, 2009

ROMANESCO

Site Sunny and sheltered

Sow March–April

Harvest October–March

Notes Sow into modules under cover, move into small pots when 2–3cm tall. At 8cm, plant out in the veg patch, 65cm apart

AS MUCH AS I LOVE cauliflower, I can't think of a single reason to grow it. There is only so much space and time to dedicate to growing and something has to give. Sow cauliflower in spring, nurture it until it's ready to plant out, protect it from slugs, cabbage white butterflies and pigeons, water when required, keep the weeds at bay and wait patiently for six months. If you happen to be there on the day it makes a beautiful head before going to seed, you have ONE lunch – and lovely as it is, it tastes very like the lunch you would have if you'd bought your cauliflower.

Romanesco is altogether different. It would earn a place in the veg patch for its beauty alone. It looks like sea coral would if it grew on land and wore teddy boy's socks. Like cauliflower, it grows into a decent open handful, but where cauliflower and calabrese have rounded pads, Romanesco has spires, each arranged in a series of self-similar logarithmic spirals – meaning that however you look at it – whole, at one of the sub-peaks or even closer – you see a spiralling peak made up of spiralling

manesco

peaks. Romanesco is quite something. It has a nuttier, brighter flavour than cauliflower and calabrese, a crisper texture, it bolts only if left for weeks on end once perfectly headed, and it is as beautiful as anything, edible or otherwise, in the garden.

There are two secrets to growing brassicas like Romanesco: they hate to be checked in any way while growing so I don't sow them too early as the frosts will knock them back when they're planted out; and I make a point of potting them on or planting out before they get too big, as constrained roots will slow their growth.

It is as much a pleasure to cook with as it is to look at. A whole head simmered for a couple of minutes only, plunged into cold water to fix the colour, served whole, dressed with oil, lemon and pepper is a great side. It's that nuttiness, along with its willingness to give in when cooked in oil, stock or chopped tomatoes that make it such a fine partner to pasta. I shred and cook it in oil, stock or tomatoes, usually with plenty of chilli or garlic, sultanas, lemon and parsley, and a pasta that will scoop it up – more often than not, orecchiette.

Cauliflower pakoras with raita (page 58)

Roasted Romanesco, shallots & celeriac (page 77)

Romanesco, apple & hazelnut salad with blue cheese dressing (page 348)

BRUSSELS SPROUTS

Site Sunny and sheltered

Sow February–April under cover in Jiffy 7s, potting on once established. Plant out when 10–15cm tall, allowing 60cm between plants

Harvest October–April

Notes Don't sow too early or the frosts may check them. Plant out May–June. Undersow with nasturtiums to retain water

'NEVER GROW ANYTHING that takes longer until it's ready than a baby'. Every year I fall foul of my grower friend Michael Michaud's advice about annual veg. I grow a couple of rows of Brussels in the veg patch every year – and I'd grow more but he's right: they take up so much space for such a long period.

To compensate, I get the best value I can from them, shredding the sprouts for coleslaw or pulling them apart into individual leaves for crisps. I rarely eat the sprouts whole as a side veg – I love them like that, especially briefly blanched and pushed around a pan with bacon and/or chestnuts, perhaps with a little cream – but they'd be gone in a couple of meals.

The mini-cabbage that forms on the top of the plant is a gloriously tasty thing, yet it is rarely available in the shops and largely ignored by allotmenters. I'm not sure why – perhaps it's the horticultural equivalent of our reluctance to go anywhere unless there's a sign pointing us in that direction – we're all too busy concentrating on the sprouts to notice them.

This little cabbage has all the sweet nuttiness of the sprouts but less of the gentle bitterness that I love, but many don't. Slice the cabbage from the top when the sprouts are growing strongly and not only will you have a delicious harvest, the sprouts will then mature all at once rather than gradually – handy if you're hosting a big family Christmas – although how long they take to mature depends on the weather and the variety.

The sprouts themselves are much more versatile than many suspect. Sliced thinly and raw, they make a fine third of a simple coleslaw with red cabbage and celeriac; peeled, releasing each leaf from the sprout, and roasted briefly, they are sensational; and roasted, steamed, or briefly boiled and buttered, I could eat them all day.

Brussels, celeriac & cabbage slaw (page 78)

Caraway sprout tops with bacon & apple (page 345)

Sprout crisps (page 350)

russels tops

Salsify

SALSIFY WAS THE FIRST THING I grew without having tasted it before. I read about it in *Jane Grigson's Vegetable Book*, found seed (at last) in a seed catalogue, and that first taste was even better than her description. The flavour is somewhere between artichoke hearts and asparagus with a hint of the seashore in there too, though their alternative name 'underground oyster' is stretching things a little too seaward for me.

That first meal of salsify convinced me that every year I should grow something I hadn't eaten before, ideally that I hadn't heard of, and I've done that ever since. Both salsify and the black-skinned relative, scorzonera, are sown in spring, growing into long, thin roots that drive steadily into the ground, often developing late enough in the season to test the gardener's confidence. They can get to 40cm easily, which, along with their tendency to snap, makes them a tricky little harvest. Don't be tempted to pull them, unless you'd like a short stump in your hand and a muddy backside – they need lifting with a fork. This tiny faff is all that is between you and a flavour that is almost taken for granted in Italy and France but unbuyable this side of the Channel.

In the kitchen, I prepare these roots the same almost every time. Boiled for 10–15 minutes until al dente then plunged into cold water, the skin slips easily off the root. From there, they'll either be cooked in a frying pan with butter, cream, parsley and Parmesan as a side dish, or form the heart of a gratin.

SALSIFY AND SCORZONERA

Site Good, deep soil

Sow Direct April–May, 15cm apart and 1cm deep

Harvest October–December

Notes Sow direct, 1cm down, 15cm apart

Root crisps (page 60)
Salsify gratin (page 344)

I'D LIKE TO TELL YOU where and how I grow herb fennel, but in truth, having sown it once, I do nothing: it self-seeds readily, spreading over the ground like spilt milk. A single plant at the end of the garden has become a patch that grows tall, catching the sun and breeze, through the summer and into winter.

To some this desire to spread is 'invasive'; to me, it's free food – I just hoe or pull up the plants I don't want. As well as being beautiful in itself, its light green foliage and pale yellow flowers make a fine backdrop for other plants, so I let it go pretty much where it likes.

A few seeds sown direct in spring, or in modules to plant out, will virtually grow themselves, reaching as high as 2.5 metres by midsummer. I pinch the aromatic leaves off as I need them – a little goes a long way, just a pinch will brighten up a leafy salad – and when the cold strikes, I don't flatten them. The frosts leach the green out of the plants, leaving pale dry skeletons with clutches of seeds at their fingertips.

The best of fennel's flavour is carried in these tiny ribbed torpedos, giving the anise warmth to the five spice I make with the last of the Szechuan pepper harvest. It makes a fantastic flavoured fudge – try it in place of the lavender in my fudge recipe. And, having unthinkingly dipped the last sticky apple of a batch into a bowlful of seeds, I can recommend it as a fabulous embellishment on the classic toffee apple.

HERB FENNEL

Site Favours well drained but ok in most soils

Sow Direct in spring, or self-sown

Harvest All year

Notes A few seeds with hot water – very refreshing

Fennel toffee apples (page 374)
Lavender & walnut fudge (page 179)

KIWI FRUIT

Site Sunny and sheltered

Harvest October–January

Notes Prune in winter and in summer snip sub-laterals back a little – to stop growing tips using energy up in making more growth than fruit

Kiwi cranachan (page 362)

DECEMBER SEEMS LIKE the least likely month to be enjoying something that tastes as tropical as a beautifully ripe kiwi, but there they are, still attached to the leafless plants. They're picked this late to let them ripen fully – so late it seems like they must turn to mush in the cold.

Leave the fruit too long and they will go beyond their moment – softening in the frosts and gaining a peculiarly alcoholic edge which does them no favours at all, but get them just right and they're heavenly – a fresh, yet deep, strawberry/wine/pineapple flavour, altogether lovelier than those in the shops.

There are two sorts: regular kiwis and dwarf kiwis. A full-sized kiwi needs a differently sexed partner for pollination (in Kiwiland, one male will pollinate eight females) and they can spread like few other plants – easily making 20 metres once established. The trick is to limit their growth, as you do with grape vines, to concentrate the plant's energies on producing fruit rather than a wall of leaves. Imagine them as a huge espalier, with arms (laterals) radiating from the main stem, keeping short stems (sublaterals) that grow from the arms pruned to 20cm or so – it is here that most flowering and fruiting occurs.

Treat the dwarf kiwis in the same way, or allow them to ramble a little less controlled, as they are only likely to get to 2–3 metres in spread. These smaller varieties are self-fertile too, so one plant is fine, perfect for a small garden or patio.

Full-sized kiwis can take time to establish and fruit, so I planted mine in the polytunnel for the extra warmth; we have dwarf kiwis in the perennial garden and a sheltered, sunny spot in the garden and they fruit every year.

After a glorious summer and autumn, and if your plant is in the finest of sheltered, south-facing spots, the fruit may ripen from October onwards. In cool years, allow them until the Christmas run-in.

We have two of the dwarf kiwis growing in pots by the house, in the sunniest corner, which means that at least once a day, Candida, Nell or I will remember to check them for ripeness on the way to the chickens or taking the dog for a walk.

The fruit of the regular kiwi are as you'd expect, though more succulent and intensely flavoured than shop-bought; the dwarf produces grape-sized kiwis that you don't actually have to peel – unlikely as it sounds, the furry skin dissolves in the mouth without a hint of a tickle. They'll keep for a few weeks in a cool room, but it's difficult not to eat them fresh, like sweets, from the plant. They make a fine cranachan too.

warf kiwis: Jenny

Recipes for

October, November & December

Borlottis with mussels

The creaminess of the borlottis is perfect here – they take up enough of the surrounding flavours without loosing their own taste and creaminess. The wine can be medium or dry, and coriander works well instead of parsley if you fancy that.

Serves 4

500g fresh borlotti beans (or use soaked dried borlottis, or tinned)

2 bay leaves

A small handful of thyme sprigs

50ml olive oil

300g shallots, sliced

8 garlic cloves, finely chopped

160ml white wine

900g mussels, cleaned

A large handful of parsley, finely chopped

A good pinch of paprika

A good pinch of chilli flakes or powder

Sea salt and freshly ground black pepper

First, cook the fresh (or dried) borlotti beans. Place them in a pan, add the bay leaves and thyme and just cover with water. Bring to the boil, then lower the heat and cook at an idle simmer for 25 minutes (allow at least 45 minutes for dried beans). Try one of the beans – it should be firm but cooked. Allow another few minutes if they need it.

While the borlottis are cooking, warm the olive oil in a large wide pan (that has a tight-fitting lid) and cook the shallots over a medium-low heat, stirring frequently, until soft. Add the garlic and cook for a few minutes more. Stir in the wine.

Drain the borlottis, discarding the herbs, and add them to the shallots. (If using tinned beans, add them at this stage.) Stir well. Add the mussels and season well with salt and pepper. Put the lid on and turn up the heat a little. Steam the mussels for 4–5 minutes, shaking the pan every minute or so.

Remove from the heat and stir through the parsley. Taste and season if necessary – I'd recommend lots of pepper. Ladle into bowls and sprinkle with the paprika and chilli.

Curried squash & mussel soup

The combination of spices, squash and mussels is a special one; even without the mussels this soup is very good. You can use any squash, though you may want to tweak the seasoning if you opt for one that's much sweeter than a butternut squash. The soup can be made a day ahead, leaving just the mussels to cook and add just before serving.

Serves 4

1kg squash

25g unsalted butter

2 shallots, finely chopped

1 leek, well washed and finely sliced

1 tsp ground cumin

1 tsp ground coriander

1 tsp ground turmeric

1 tsp mild chilli powder

1 tsp garam masala

600ml chicken or vegetable stock

350ml dry white wine

A small handful of thyme, leaves only

800g mussels, cleaned

A handful of coriander

Sea salt and freshly ground black pepper

Peel, deseed and coarsely grate the squash.

Melt the butter in a large pan over a medium heat and cook the shallots and leek gently, stirring frequently, until softened. Stir in the spices and cook for a couple of minutes. Add the squash, then pour in the stock and stir well. Cover and simmer gently for 25 minutes.

Allow the soup to cool just a little, then purée in a blender until smooth. Return to the pan and keep hot over a low heat.

Heat the wine with the thyme in another large pan (that has a tight-fitting lid) and bring to a simmer. Add the mussels and season well with salt and pepper. Put the lid on, turn up the heat a little and steam the mussels for 4–5 minutes, shaking the pan every minute or so. Meanwhile, chop most of the coriander. Remove all but four of the mussels from their shells.

Add the chopped coriander to the soup, taste and season if necessary. Share the shelled mussels between warmed deep bowls. Ladle the soup over the mussels and scatter over the remaining coriander. Add a mussel in shell to each bowl and serve.

Pot-roast chicken with grapes in milk

I love chicken cooked in milk. The results are unfailingly succulent. This recipe is also a nod to chicken véronique, that old favourite where chicken is cooked with grapes. You can lean the core recipe any way you fancy: the sweet white wine, herbs, olives and grapes can be replaced with cider, lemon, lemon thyme and apples, or whatever you like.

Serves 4

1 free-range chicken, about 1.6kg
90g butter
A few splashes of olive oil
A handful of thyme sprigs
A dozen or so sage leaves
2 bay leaves
12 garlic cloves
16 black olives
200ml sweet white wine
About 500ml milk
50ml double cream
A little beurre manié (see below), if needed
400g grapes (ideally seedless, but I'm not fussy)
A handful of parsley, chopped
Sea salt and freshly ground black pepper

Preheat the oven to 200°C/Gas 6.

Season the chicken generously, inside and out, with salt and pepper. In a flameproof casserole to suit the size of the chicken, warm the butter with the olive oil until it begins to shimmer. Add the chicken and colour on all sides until golden. Put the bird breast side up in the casserole.

Scatter the thyme, sage, bay leaves, garlic cloves and olives around the chicken. Pour in the wine and enough milk to come halfway up the bird. Cover and cook in the oven for 20 minutes, then lower the oven setting to 180°C/Gas 4 and cook for a further 1 hour 10 minutes or until cooked through, basting the bird a few times. To check whether it is ready, pierce the join between leg and body and the juices should run clear.

Lift the chicken out onto a plate and cover it with foil. The wine usually causes the milk to split; this is fine.

Return the pan to a medium heat and whisk in the cream. If you'd like the sauce a little thicker, you can thicken it with beurre manié (see below). Add the grapes and simmer gently for a further 2 minutes. Taste the sauce and adjust the seasoning if need be, then scatter over the parsley.

I usually pull the meat off the carcass into the sauce, rather than carve, and often as not we'll eat it with mash and greens.

Beurre manié
This can be used to thicken any sauce or cooking liquor that is too thin. Using a fork, cream together a knob of soft butter and 2 tsp plain flour to make a soft paste. Whisk into the sauce a little at a time until the sauce is the required thickness.

Chicken, pork & borlotti stew

If I had a paella pan rather than having lent it to someone a while ago, this might well have been a paella. As it is, a large cast-iron pan worked marvellously. I've made this with fish, chicken and prawns and I'm sure it would be great with rabbit – it's very adaptable to whatever's in season. Lemon thyme lends a little freshness, though you can substitute it with standard thyme if you'd rather, and I've used green beans in place of the borlottis earlier in the year.

Serves 4

4–5 tbsp olive oil

3 chicken legs, each jointed into two

500g shoulder of pork, diced

A splash of Marsala

1 Romanesco, broken into florets

1 tsp paprika

1 tsp smoked paprika

A good pinch of saffron threads

A small handful of lemon thyme sprigs

230g fresh borlotti beans (or use cooked dried, see page 62, or tinned beans)

400g tin chopped tomatoes

500g pearled spelt, risotto rice or paella rice

A handful of parsley, finely chopped

Juice of ½ lemon

Sea salt and freshly ground black pepper

Warm the olive oil in a large pan over a moderate-high heat. Cook the chicken pieces, seasoning as you go, browning them on all sides, then lift out with a slotted spoon onto kitchen paper to drain.

Cook the pork pieces in the same way, then return the chicken to the pan. Splash the base of the pan with Marsala to deglaze, using a wooden spoon to dislodge and dissolve any burnt nuggets.

Add the Romanesco, both paprikas, saffron, lemon thyme, borlottis and tomatoes and mix well. Add just enough water to cover everything – it should be around 1.4 litres. Simmer, uncovered, for 45 minutes.

Stir in the spelt and cook for a further 15–20 minutes – the spelt (or rice, if using) should be tender but still firm to the bite. Add a little water if you need to as it cooks.

Once cooked, remove from the heat and take out the thyme. Stir in the parsley and season with salt and pepper as you like. Squeeze over the lemon juice and serve.

Sorrel pie

You'd be forgiven for thinking that the sourness of the cream and the sharp edge of the sorrel might be too much here, but they work perfectly with the cheese and the crunch of the pastry. You can substitute chard, spinach or Good King Henry for the sorrel if you fancy.

If using frozen filo (and who doesn't), take it out from the freezer early but don't unwrap it as it dries out rapidly, making it difficult to separate the flimsy sheets.

Serves 6

450g young sorrel leaves

300g Lancashire or other crumbly cheese, such as feta

3 free-range eggs

250g soured cream

2 tbsp cornflour

10 large sheets of filo pastry

Vegetable oil, for brushing

Sea salt and freshly ground black pepper

Preheat the oven to 180°C/Gas 4.

Wash and shred the sorrel, then wilt it thoroughly in a pan over a moderate heat with just the water that clings to the leaves after washing.

Break the cheese into small pieces and place in a bowl. Add the eggs, sorrel, soured cream and cornflour. Mix well and season to taste – you may not need much or any salt, depending on the saltiness of the cheese.

Lightly oil the base of a shallow baking tin, about 30 x 30cm. Cover the base with a sheet of filo and brush with oil. Add two more sheets, lightly brushing each with oil.

Now spoon in half of the cheesy mixture, spreading it evenly with the back of a spoon. Add three more sheets of filo, oiling between each, then spoon on the rest of the filling.

Top with the remaining four sheets of filo pastry, oiling between each and brushing the top layer of filo with oil. Bake for about 35 minutes, until lightly coloured and crisp.

Slow-roast five-spice pork belly

A lazy recipe where the wonderfully fatty belly melts with long, slow cooking, while the lentils and onions cook beneath. It's a very forgiving process – you can turn the heat down a little and extend the cooking time to the working day or overnight, whatever suits. I quite like the lentils dryish, but you can always add a little more cider or water late on if you like, and/or stir through a spoonful of crème fraîche just before you serve.

Stir-fried chard leaves and pickled chard stalks are wonderful with this, but kale or other greens are almost as good.

Serves 4

1kg ribless pork belly, skin scored

3–4 tbsp five-spice powder (see page 267)

200g Puy lentils, well rinsed

4 red onions, cut into wedges

5 garlic cloves, finely chopped

A handful of thyme sprigs

500ml dry cider

1 tbsp sea salt

Preheat the oven to 130°C/Gas ½–1.

Using a sharp knife, slice the skin off the pork belly in one piece and place it in the fridge. Rub the surface of the meat with the five-spice and leave it to marinate for an hour or two.

Make an inch-high platform with the lentils, onions, garlic and thyme in a roasting pan large enough to accommodate the pork. Put the pork on top and slowly pour in the cider. Make a lid for the roasting pan from foil and place it over the pork, sealing it under the rim of the roasting tin.

Cook for 6 hours or so, checking after 5 hours to see if the lentils have dried out at all and you need to add a little water. Once cooked, remove from the oven and leave to rest, still covered with foil.

Preheat the grill to high. Place the scored pork skin on a baking tray and rub with the salt. Place under the hot grill until it blisters into crackling.

I like to serve the pork and crackling with stir-fried chard leaves (page 80), pickled chard stems (page 82) and mash.

Squash, shallot & mushroom tart

A simple early autumn lunch or supper that takes little effort to prepare. It can be altered to suit what you have to hand – try a handful of walnut pieces, blue cheese instead of goat's, red onions instead of shallots. A good pokey salad that includes rocket and/or oriental leaves such as Green In Snow goes especially well with this.

Serves 4

440g peeled, deseeded squash

240g shallots, peeled and halved vertically

3 tbsp olive oil

20 or so sage leaves

A good pinch of chilli powder

1 sheet of ready-rolled all-butter puff pastry, about 320g

130g large, firm mushrooms, thickly sliced

120g hard goat's cheese, such as Village Green, crumbled into smallish pieces

A few tbsp parsley pesto (page 165) or good basil pesto

Sea salt and freshly ground black pepper

Heat the oven to 190°C/Gas 5.

Cut the squash into 1cm thick half-moon slices and spread out on a large baking tray with the shallots. Spoon over the olive oil and season well with salt and pepper. Scatter over the sage leaves and dust with chilli powder. Roast for 30 minutes or so – the squash should be firm but cooked, the shallots soft but not burnt. Allow a little longer if needed, then remove and set aside to cool.

Turn up the oven to 200°C/Gas 6.

Roll the pastry out to fit a lightly oiled baking tray (20 x 30cm is ideal). Lay the pastry on the tray and score a border 2cm from the edge on all sides, taking care not to cut completely through the pastry. Avoiding the border, pierce the pastry every few centimetres or so with a fork to stop it rising to much during cooking.

Arrange the squash and shallots on the pastry within the border and scatter over the mushroom slices and cheese. Splash with pesto and season with salt and pepper to taste. Bake for 20 minutes, until the pastry border is risen and golden.

Salsify gratin

It's good to have a gratin recipe up your sleeve to adapt to the seasons and whatever you happen to fancy eating, and here's mine. It works beautifully with salsify, as well as Jerusalem artichokes, potato, or even beetroot, and with the spinach replaced by other leaves, including most of the brassicas – shredded Brussels sprout tops especially.

Serves 4

35g unsalted butter, softened, plus extra for greasing

Juice of 1 lemon

600g salsify or scorzonera

20ml olive oil

2 medium onions, finely sliced

3 garlic cloves, finely chopped

A good glug of Marsala or sherry

500ml vegetable or chicken stock

1 bay leaf

A small handful of thyme sprigs

30g plain flour

150ml double cream

A good grating of fresh nutmeg

120g spinach leaves

60g coarse breadcrumbs

50g crushed hazelnuts

60g Cheddar, grated (optional)

Sea salt and freshly ground black pepper

Preheat the oven to 200°C/Gas 6.

Butter a 25cm oven dish.

Three-quarters fill a bowl with water and add the lemon juice. Under slowly running cold water, peel each salsify root, cut into 5 x 1cm batons and drop into the lemony water to prevent them discolouring.

Heat the olive oil in a large pan and gently fry the onions until softened, without browning. Add the garlic and cook for a few minutes more. Add the Marsala to loosen and flavour the onions, and then add the stock, bay leaf and thyme. Bring to a simmer.

Drain the salsify and add to the pan. Cook until it is just tender but still firm – this can take 5–20 minutes depending on the age of the salsify, so test every few minutes with the tip of a sharp knife. Once tender, lift out and place in the buttered dish.

Meanwhile, work the butter and flour together with a fork to a paste (beurre manié). Remove the herbs from the stock and add a quarter of the beurre manié to the stock, whisking constantly over the heat to thicken the stock. Add more of the paste, a little at a time, whisking constantly, until the stock is the thickness of single cream.

Stir in the double cream, season with salt, pepper and nutmeg to taste and add the spinach. Simmer briefly until the spinach has wilted. Remove from the heat and pour over the salsify in the dish.

Combine the breadcrumbs, nuts and cheese, if using, and sprinkle evenly over the surface. Bake for around 20 minutes until golden brown.

Caraway sprout tops with bacon & apple

Sprout tops are one of my favourite and most flavoursome vegetables. With a texture of spring greens alongside a sweet nuttiness, they are delicious and perhaps even more versatile than the sprouts themselves. You can cook them in advance and plunge them into cold water to fix the colour and stop them cooking further, then mix with the other cooked ingredients and warm through to serve. This is a fine lunch or a great side.

Serves 2

2 good-sized Brussels sprout tops

3 tbsp olive oil

1 small red onion, thinly sliced

200g piece of smoked or unsmoked streaky bacon, rind removed and cut into roughly 1cm cubes

1 apple

1 tsp caraway seeds

A good grating of fresh nutmeg

Juice of ½ lemon

Sea salt and freshly ground black pepper

Shred and steam the sprout tops for 3–5 minutes until just tender.

Warm the olive oil in a frying pan over a medium heat and fry the onion until soft. Add the bacon and cook until lightly browned. Pour off excess oil from the pan.

In the meantime, peel, core and grate the apple, then add to the pan with the caraway seeds and nutmeg. Cook, stirring occasionally, for a minute or two. Add the just-tender sprout tops and briefly warm through, stirring everything together.

Squeeze the lemon juice over, season with salt and pepper as you like and serve straight away.

Ocas bravas

The tapas bar at the end of my road when I lived in London saw far too much of my money – there simply wasn't a time of day or night when my stomach wasn't happy to welcome patatas bravas, the famous Spanish spicy potato dish. This recipe replaces the potatoes with oca, which gives it a hint of lemon but works beautifully with waxy potatoes too.

Serves 4

For the oca

250g oca tubers

3 tbsp olive oil

2 sprigs of rosemary

2 garlic cloves, finely chopped

1 tsp sweet paprika

1 tsp sea salt

For the bravas sauce

2 tbsp olive oil

1 onion, finely sliced

3 garlic cloves, finely chopped

1 lively red chilli, deseeded and finely chopped

1 tsp smoked paprika

1 tbsp sherry vinegar

400g tin chopped tomatoes

A pinch of sugar

To serve

A handful of parsley, chopped

Simmer the oca briefly in water to cover until just hinting at tenderness, 5–15 minutes depending on age. Drain and allow to cool. Once cool enough to handle, cut larger oca into pieces.

For the bravas sauce, heat the olive oil in a pan over a medium heat and cook the onion, stirring frequently, until soft. Add the garlic and chilli, and cook for a further few minutes. Stir in the paprika, then the sherry vinegar and simmer for a minute. Now stir in the tomatoes, sugar and a good pinch of salt and simmer for 5 minutes. Remove from the heat and blitz, using a blender, to a sauce, retaining some texture. Keep warm over a gentle heat while the oca is frying.

Heat the olive oil in a frying pan and fry the oca with the rosemary over a moderate heat until crisp and lightly golden, adding the garlic for the last minute or two. Lift the oca out using a slotted spoon and drain on kitchen paper.

Arrange the oca in a ring on a plate and dust with the paprika and sea salt. Pour the bravas sauce into the centre, rather than over the oca, to ensure the oca keeps crisp. Scatter over the chopped parsley and serve.

Romanesco, apple & hazelnut salad with blue cheese dressing

Parsley is much underused as a salad leaf. If the leaves are young and tender, it works especially well with beetroot, apple and salty meats, as well as sparingly in a leafy salad. Here, it joins the dots between the ingredients perfectly.

Serves 3–4

80g hazelnuts

2 tsp olive oil

60g pancetta, cut into cubes

350g Romanesco

2 sharp green apples

A handful of flat-leaf parsley, leaves only

For the blue cheese dressing

50g blue cheese, such as Cropwell Bishop Stilton

A little milk

½ handful of chives, chopped

Juice of ½ lemon

Toast the hazelnuts in a dry frying pan over a medium heat until lightly coloured, then tip into a tea towel and break up a little with a rolling pin.

Add the olive oil to the frying pan and cook the pancetta cubes over a medium heat until lightly crispy. Drain on kitchen paper.

Break the Romanesco into florets and cook in boiling water for 2 minutes, then drain and plunge them into ice-cold water to stop the cooking and fix the colour.

Quarter, core and slice the apples into half-moon slices, about 3mm thick.

For the dressing, break the cheese into pieces and mash in a bowl with just enough milk to make a paste. Add the chives and lemon juice, and work until evenly combined.

Arrange the Romanesco florets and apple slices on a serving dish. Scatter over the parsley leaves, crushed hazelnuts and pancetta, then spoon the dressing over everything.

Sprout crisps

As much as I love sprouts as a buttery side, in coleslaw (see page 78) or pushed around a pan with bacon or chestnuts, this may be my favourite way with them. Try it with kale leaves too – they are superb. It's hardly a recipe, it's so simple.

Serves 2–3 as a snack

12 Brussels sprouts

2 tsp olive oil

1 tsp salt

Freshly ground black pepper

Preheat the oven to 180°C/Gas 4.

Strip off any discoloured or damaged leaves, then slice off the base of each sprout. The outer leaves should, for the most part, fall away easily; set these aside. Slice another coin from the base, and pull away more leaves. Continue until the centre stays intact – have a nibble; the cores are deliciously fresh and nutty raw. Repeat for all the sprouts.

Place the sprout leaves in a bowl, add the olive oil, salt and pepper and toss until all the leaves are well coated.

Spread out the leaves on baking sheets in a single layer and roast in the oven. You are after a light crispiness and a gentle golden tinge to the green, not black bits. Check after 3–4 minutes, removing any crisps that fit the bill, roasting the rest a little longer until they are all done.

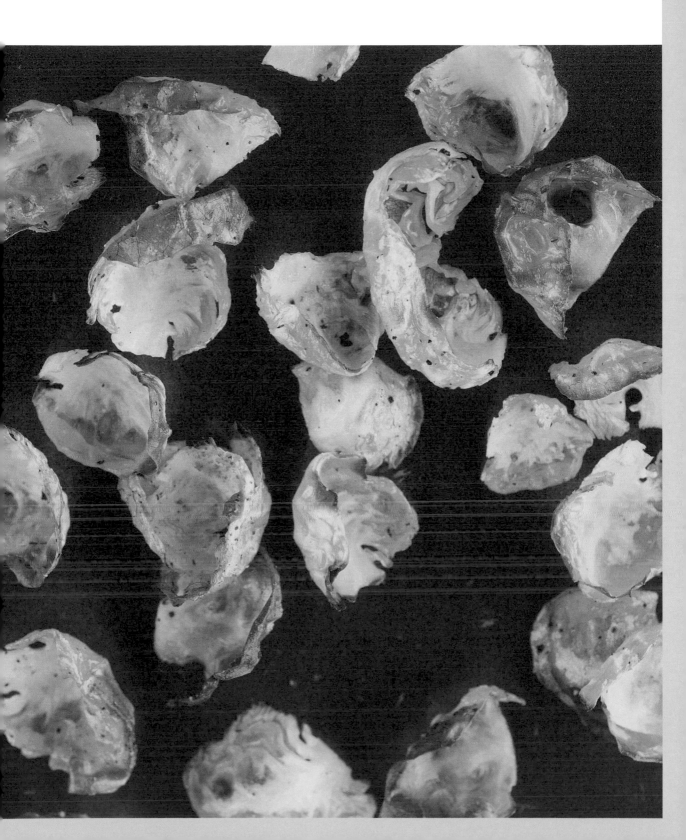

Spiced almonds

If you're looking to put on a few pounds I can recommend these spicy nuts as a fairly swift way of achieving your goal. Not only ridiculously moreish, they also pair up stupendously well with a cold beer. They are a perfect football snack, which gives you 90 minutes (plus injury time) of fairly hefty calorie intake.

Serves 2–3 as a snack

2 tbsp light brown sugar

1 tsp ground cumin

1 tsp hot paprika

1 tsp ground cinnamon

1 tsp salt

1½ tbsp olive oil

200g shelled almonds

¼ tsp cayenne pepper

Preheat the oven to 170°C/Gas 3.

Mix the brown sugar, cumin, paprika, cinnamon and salt together in a large bowl.

Warm the olive oil gently in a pan, then add the almonds, turning to coat them in the oil. Toss over the heat until the nuts are lightly coloured.

Tip the almonds into the bowl of spicy sugar, toss well to coat evenly, then spread out on the prepared baking sheet. Bake for 10 minutes or so, checking after 7 minutes just in case – they can quickly catch and burn.

Let the almonds cool, at least a little, before serving, sprinkled lightly with the cayenne.

Pickled apples

I really ought to pickle more fruit. The pickling blend of sharp, sweet and aromatics suits so many, and none more than apples. This recipe is vague – the weight of apples needed depends on the variety, and you may prefer a sweeter flavour, so do adjust the core recipe as you like. It's particularly good alongside pork or hot-smoked mackerel.

Makes about 700g

700g apples

For the pickling liquor

120g soft light brown sugar

1 tsp salt

500ml cider vinegar

1 cinnamon stick

1 tsp whole allspice

2 cloves

½ tsp Szechuan peppercorns or black peppercorns

1 star anise

1 bay leaf

For the pickling liquor, dissolve the sugar and salt in the cider vinegar in a pan over a medium heat. Add the spices and bay leaf, bring to the boil, then lower the heat and simmer for 10 minutes or so. Remove from the heat and allow to cool.

While the liquid is cooling, quarter, core, peel and thinly slice a couple of the apples into 2mm thick slices. Put into a sterilised jar (see page 170) and pour on enough of the spicy vinegar to just cover the apple slices.

Peel, core and slice the remaining apples, add them to the jar and cover with spicy vinegar. I usually leave the spices in the jar to allow the flavour to intensify a little.

Seal the jar and keep in a cool, dark place. Eat within a week or so; thereafter the apples will gradually lose some of their quality.

Quince cheese

Known as membrillo in Spain, this sweet, firm delight is typically served with cheese, game or cured meats. Don't tell the Spanish, but it can also pass as a posh fruit pastille – let a small piece, rolled in sugar, dissolve on your tongue. It's a fabulous filling for doughnuts (see page 368), too.

Quince paste is easy to make and lasts for months, certainly over a year, in an airtight container in the fridge. You can use any number of quinces as the ingredients are few and the weight of sugar equal to that of the purée. Don't peel the quince – firstly, it's a pain as they are so hard; secondly, the skin adds pectin to the pulp, helping it to set.

Makes about 90 slices

Juice of 1 lemon

8 quinces

500g caster sugar, give or take

A few drops of sunflower oil

Caster sugar for dusting

One-third fill a large saucepan with water and add the lemon juice.

Quarter and core the quince, but don't peel them. Immediately submerge them in the lemony water to prevent them from discolouring. If needed, add a little water so that the fruit is just covered.

Bring to a gentle simmer and cook until the quince are nicely soft – this can be anywhere from 30 minutes to 1½ hours, depending on the size and ripeness of the fruit. Drain the quince and pass them through a fine sieve or mouli into a measuring jug to give a smooth purée, free of skin and any grainy bits. Now stir in an equal volume of sugar as there is purée.

Return the mixture to the cleaned saucepan and bring to a simmer over a medium heat, stirring constantly. Don't let the heat get too high unless you are wearing chain mail – the purée with thicken as it cooks and may spit as it bubbles. Keep cooking and stirring until you can draw a spoon across the bottom of the pan and the purée takes a moment to fill the channel behind it.

Lightly oil a dish or tin, about 30 x 20cm. Pour in the quince purée to a depth of 1–2cm. Leave to cool, then cover and allow to set overnight.

Carefully ease the quince cheese out of the dish onto a board and dust with caster sugar. Cut into slices or squares to serve.

Poached & roasted quince

This is a lovely way to enhance the natural fragrance and colour of quince. The poaching liquid can be wine, sherry, port or even water rather than cider, but I have a soft spot for the local brew. Simmer the quince a little longer if you are eating them unroasted – they keep their shape well rather than collapsing when cooked.

Serves 4

6 tbsp caster sugar

700ml cider (or wine if you prefer)

5 cloves

8cm cinnamon stick

2 large or 4 small quince

3 tbsp honey

A good glug of Marsala or sweet sherry

Put the sugar and cider into a saucepan and bring slowly to a simmer, then add the cloves and cinnamon.

Peel, halve and core the quince and immediately immerse each half in the cider to prevent them discolouring. Let the fruit simmer until tender –test with the point of a sharp knife. This can take anywhere from 30 minutes to an hour, depending on their size and state of ripeness.

Preheat the oven to 180°C/Gas 4.

When cooked, lift the quince out with a slotted spoon and place them in a shallow baking dish. Combine 130ml of the sugary cider (along with the cloves and cinnamon) with the honey. Pour over the fruit and bake for 20 minutes.

Splash the Marsala over the fruit and stir to deglaze and incorporate any sticky bits in the dish. Cook for another 10–20 minutes until the quince are beautifully tender. Serve with the cider syrup and cream or yoghurt.

Quince granita
Don't throw your poaching liquor away. Strain and freeze it to make a glorious granita.

Medlar sticky toffee pudding

Other than the left-footed goal I scored from outside the box on the only time I played outfield for my primary school, this may be the pinnacle of my wintry achievements. You can be sure I wouldn't mess with something as perfect as a sticky toffee pudding and make it public if it wasn't special. Medlars' wonderful datey-ness pairs perfectly with the walnuts and the toffee, making this one of those wintry desserts that is so appealing in the cold weather. The brief grilling at the end is by no means essential, but it turns the top beautifully fudgy.

Serves 6

For the sauce

125g unsalted butter

70g golden caster sugar

50g dark muscovado sugar

170ml double cream

For the cake

60g unsalted butter, softened

85g golden caster sugar

70g dark muscovado sugar

2 eggs

180g plain flour

1 tsp baking powder

1 tsp bicarbonate of soda

1 tsp ground cloves

½ tsp salt

200g medlar pulp (see page 312)

85g walnuts, roughly crushed

Preheat the oven to 180°C/Gas 4.

Lightly butter a baking dish, approximately 24 x 20cm.

For the sauce, put all the ingredients in a pan and heat gently until the butter melts. Turn the heat up and boil for 5 minutes, stirring frequently, until the sauce is thick enough to coat the back of a spoon. Pour a little over half of the sauce into the baking dish, allow to cool, then refrigerate to firm up.

For the cake, beat the butter and both sugars together, then add the eggs, one at a time, beating well to combine. Sift the flour, baking powder, bicarbonate of soda, cloves and salt over the mixture and stir until evenly incorporated. Thoroughly stir in the medlar pulp and crushed walnuts.

Spoon the cake mixture into the baking dish, over the toffee sauce. Bake for 30 minutes until a skewer inserted into the centre comes out clean.

Preheat the grill to medium. Make holes in the cake with the tip of a knife – just large enough to allow the sauce to soak into the sponge. Pour the remaining sauce on top of the cake and grill for just long enough to crisp the top a little.

Serve with a great deal of double cream or vanilla ice cream.

Spiced fudgy squash cake

With its sweet fudginess, this is almost a cheesecake – you can make it even more of one by putting a biscuit base of crushed ginger nuts (200g crushed biscuits mixed with 100g melted butter) beneath it if you fancy, though it's perfectly delicious without. It's very good cold too.

If the squash is a tricky one to peel, it's fine to cook it in its skin and peel away the skin afterwards.

Serves 6

1.2kg squash
150g caster sugar
3 tbsp honey
2 free-range eggs, lightly beaten
120g ground almonds
1 tsp ground cinnamon
1 tsp ground ginger
60g blanched almonds
30g soft light brown sugar

Preheat the oven to 190°C/Gas 5.

Peel and deseed the squash, removing all the fibres; you need about 750g prepared weight. Cut the squash into slices, 1–2cm thick, and place in a wide pan with about 300ml water. Bring up to the boil, then lower the heat to an idle simmer. Cover and cook for 15 minutes or so until the squash is tender. Half-steaming, half-boiling, it may take a little longer, depending on the variety.

Drain the cooked squash thoroughly and mash until smooth. Return the purée to the pan and stir over a low heat for a few minutes to drive off any water. Stir in the caster sugar and honey and cook for a couple of minutes. Remove from the heat and let cool slightly.

Stir the eggs, ground almonds and spices into the squash purée. Spoon into a small baking dish, about 20 x 15cm, and smooth the top with a palette knife.

Briefly blitz the almonds and brown sugar together in a blender to make a crumble. Sprinkle over the top of the squash and bake for 45 minutes or so – it should be very lightly golden.

Allow the cake to cool a little before serving. I like it with cream.

Kiwi cranachan

I may well have made this pudding with every fruit we grow here. The blend of whisky, cream and toasted oats is ridiculously addictive and I've yet to discover a fruit that doesn't work with it. A purée of early, sharp gooseberries does as well as blackberries at the end of summer, and here I am at Christmas finding the kiwis give me an excuse to keep eating it. You might want to adjust the caster sugar either way, depending on the sweetness of the fruit you're using.

Serves 4

40g rolled or porridge oats

6 kiwi fruit

300ml double cream

2–3 tbsp whisky

3 tbsp caster sugar

4 tbsp runny honey

Gently toast the oats in a dry frying pan over a medium heat until golden, flipping frequently to prevent burning. Tip onto a plate to cool.

Peel the kiwi fruit and blitz the fruit in a blender until fairly smooth.

Whisk the cream, whisky and sugar together until the cream forms soft peaks. Gently fold in the honey, kiwi purée and half the oats. I prefer them only partly incorporated – a ripple rather than a blend.

Spoon the mixture into glasses, top with the remaining oats and serve immediately. If you are making this ahead, refrigerate and add the oats topping just before serving.

Autumn into winter fruit tart

A gorgeous tart that can be adapted to whatever fruit you have. If you don't grow autumn olive, either up the weight of grapes or substitute with any fruit you like, as long as you keep to the 500g total. Strawberries with a little elderflower cordial, and gooseberries, are the other variations I make most often earlier in the year. Ease back on the caster sugar in the filling if using sweet fruit, or nudge it up 10g if making the tart with early gooseberries.

Serves 6

For the pastry

100g plain flour

A pinch of salt

1 tsp fennel seeds, ground

40g caster sugar

130g cold unsalted butter, cut into small cubes

1 large free-range egg, lightly beaten

For the filling

100g autumn olive

40ml double cream

60ml natural yoghurt

2 free-range egg yolks

1 tsp balsamic vinegar

50g caster sugar

400g grapes

A few tsp light brown sugar

Preheat the oven to 180°C/Gas 4.

For the pastry, put the flour, salt, fennel and sugar in a food processor and pulse for a moment to combine. Add the butter and whiz briefly until the mixture resembles fine breadcrumbs. Add about two-thirds of the egg and process briefly, until the dough just starts to come together, adding more if needed. Gather the dough into a ball with your hands, divide in two and flatten each slightly into a disc. Wrap in cling film and refrigerate for 30 minutes. (You only need one portion for the tart so freeze the other.)

Lightly butter and flour a 22–24cm loose-bottomed tart tin. On a lightly floured surface, roll out the pastry to a 5mm thickness and line the tart tin with it, easing the pastry into the corners. Roll your rolling pin over the top of the tin to cut off the excess pastry. Prick the base well with a fork.

Now line the pastry case with a piece of baking parchment and baking beans and bake for 10 minutes. Remove the paper and beans, brush the pastry with beaten egg and bake for another 7 minutes.

For the filling, blitz the autumn olive in a blender, then push the pulp through a sieve to remove the seeds.

Whisk the cream, yoghurt, egg yolks, balsamic vinegar and sugar together in a bowl. Scatter the grapes fairly evenly in the pastry case and pour in the custard. Dot with the autumn olive purée and sprinkle with the light brown sugar. Bake for about 35 minutes, until the custard is set.

Allow the tart to rest for 10 minutes, before removing the side of the tart tin and placing the tart on a wire rack to cool.

Walnut tart

This is delicious with coffee. And happily, it's at least as good the next day as on the day it is cooked. The fennel in the pastry and the cinnamon in the filling don't overpower in any way – walnuts seem to have an affinity with both flavours. I like to eat this tart with double cream or yoghurt.

Serves 6

For the pastry

100g plain flour
A pinch of salt
1 tsp fennel seeds, ground
40g caster sugar
130g cold unsalted butter, cut into small cubes
1 large free-range egg, lightly beaten

For the filling

240g caster sugar
180ml double cream
2 tbsp good honey
1 tsp ground cinnamon
200g walnuts

Preheat the oven to 180°C/Gas 4.

For the pastry, put the flour, salt, fennel and sugar in a food processor and pulse for a moment to combine. Add the butter and whiz briefly until the mixture resembles fine breadcrumbs. Add about two-thirds of the egg and process briefly, until the dough just starts to come together, adding more if needed. Gather the dough into a ball with your hands, divide in two and flatten each slightly into a disc. Wrap in cling film and refrigerate for 30 minutes. (You only need one portion for the tart so freeze the other.)

For the filling, warm a pan over a medium heat, add the sugar and allow it to melt. When the sugar starts to turn to caramel, stir briefly. Stir once or twice more until all the sugar becomes caramel. Over the heat, slowly and carefully pour in the cream, stirring as you do so – it will form ribbons but keep pouring and stirring and it will become smooth. Stir in the honey, cinnamon and nuts. Leave to cool slightly while you make the pastry case.

Lightly butter and flour a 22–24cm loose-bottomed tart tin. On a lightly floured surface, roll out the pastry to a 5mm thickness and line the tart tin with it, easing the pastry into the corners. Roll your rolling pin over the top of the tin to cut off the excess pastry. Prick the base well with a fork.

Now line the pastry case with a piece of baking parchment and baking beans and bake for 10 minutes. Remove the paper and beans, brush the pastry with beaten egg and bake for another 7 minutes.

Spoon the caramel walnuts evenly in the pastry case and bake the tart in the centre of the oven for about 30 minutes.

Allow to rest for 10 minutes, before removing the side of the tin and placing the tart on a wire rack to cool.

Baklava

I first ate baklava 25 years ago in Istanbul. I tried half a dozen different varieties at one stall – different nuts, syrups and flavourings – and I'm glad I did, as it gave me the energy to outrun a group of men who inexplicably started chasing me through the streets. I had long hair then: perhaps they thought I was Mick Hucknall and were upset at the direction that his album had taken. It didn't put me off baklava though, nor experimenting with different varieties – try it with pistachios and/or rose or orange flower water instead of the lemon juice.

Makes about 50 pieces

6 cardamom pods, seeds only

4 tbsp granulated sugar

440g walnuts, smashed or chopped into small pieces

2 tsp ground cinnamon

230g unsalted butter, melted

12 sheets of filo pastry

For the syrup

100g dark muscovado sugar

300g caster sugar

250ml water

1 tbsp lemon juice

Finely grated zest of ½ orange

To finish

40g shelled walnuts, finely crushed

Preheat the oven to 180°C/Gas 4.

Pound the cardamom seeds together with the sugar, using a pestle and mortar. Mix thoroughly with the walnuts and cinnamon.

Lightly butter a baking tray, about 18 x 28cm. Place a sheet of filo pastry in the tray and brush with melted butter. Lay a second filo sheet on top of the first, brush with butter and repeat until 6 sheets of filo are used.

Spread the spicy nuts over the pastry and layer the other 6 sheets of filo on top, brushing each with butter as before. Now score the pastry into 5 x 3cm rectangles, cutting deep enough to just reach the filling.

Bake in the centre of the oven for 20 minutes, then lower the setting to 150°C/Gas 2 and bake for another 30 minutes until the pastry is golden.

Meanwhile, make the syrup. Warm the sugars and water in a pan over a medium heat, stirring to dissolve the sugar. Add the lemon juice and orange zest and simmer for around 15 minutes to form a runny syrup.

Once the baklava is cooked, remove from the oven and leave it to stand for 5 minutes. Pour the syrup over the warm baklava and sprinkle over the finely crushed walnuts. Leave to cool.

Using the initial cuts through the pastry as a guide, cut the baklava into rectangles and try not to eat too many at once.

Quince doughnuts

To paraphrase Samuel Johnson, 'When you are tired of doughnuts, you are tired of life.' And homemade doughnuts surpass even the finest you can buy. The filling can be whatever takes your fancy – cold custard, raspberry jam, puréed rhubarb – even a square of quince cheese (my favourite).

Makes 8

300g strong white bread flour, plus a handful for dusting
14g active dried yeast
1 tsp salt
85g caster sugar
125ml whole milk
90ml warm water
50g unsalted butter
2 free-range eggs, beaten
1 tsp vanilla extract
Quince cheese (page 354), for the filling
Sunflower oil for deep-frying
1 tbsp ground cinnamon, or more to taste

Sift the flour into the bowl of an electric mixer, fitted with the dough hook. Add the yeast, salt and 35g sugar and mix briefly.

Warm the milk and water slowly in a pan, then add the butter and warm gently until melted. With the mixer on a slow speed, gradually add the warm liquid, then the eggs and vanilla. Once a dough is formed, turn the speed up one notch and let the machine knead the dough for 10 minutes or so. (Or mix the dough by hand, then knead on a floured surface.)

Transfer the dough to a lightly oiled bowl and cover with cling film or a damp tea towel. Leave somewhere fairly warm to rise until doubled in size. This will take about an hour, depending on the temperature.

Pat the risen dough firmly a few times to knock out most of the air. On a lightly floured surface, divide into 8 equal pieces and shape into fat discs. Put a generous cube of quince cheese in the centre of each disc and fold the dough over the filling to enclose it. Work each into a ball with your hands. Cover with a damp tea towel and leave to prove for 25 minutes.

Pour the oil for deep-frying into a suitable large, deep, heavy pan, making sure it comes no more than one-third up the side of the pan. Slowly heat to 160°C (check with a cook's thermometer), or until a cube of bread dropped into the oil turns golden in a minute or so. Meanwhile, mix the remaining 50g sugar with the cinnamon; set aside.

You will need to deep-fry the doughnuts in batches. Lower into the oil with a spoon and cook, turning regularly, for about 7 minutes until evenly golden. Lift out with a slotted spoon onto kitchen paper.

Allow to drain for a minute, then roll the doughnuts in the cinnamon sugar until nicely dusted. Serve while still warm.

Fennel sugar plums

The first time I made sugar plums, I dropped one and it almost hit the dog on the back of the head, he was so fast in snaffling it. Everyone, even Harris, likes sugar plums it seems. The spices give it just the right amount of autumn for October and few things go so well with a coffee.

Makes about 8

200g shelled walnuts

70g pitted dates, chopped

70g dried apricots, chopped

70g prunes, chopped

Finely grated zest of 1 orange

½ tsp salt

1½ tsp ground cinnamon

½ tsp freshly grated nutmeg

½ tsp ground allspice

¼ tsp ground coriander

For the fennel sugar

1½ tsp fennel seeds

3 tbsp caster sugar

Briefly zap the nuts in a food processor to break them up into small pieces. Add the dates, apricots, prunes, orange zest, salt and spices and pulse to blend until minced together to form a thick paste. Transfer to a bowl and allow to rest for a few minutes.

Meanwhile, for the fennel sugar, pound the fennel seeds with a pestle and mortar until they start to break apart, then mix with the sugar.

Roll the walnut and fruit paste in your hands into sugar plum balls, each about the size of a table tennis ball. Shower with fennel sugar and eat at once. Or store in the fridge for a few days if you've any willpower.

Almond biscuits

A beautifully light, easy-to-make nibble that is good with ice cream, sorbet or just a coffee. If you like you can sprinkle a few flaked almonds on top of the biscuits just before baking.

Makes about 20

60g ground almonds

25g plain flour

A pinch of salt

2 free-range egg whites

100g golden caster sugar

65g unsalted butter, melted and cooled

Preheat the oven to 180°C/Gas 4.

Mix the ground almonds, flour and salt together in a bowl.

Briefly whisk the egg whites in another bowl to loosen them a little. Add the sugar and whisk until just frothy, then fold in the ground almond mixture and the melted butter until evenly combined.

Line a large baking tray (or two) with baking parchment and dollop on teaspoonfuls of batter, leaving a few centimetres between them to allow for them to spread a little as they cook.

Bake for 6–8 minutes until the biscuits are just turning golden around the edges. Let them rest for a minute or two before easing them off the paper and placing on a wire rack to cool.

Fennel toffee apples

What better way to use a few late-season apples than cover them in toffee? Sprinkle them with a few fennel seeds is the answer. That gentle aniseed sets them alight, it's so good. Caraway works well too, as do crushed sweet cicely seeds. You need to work quickly to twist the apple to coat them in toffee – it's a dull fact that the toffee gets quickly immobile until you sit the apple on parchment paper when half seems to happy to slip off the fruit. You can always re-dip, as my daughter Nell insists I do, to give the top an extra coating.

Makes 8

A few drops of vegetable oil

8 apples

350g caster sugar

170ml water

1 tsp white wine vinegar

3 tbsp golden syrup

A sprinkling of fennel seeds

Lightly oil a sheet of baking parchment. Wash the apples with warm water if they are waxy and dry thoroughly. Push a lollypop stick into the end of each one.

Put the sugar, water, wine vinegar and golden syrup in a large pan and bring slowly to a simmer, stirring just enough to dissolve the sugar and syrup. Turn up the heat slightly and let the syrup boil, without stirring, until it darkens, turning a soft walnut colour.

Turn the heat off. Dip each apple in the toffee, twisting and tipping the apple to allow the toffee to cover it completely. Dip it again if needs be, then sprinkle with fennel seeds. Place the apples on the parchment and leave to set.

Grape, beetroot & mint smoothie

If I've overdone the cooked breakfasts, I'll have a few days of breakfast smoothies in the hope of pacifying the paunch gods. Once you get past the usual (and delicious) berry and banana smoothies, there are some fine combinations to be discovered. Even if you're no fan of beetroot, try this one – it adds so much without making anything particularly beetrooty.

Serves 1

300g white grapes

1 cooked, skinned medium-large beetroot

Juice of ½ lime

A handful of mint leaves, chopped

A sprinkle of Greek basil leaves (optional)

Place all the ingredients in a blender and blitz until smooth. Pass the smoothie through a medium sieve to remove any tiny bits of grape skin if you like it totally smooth.

Mulled cider

Few things welcome in the frosts like mulled cider. As with punch, mulled cider has been much abused: at its finest, the spices build on the fabulous appley-ness of cider; at its worst, the cider is swamped by a wash of pot pourri. The key is to use a good cider and fresh spices – and don't over-sweeten. Honey's warmth works better than sugar in my view.

This makes one relaxing goblet – multiply up to a bucketful for Halloween and Bonfire Night.

Per person

250ml dry cider

1 clove

1 star anise

2 allspice berries

2–3 lemon verbena leaves (optional)

A good grating of fresh nutmeg

4–5cm piece of cinnamon stick

A few strips of unwaxed lemon zest

1–2 tsp honey (optional)

Pour the cider into a pan, add all the other ingredients except the honey and bring to a simmer. Allow to simmer for 8 minutes or so. Turn off the heat. Taste and stir in a little honey if you think it needs it.

Resources

Seeds and seedlings

Otter Farm
shop.otterfarm.co.uk

Heritage Seed Library
gardenorganic.org.uk/hsl
024 7630 3517

The Real Seed Catalogue
realseeds.co.uk
01239 821107

Edulis
edulis.co.uk
01635 578113

Agroforestry Research Trust
agroforestry.co.uk
01803 840776

Pennard Plants
pennardplants.com
01749 860039

Sarah Raven
sarahraven.com
0845 092 0283

Delfland Nurseries
organicplants.co.uk
01354 740553

Sea Spring Seeds
seaspringseeds.co.uk
01308 897898

Ann Miller's Speciality Mushrooms
annforfungi.co.uk
01467 671315

Other supplies

Green Gardener
greengardener.co.uk
01493 750061
*Range of biological pest control,
plus general veg patch supplies*

Greenhouse Sensation
greenhousesensation.co.uk
0845 602 3774
Propagators and more

Harrod Horticultural
harrodhorticultural.com
0845 402 5300
Fruit cages and more

UK Juicers
ukjuicers.com/dehydrators
01904 757070
*Excellent dehydrators for drying/
preserving harvests*

Wood Ovens
woodovens.net
01636 678653
*Supplier of good-quality outdoor
wood-fired ovens*

Hot Smoked
hotsmoked.co.uk
01398 351604
Hot and cold smokers

Omlet
omlet.co.uk
0845 450 2056
*Good source of chicken supplies,
including housing*

Useful organisations

GIY
giyinternational.org
*The international community
of food growers*

Garden Organic
gardenorganic.org.uk
024 7630 3517
*A charity (formerly the HDRA)
dedicated to organic growing.
Well worth joining to give you
access to a wealth of advice. Also
an excellent source for seeds and
everything to do with growing*

Royal Horticultural Society
rhs.org.uk
0845 062 1111
*A great source of advice, with
numerous excellent gardens to visit;
also offers a soil analysis service*

Slow Food
slowfood.org.uk
020 7099 1132
*Promoting the locality, diversity
and enjoyment of food*

Index

Page numbers in *italic* refer to the illustrations

For Candida & Nell

Acknowledgements

A few years ago, when my chin was on the desk and I was wondering if I hadn't bitten off a little too much, an email pinged into my inbox. It was from someone called Trent Peterson. I'd always meant to become friends with someone with a surname for a first name so this was good. He knew about vineyards and wondered if there was some work here. He was only here a day or so a week for 18 months but he made a huge difference, leaving his mark on the place and on us. Paul Collins, Stuart Woolger, Kate Colwell and Ali Thompson came later and have all made the place a happier and more productive one. The Riddles, the Beekens, David George, the Beales, Rodney Pring and the ever-youthful Vivian Bolt have all been the right person at the right time more often than once. To all of you, thank you.

Thanks, also, to Chris, Mike and Jayne at the nursery.

I am enormously grateful to Richard Atkinson and Natalie Bellos at Bloomsbury Publishing for their enthusiasm for the idea, and to Natalie for her dedication and skill in overseeing the creation of such a beautiful book with Xa Shaw Stewart. To Janet Illsley, thank you so much for your sensitive editing and vision; to Andrew Lyons, for such beautiful illustrations; to the very talented Jason Ingram, for the three pics of me where I don't look as gormless as usual; to Matt Cox, the brilliant designer, who somehow got the idea and feel of Otter Farm from Day 1, thank you.

As ever, I owe much to my agent: thank you, Caroline Michel at PFD, who couldn't be more enthusiastic or tireless.

To Candida and Nell, thank you for turning Otter Farm from an interesting venture into somewhere so rewarding and lovely to live – and for giving it all meaning.

First published in Great Britain 2014

Text © Mark Diacono 2014
Photography © Mark Diacono 2014,
except pages 2–3, 8 and 202 © Jason Ingram 2014
Illustrations © Andrew Lyons 2014

The moral right of the author has been asserted

Bloomsbury Publishing Plc
50 Bedford Square
London WC1B 3DP

bloomsbury.com

Bloomsbury is a trademark of Bloomsbury Publishing Plc

Bloomsbury Publishing, London, New Delhi, New York and Sydney

A CIP catalogue record for this book is available from the British Library

ISBN 978 1 4088 2861 8

10 9 8 7 6 5 4 3 2 1

Project editor: Janet Illsley
Designer: Matt Cox at Newman and Eastwood

Printed and bound in China by C&C Offset Printing Co. Ltd.

All papers used by Bloomsbury Publishing are natural, recyclable products made from wood grown in well-managed forests. The manufacturing processes conform to the environmental regulations of the country of origin

Otter Farm